Software Product Management and

"These two seasoned practitioners have masterfully distilled the essence of the software business and the art and craft of the increasingly important and challenging field of software product management. Worthwhile to any who want an appreciation of the evolving world of product management, seasoned veteran and new entrant alike."

Richard Campione, Senior Vice President, Business Suite Solution Management & CRM On Demand, SAP, Germany/USA

"Mr. Kittlaus and Mr. Clough have used their considerable knowledge and experience to succinctly lay out the value chain that is essential to the development of a financially healthy software company. If you want to understand how to turn software technology into a long-term profitable company this is the book to read."

Paul Kaplan, Vice President, Worldwide Enterprise Software Sales, Software Group, IBM, USA

"This book on Software Product Management and Pricing is the first book that treats the business of software in a systematical way. Although software products were already shipped in the seventies of the last century, there are hardly any books providing an overview of all issues a company faces when playing a role in this industry. Product management and pricing are key processes, and this book informs the reader of the essentials. It is a must-read for anyone involved in software products, be it in business or in research."

Prof. Dr. Sjaak Brinkkemper, Information and Computing Sciences, Utrecht University, Netherlands

"This compendium covers all facets of the software business using the advanced professionalism of the industry's global players as its standard. The authors have managed to combine professional accuracy with helpful practical examples and valuable references for further reading. Highly recommended, in particular for managers in corporate IT and software vendor organizations!"

Wilhelm Gans, CTO, DSV Group (German Savings Banks Organization), Germany

"A comprehensive book on best practices for software product management and pricing. It provides a deep insight into strategy and tactics of software organizations in a time of growing complexity and new challenges like Software as a Service."

Udo Hertz, Director of Information Management Development, IBM Germany Research & Development, Germany

Hans-Bernd Kittlaus • Peter N. Clough

Software Product Management and Pricing

Key Success Factors for Software Organizations

 Springer

Hans-Bernd Kittlaus
InnoTivum Consulting
Im Sand 86
D-53619 Rheinbreitbach
Germany
hbk@innotivum.com

Peter N. Clough
InnoTivum Consulting
9 Light Horse Lane
Pound Ridge, NY 10576
USA
pnc@innotivum.com

ISBN 978-3-642-09570-2   e-ISBN 978-3-540-76987-3

Cover design: KuenkelLopka GmbH

Printed on acid-free paper

9 8 7 6 5 4 3 2 1

springer.com

Preface

Amazingly, in a time in which book fairs are overflowing with a multitude of new publications, there are important topics which are not yet addressed in literature. Software product management used to be one of these, software pricing still is. When we first dealt with these subjects in IBM in the 1980s, it was like occult science with a few insiders who did not share their secrets with others, let alone reveal it to third parties. There was no literature on the subject.

Through a laborious learning-by-doing process, we gradually became insiders ourselves. Peter Clough worked on IBM's software pricing and terms for over 20 years, the executive from 2002 to 2008 who designed the pricing for the largest software deals, before he started his own consulting business. Hans-Bernd Kittlaus was responsible for IBM's European product management for database and application development projects before he made his first attempt, as director of the German savings banks organisation at the end of the 1990s, to take the concept of software product management into an organisation with thousands of application developers. There was still no literature. In 2004 he co-authored one of the first books on software product management ([KiRaSch04]) and started to consult software vendors and corporate IT organizations on the subject. The book in your hands provides an updated comprehensive view of software product management and the first extensive publication on software pricing that we are aware of. We hope you find the work both thought-provoking and useful. On www.innotivum.com you can find updates and additional information. The judgement of our success we leave to you and look forward to your criticism and praise at "info@innotivum.com".

We would like to thank our many former customers and IBM colleagues who formed the crucible in which many of our ideas were shaped (sometimes by agreement, sometimes by criticism, almost always by wisdom) over many years. We would also like to recognize Christoph Rau and Juergen Schulz, Hans-Bernd's co-authors of his previous book on software product management ([KiRaSch04]), for all the work that they put into it and that helped with this publication. We thank Hermann Engesser and Dorothea Glaunsinger from Springer-Verlag for the good cooperation. Our special thanks go to Richard Campione, Senior Vice President of Suite Solution Management, SAP AG, an industry leader highly experienced in software product management in a broad array of software companies, for sharing his insight and experience and to Paul Kaplan, IBM Software Group Vice President of Worldwide Software Enterprise Sales, for his thoughtful reading of and many insightful suggestions for the chapter on Pricing. We also thank Karl A. Wagner, Director and Head of ARIS R&D, Product and Solution Management, and his product managers Georg Wilhelm und Uwe Roediger of IDS Scheer AG, for some very helpful discussions. We thank Sjaak Brinkkemper and Inge van de Weerd, Utrecht University, Netherlands, and Gartner, Inc. for giving us some graphical images for publication. Thanks also to Strategic Pricing Group, Thomas Nagle, and John Hogan for allowing us to reproduce their Strategic Pricing Pyramid. Last but not least, special thanks go to our better halves for accepting the fits of writing and writer's block without complaint and for their moral support.

Rheinbreitbach, Germany   *Hans-Bernd Kittlaus*
Pound Ridge, New York, USA   *Peter N. Clough*
September 2008

Contents

Chapter 1
Introduction

People have been talking of software crises since the 1960s. They were referring to the disparity between expectations and actual achievements in productivity and in the quality of the software being provided, as observed by both software vendors and corporate users. Nevertheless, the industry has for the most part been doing brilliantly for decades. The first real crisis in the software industry occurred when the Internet bubble burst in 2000. Many publicly traded software companies had to declare insolvency, others were taken over. This development can be considered an overdue consolidation following an exaggerated boom phase. However, it also reveals the immense risks of a difficult business with a rapid succession of techno-logical changes, little standardization, and a lot of irrational hype. Compared to more traditional industries, the software industry is still quite immature.

Corporate users became disillusioned after having made enormous IT invest-ments during the boom period. The "soft" in software was often misinterpreted as meaning "everything is feasible". A vast number of large projects, including retail banking and securities applications, failed completely in the finance indus-try. The time and money invested in other projects sometimes either got com-pletely out of control or did not produce the anticipated return on investment or both. In this case we should not conclude that all IT expenditures are excessive, and throw the baby out with the bathwater, however. The question is not whether money should still be invested in IT, but rather how such investments can lead to the desired sustainable commercial success. This is exactly what systematic software product management aims to do.

Product management is a discipline that has been utilized by many industries for decades, above all the consumer goods industry. The invention of product manage-ment as an explicit management concept is attributed to Procter & Gamble. In 1931 the company assigned one product manager to each of two competing soap prod-ucts (see [Gorche05]). Since then, this basic idea has become widespread. In fact, it makes sense for any company to manage explicitly the products that generate its revenue and that, as assets, represent the company's sustainable value. But what does product management actually mean? Unfortunately, a general answer can only be given for parts of this question, since practice has shown that the activities of the product manager depend largely on the type of product involved, the culture, his-tory, and organization of the company, and the target and reward system. Basically,

H.-B. Kittlaus and P.N. Clough, *Software Product Management and Pricing.*
© Springer-Verlag Berlin Heidelberg 2009

it means managing and coordinating all relevant areas inside and outside the company with the aim of sustainably optimizing product success. Within the company, product management specifically concerns itself with development, production, marketing, operations and logistics as well as pricing or market analysis.

In several decades of experience in the software industry, the authors have come to realize that the knowledge and experience acquired in other business areas and with other types of products are only partially transferable to software. A software product manager's job is basically characterized by the specific features of the software involved. Most conspicuous are the limited importance of production and logistics and the great importance of requirements management, which allows frequent changes to be made to the product during its lifetime. The authors are of the opinion that software is the most complex product of human invention that we know of (see chapter 2) and that the management of software products is thus special and uniquely demanding on the persons responsible for this task.

One of the responsibilities of a software product manager is making sure that the pricing of his product continues to be appropriate over time in relation to changes in the market and in product plans. Most often, the product manager cannot make pricing decisions on his own. In large software vendor organizations, there are usually pricing units that are organizationally separated from product management. With smaller software vendors and corporate IT organizations, executive management reserves the right to make pricing decisions. Therefore, we treat software pricing in a separate chapter in this book (chapter 5), but emphasize the tight connection and interdependence between product management and pricing decisions.

Corporate IT organizations (see the explanation of this term at the end of this chapter) have recently come to view software products somewhat differently than they used to. Since they are increasingly being viewed as separate units in a business sense, e.g. due to outsourcing or internal cost allocation, it has become apparent that software products need to be explicitly managed as crucial assets. The realization that companies from non-IT industries are suddenly becoming "standard software suppliers" for their customers by providing Java Applets on their Web site may also have contributed to this development. As software product management is not implemented as consistently among corporate IT organizations as it is among software vendors, there is potential for improvement in this area.

In the last five years, a number of books have been published on software product management and the software industry in general that provide help for beginners to learn the trade (see Appendix C). This book is intended to provide an integrated view of software product management and pricing for both software vendors and corporate IT organizations. We consider the similarities between these two types of organizations which are induced by the specifics of software as a product as more significant than differences in organizational views. Nevertheless, the differences must be taken into consideration by setting different priorities regarding the individual tasks (see chapter 6). The target group of this book is everyone involved in software product management and pricing at software vendors and corporate IT organizations, especially top management at organizations striving for more explicit management of their software assets. Naturally we also appreciate our academic readers, although this book is not meant to be an academic monograph or a textbook.

Clear boundaries are needed to be able to address the breadth of this topic. Despite important interfaces between development and software product management, neither the topics of software development methods and management nor project management will be discussed here. We have also omitted operations and consulting issues. We want to clarify at this point that we are not talking about software license management, i.e. appropriate bookkeeping, administration, and payment for the software licenses acquired and used in a company, nor software product line management, i.e. the management of development variants based on the same product platform (e.g. adaptations of a mobile phone operating system to the various mobile phone models that it supports).

In chapter 2 we attempt the difficult task of setting a universally applicable definition of the term "software product" and discussing important characteristics of such products. Chapter 3 examines software as a business. Chapter 4 describes the elements of software product management. It deals in great detail with all facets of the subject from market positioning to licensing models. The focus of chapter 5 is on software pricing. The incorporation of software product management and pricing as part of the organizational structure of software vendors and corporate IT organizations is the topic of chapter 6. This chapter addresses the interplay and the boundaries between software product management and business strategy, product portfolio management, management of product platforms and product families as well as pricing, development, marketing, operations and consulting. On this basis, structural organizational alternatives and specific priorities of the elements of software product management and pricing are presented for different types of companies and products. The book ends with a summary and outlook in Chapter 7. In Appendices A and B examples of job descriptions for both software product manager and pricing manager are given. As mentioned above, there is plenty of literature available about product management, but few books that are useful for software product management, and hardly any for software pricing. In Appendix C we provide an overview of the books we find helpful. Appendix D lists the definitions of all relevant terms used.

Before we begin our in-depth discussion of software products, we need to clarify several conventions used throughout this book. Terms such as "manager" or "director" are meant to be gender-neutral, that is they refer equally to female and male persons. While women increasingly participate in IT management, we have chosen a convention of referring to such positions using the male pronoun. This is not intended to be in any way discriminatory and was chosen simply for the purposes of easier readability. We use terms like development or marketing with small characters when we mean the activity, with capital characters when we mean the organizational unit.

We use the term "software vendor" when we mean companies whose primary business is the development and/or provision of software for commercial purposes for a relatively large number of consumer and/or business customers. Examples are

Microsoft, SAP, Oracle, IBM, or Google. We use the term "corporate IT organization" for organizational units that are part of companies in all industries and whose
primary mission is to provide software or IT support for the parent company or
corporation which we call "corporate user". In that sense, software vendors are
corporate users with regard to their internal IT.

The term "service" has many different meanings (see Webster's Dictionary) at
least three of which are relevant for this book:

- Useful labor that does not produce a tangible commodity (as in "professional
  services")
- A provision for maintenance and repair (as in "software maintenance service")
- The technical provision of a function through a software component that can be
  accessed by another software component, often over a network and executed on
  a remote server (as in "web services")

Whenever we use the term "service" in this book, we try to make it clear which
meaning is intended.

When we use the term "controlling" we mean "performing the functions of a
(business or financial) controller".

With these rather prosaic clarifications out of the way, we can jump right into
the secrets of software product management and pricing.

Chapter 2
Software Products: Terms and Characteristics

Software is an intangible economic good, with no physical form, its utility or value not even perceptible in another form. So only the functionality of software is perceptible e.g. via a user interface, or as the result of a controlled transaction via software, e.g. as an account movement. What exactly constitutes a software product is often rather subjective. As with many highly technical products, many people do not understand how software products work. Software is therefore in the truest sense of the word "intangible." Software thus contrasts greatly with other investments or acquisitions of consumer goods. In particular the customer does not really acquire the product when buying software, rather very specific, precisely defined rights of use in a license contract. However, investments in software today represent a larger proportion of spending for IT infrastructure than investments in hardware, and software contracts with large companies often amount to multiple million of dollars.

Software belongs not to the three classic economic factors of capital, land, and labor, but in the new fourth category of "knowledge." Software is the manifestation of human know-how in bits and bytes and in this form also possesses the invaluable advantage (and simultaneous disadvantage), that it can be easily copied and quickly circulated over any distance. The right software, ideally applied, can represent a more important strategic competitive advantage in today's economic life than all the other factors. Software can be crucial for competitiveness in production processes, functionality, the availability of service products, and thus for a company's success or failure on the market. But what is a software product and what is it not – or not yet? What role does the price play? How should we classify services that are offered on the basis of software?

We find it reasonable not to limit the term "software product" to the world of software vendors, but also to use it in the world of corporate IT organizations. Is, for example, an online account with a direct bank, a mobile phone in combination with a special mobile phone tariff or the membership to a chat community a software product? In this chapter we attempt to define the term "software product" and to discuss certain features of software and their relevance for products and product management.

Marketing generally defines the term "product" as follows: "a product is anything that can be offered to a market for attention, acquisition, or consumption that might satisfy a want or a need." (See [KotArm07]).

H.-B. Kittlaus and P.N. Clough, *Software Product Management and Pricing.*
© Springer-Verlag Berlin Heidelberg 2009

In our definition we avoid the market term (which focuses the conceptualization too much on a "mass market" for our purposes) and prefer to put the relationship between two parties in the foreground, so that individual developments and internal customer/supplier relationships can be included.

Product = Combination of (material and/or intangible) goods and services, which one party (called vendor) combines in support of their commercial interests, to transfer defined rights to a second party (called customer).

Software product = Product whose primary component is software.

The word "party" indicates that we are not necessarily dealing with a corporate entity. It can also be areas within a company or an individual person. The phrase "in support of their commercial interests" should make clear that it refers to business but does not necessarily lead to a payment. There is also a commercial interest behind Open Source even if only to harm the established software vendors. Even a product free of charge (e.g. the Microsoft PowerPoint Viewer) has a commercial goal – to increase market penetration of another product from the same software vendor which is subject to a fee. The phrase "defined rights" expresses that there is some room for variation here, e.g. right of use (possibly with restrictions), property right, right to resale etc. Details are typically defined in the software vendor's licensing terms or in an individual contract between the parties concerned.

This product definition should also express that something can already be a product when it has not yet been bought by a customer; that is it does not become a product through the buying process, but through the intention to sell it. In establishing the boundaries of what a software product is and is not, we have knowingly chosen a "flexible" phrase: the word "primary" should make it clear that there is room for discretion.

A mobile phone is not a software product according to our definition (rather a telecommunication product), even if software is an important part and may have absorbed a large proportion of the development costs. In this case we would be talking about embedded software, which "serves" the function of making phone calls and is therefore an underlying part of the whole product, which cannot be bought separately. We define:

Embedded software = A piece of software that is not sold as a stand-alone software product, but is integrated in a non-software product.

Embedded software does not manage and operate only a computer or a processor, but rather is embedded in a technical system which consists of other components as well, which allow the whole thing to become a product. This can be the software for programming and managing a machine, but also diagnosis software for finding errors in an automobile or software for servicing a dialysis machine in medicine. These programs serve highly specialized interfaces, which are typically very closely integrated with hardware. Therefore the requirements and the product management are driven by the functionality of the complete system. According to our definition from the beginning of this chapter, since embedded software is not a stand-alone software product, it will not be discussed further in this book.

Another important term in this context is "OEM product". OEM stands for Original Equipment Manufacturer. The term was originally coined in the hardware business and later transferred into the software world. It means that one manufacturer sells one of his products to another manufacturer who uses it as a component in one of his products without showing its origin openly. We define:

OEM software product = software product of software vendor A that is used by company B as a component under the covers of one of B's products.

Notice that B's product can be, but does not have to be a software product. A vendor is usually willing to sell his products as OEM products at a significantly reduced price in order to increase the volume. We will discuss the pro's and con's of this approach in chapter 5.

Let's look at some more examples. A games console is also not a software product (rather a games product). The same arguments are valid here as for the mobile phone. A game for this console – purchased separately, separately packaged with its own price and own terms of licensing – is obviously a software product, however.

An online account is not a software product according to this definition, rather it is a banking product realized with help of software (products) within the bank. The customer receives online access to his account from his bank, which allows him to carry out bank transactions (bank balance enquiries, transfers, establishment of standing orders etc.) at home or wherever he happens to be. The software is only useful and usable in connection with the account. So the account is the primary component.

A search offering like Google qualifies as a software product even though that may be contrary to some people's intuitive understanding. It does fulfill all the criteria of our definition: there is a commercial interest, the customer gets the right to use it, and its primary component is software. This approach is close to the "Software as a Service" model (SaaS) that we will discuss in more detail. Google's case is special since the price is zero, but Google makes significant profit with the advertisements displayed with the search results.

2.1 External and Internal Views on a (Software) Product

By changing the perspective or the point of view, a "non-software product" can very quickly become a "pure" software product. Let us keep the example of the online account from the last chapter: The online account is seen as a bank product through the eyes of the bank's end customer or the bank's executive board. For this purpose, there may be a product manager in the bank's organization, who works on the customers' requirements and generally makes sure that the bank has a consistent and competitive home banking offer for its customers.

The online account is realized internally via several hardware, software and service components, which can originate from various sources. Let us accept that the product is realized by the components online application, HBCI (Home Banking Computer Interface) server and a call center. Furthermore:

- The online application is created by Application Development as part of the corporate IT organization.
- The HBCI server is bought as standard software and integrated with the online applications by the corporate IT organization, tested and put into production.
- The call center is outsourced to an external service provider.

From the point of view of the corporate IT organization, the "online application" component is a software product. Since it was developed internally, an internal software product management is needed that receives – at least functional requirements – from the product manager of the bank product "online account". Furthermore, the bank may decide to sell this software product to other banks, which would underline the necessity of an explicit software product management.

For the standard product "HBCI Server" on the other hand, the bank is a customer of a software vendor. Since the product does not fulfill all of the bank's specific requirements from the perspective of the IT organization, corresponding requirements are given to the product manager of the software vendor who has to commit to their implementation.

The call center, including infrastructure and agents, was completely handed over to an external service provider. Service level agreements (e.g. average and maximum time that the customer is supposed to spend in the queue) were negotiated and secured contractually; no requirements were placed on individual software products.

The external service provider implements the call center for the bank via hardware and software as well as personnel recruitment. This includes components such as ACD (Automatic Call Distribution), CTI (Computer Telephone Integration), and IVR (Interactive Voice Response) Units, call recording etc. As the service provider offers call center solutions for many firms, this is one of their main products from their point of view, and therefore they assign a product manager who manages requirements from customers (e.g. the bank) and elicits requirements against the integrated hardware and software products from other vendors.

As this example shows, which can easily be detailed even further, the definition of what a product is depends on the individual perspective. Many non-software products have software products inside. So the topic of software product management often plays a role in those product areas as well.

2.2 The Software Product as Type and the Customer-Specific Installation as Instance

To understand the term "software product," we must differentiate between type and instance. For example, the development of an automobile, e.g. of the Audi A4, defines a type. This can have a multitude of different parameters which influence the production process.

Audi A4 type
Model: *Sedan, Avant, Cabriolet*
Engine: *2.0, 3.2*
Color: *grey, white, red, beige, blue*

When ordering a specific car for a customer, the model features are specified (product configuration). In this way, during the manufacturing process an instance of the A4 type is created.

A4 for Fred Miller = Audi A4
(Model: *Sedan,*
Engine: *3.2,*
Color: *red)*

Afterwards the instance is delivered to the customer and no longer changed by the manufacturer or the customer.

The product manager for the Audi A4 is therefore responsible for the whole "type" of A4; even when there are many different models, the number is always finite and all combinations are known before production begins.

Software products can also be distributed by the manufacturer in diverse variations. However, in many cases, not only a selection of a variation before distribution is carried out, but a customer-specific customization of the software product to its environment on location. This can be carried out by the customers themselves, or with the support and advice of the software manufacturer or a consulting company.

Salary and wages type
Platform: *IBM AIX, SUN Solaris, HP-UX, Linux*
Language: *German, English, French, Italian*
Tax table: *Germany_2009, Italy_2009,*
             Switzerland_2009, Austria_2009,
             England_2009, France_2009
Medium: *CD, Download*

S&W for Vienna = Salary and wages
(Platform: *SUN Solaris,*
Language: *German,*
Tax table: *Austria_2009,*
Medium: *CD)*

If parts of the product are also distributed in source code, the product itself can be changed beyond pure customization. For this there are unpredictable numbers of possibilities, which cannot all be considered, planned, and checked by the product manager. Nor does the software vendor wish to be dependent on code for which he does not control the quality. For all these reasons, as a rule the manufacturer's guarantee relates only to items originally distributed by the vendor, but does not apply to code modified by the customer.

2.3   Product Platform, Family, and Line

For technology companies it can make sense to differentiate between product platform, product family, and individual product. McGrath defines ([McGrat01]): "A
product platform is not a product. It is a collection of the common elements, especially the underlying defining technology, implemented across a range of products.
A product platform is primarily a definition for planning, decision making, and
strategic thinking. The choice of a defining technology in platform strategy is perhaps the most critical strategic decision that a high-technology company makes."
So we define:

Product Platform = the technical foundation on which several software products are based.

An example of a product platform is the SAP core system that serves as the basis
for all SAP components. McGrath sees the product platform as key competitive
factor the management of which must be a core competency of a company. For him
a product platform must be controlled by the company. For software there can be
platforms that are not under control of the software vendor but which nevertheless
may have key influence on the success of their product. For example, for any kind
of PC software the question of the operating system platform(s) needs to be
answered. For some time the decision for Microsoft Windows was easy because of
its dominance in the market whereas several years ago IBM's OS/2 was a valid
option, and today Linux makes the decision more difficult again.

A product platform is usually not an independent product, but rather a combination of technological elements used in various products. Such a platform often constitutes an especially valuable asset and serves as a market differentiation factor. It
therefore requires very sensitive management, since errors will immediately have
serious consequences for all products based on the platform and thus for the company as a whole. An example is Wang Laboratories, which dominated the word
processing market in the late 70s with its combined hardware and software products.
Wang viewed the combination of hardware and software as a defining element of its
product platform and continued to do so – which proved to be a fatal mistake – even
after the computer market had developed and customers thus no longer wanted hardware intended solely for word processing. If Wang had, at the time, realized that the
defining element of its product platform was software and ported this software onto
the new computer platforms, Wang might still be the major supplier of word processing software today. In fact, Wang disappeared from the market, giving Microsoft the
opportunity to take over the word processing market.

A positive example on the part of commercial users is Amazon, the large
Internet e-commerce company. Amazon developed a product platform and defining technology comprised of software that today not only sets the standard for
e-commerce, but also serves as a basis for geographic and product-range-related
expansion of commercial transactions.

A platform that brings real competitive advantage may serve as a base not only
for one product, but for a family of products. The establishment of a product

family in the market, however, is motivated by pure marketing reasons. An example is IBM's DB2 family. In the 1990s, IBM combined all relational database products on the various system platforms to the DB2 product family and gave all products this name (which had previously only been used for the host product). However, this was not based on a joint code base of the individual products, even though this would have been preferable from a development perspective. In any case, customers associated the same family name with a large degree of similarity. We define:

Product Family = A group of software products which for marketing reasons are marketed as belonging together under a common family name.

A software vendor groups various products together under a "family name" which can then be marketed more efficiently than a single product. This approach suggests that the products belong together, implying that they are either technologically similar or that together they provide a solution for specific problems. The technological similarity can be a common product platform, e.g. SAP products, or a common basic technology, e.g. IBM's DB2 family. Microsoft Office is an example of a product family comprising a group of products that address specific problems, in this case office tasks, even if the components of Office have not always had a seamless relationship. The above examples illustrate that the terms "product platform" and "product family" sometimes coincide, i.e., products based on a common product platform can be – but do not have to be – marketed as a product family. Conversely, products that are marketed as a family can have – but do not have to have – a common product platform. Whether or not it is advisable to establish a family concept is primarily a marketing decision, which does, however, have an impact on the requirements for the products concerned. Customers expect products belonging to a product family to exhibit more common features in terms of integration of product combinations or interface similarities in the case of technologically similar products. A negative example is the Norton security products System Suite and Utilities, which are fundamentally one menu from which multiple unrelated programs may be invoked. If the products do not adequately meet customer integration expectations, the family concept can have a negative market impact.

The term "product line" has gained a lot of attention in the last couple of years, primarily in, but not restricted to the area of embedded software. We define:

Product Line = A group of software products which are variants of a base product governed by a common software architecture.

An example is an application software for offer calculation for craftsmen that needs to be adapted to any specialized craft it supports, like plumber, gardener, etc. Here adaptation means more than just customization, i.e. it means not just setting parameters differently, but requires changes to parts of the code of the base product. That is why in this case we do not call the base product a product platform which by definition would have to be identical for all products based on it.

All three concepts, product platform, product family and product line generally increase the complexity of software product management (see chapter 4).

2.4   Product Name, Version Numbers and Compatibility

For most software products development continues throughout its commercial (sales) lifetime. An important question in this context is if and when the development of a product results in a different product (with a new product name etc.) or simply a "new edition" of the existing product. There is no universally applicable answer to this question. Marketing aspects frequently play a more important role than technical aspects when selecting a name. It has become common to denominate software versions after a specific nomenclature, which is generally dependant on the manufacturer, however.

IBM uses a three-level hierarchy of software levels, for example:

- **Version:** Denotes a new product, which as a rule comprises crucial expansions and improvements. Furthermore, a new version is always subject to a fee and also always receives a new (internal) product number.
- **Release:** Denotes a new level of software with bigger functional or other improvements. New releases are generally free of charge for customers with a maintenance contract, and keep the product name, product number and the price model from the predecessor.
- **Modification Level:** Denotes a new status of software with limited expansions and delivery of error and cosmetic corrections to the predecessor.

An example of complete product identification is IBM z/OS Version 1 Release 9 Modification Level 5 (in short z/OS 1.9.5).

Anecdotally, customers seem to be more accepting of new version designations (a.k.a. new product) if the version is declared on an obvious boundary and the most satisfactory boundary seems to be a machine architecture and operating system change boundary.

There may be a number of motivations to rename a follow-on product. If, for example, the product currently on the market had a quality problem during introduction this may have led to an image problem in the long term, which is naturally associated with the product name. In this case, a new name may signal a new beginning and as little in common as possible with the previous product. A new name can also be necessary due to the standardization of product names in connection with a larger product portfolio or a product family like IBM's DB2 family (see above).

Frequently, further development is needed – if not mandatory – due to technological progress and changes in products which serve as a basis for the software product (prerequisites). For example, an operating system must support new hardware (processors, storage mediums, etc.). The old version of the operating system will be taken out of service at some point, so that – often with a certain time delay – a chain of upgrades is required for the system and application software products on higher layers of the technology stack. In this case, the version and release numbers underline upward compatibility of products and investment protection ensured by the vendor for its customers. Therefore, a change in the product name should always be well considered to prevent potential irritation of the customers. Naturally not all software vendors adhere to this "unwritten" law of upward compatibility, and there are enough examples in which the product name was kept and the customers experienced a nasty surprise when changing to the new version.

By upward compatibility, it is understood that:

- In changing from software version n of a product to the next version n+1, existing functions of version n continue to be supported.
- Data from version n can be transferred to and used with version n+1 without changes.
- Interfaces of version n (APIs, Interfaces for other Systems/Products) remain unchanged.

Should only parts of these conditions be fulfilled, we speak of function, data and interface compatibility.

Frequently, with a new release of a product comes an expansion and change of the underlying data model which leads to changes to the data structures. In this case, data compatibility cannot be achieved easily. A separate data migration is required, for which the software vendor should preferably provide in the form of procedures and scripts.

By downward compatibility, it is understood that:

- Data from version n+1 can be transferred to and used with version n without changes.
- Version n+1 can communicate to Version n, i.e. Version n interfaces are supported.

In contrast to the upward compatibility, downward compatibility cannot always be expected or presumed. For example, a document created with MS Word 2007, as a rule, cannot be read using an older version of MS Word and must be converted before being read to the internal format of the older version. The opposite way should not lead to any problems. (Note: in response to customer demand, Microsoft has made available add-ons to some of their old Office products which allow opening the newer file types. From personal experience we can assert, however, that there remain incompatibilities, e.g. Formatting in Excel 2007 vs. Excel 2002).

2.5   Attributes of Software Products

Software products have specific attributes, which classify software in more detail and which help to highlight certain aspects of product management, as different kinds of software products pose different questions and also demand different approaches in product management. Basic description criteria are, for example:

- Market:
  - Consumer (B2C), e.g. games software
  - Business (B2B)
    - Horizontal (i.e. across many industries): e.g. systems software, middleware
    - Vertical (i.e. industry specific): e.g. securities application for brokerage industry
- Functional areas, e.g. systems software, middleware, application
- Development focus, i.e. standard software vs. services vs. individual development
- Conditions:
  - Terms of contract, e.g. open source, freeware, shareware, priced licensing, SaaS
  - Development at a fixed price or a price according to effort

The term "services" has emerged as a new topic as the base of service-oriented software architecture, often in the form of web services. Web services are usually offered via APIs (application programming interfaces) that can be accessed over a network, such as the Internet, and executed on a remote system hosting the software that performs the requested services. The business models and marketing and operation strategies for services are currently still in the experimentation stages, even though the concept has been around for quite a while.

In every software installation, there are three basic types of software products: 1) the operating system, 2) middleware, and 3) applications. The operating system provides a standard base of system facilities (e.g. the ability to read and write to storage) and takes care of interactions with the hardware. The term "middleware" refers to the software that connects software components and sits "in the middle" between the operating system and the applications. It includes web servers, application servers, database systems and transaction monitors. Finally applications are written to perform functions requested by end users, so that they can accomplish useful business or personal tasks with their computers.

An especially important differentiator of products is triggered by market criteria, i.e. the question, is the customer a company (Business-to-Business or B2B) or a consumer, i.e. packaged software products for the mass market, which appeal to individual end users (Business-to-Consumer or B2C). Mostly, this refers to PC or games software.

Of course, there are overlaps between B2B and B2C. The best examples are PC operating systems, security products, and office products. Usually packaging and pricing differ for these target markets. While PC products for the end user market are typically sold at the list price as so-called shrink-wrapped products with all the corresponding media (software on CD, printed documents) or via download on the internet, the same software is offered to a company with a multi-user or enterprise license with just one copy of the media or download rights at an individually negotiated or volume offering price. Furthermore, many vendors, e.g. Microsoft, create variations of their base PC software products by limiting functionality. Thus they can sell it at different price points in the end user market.

There are clear differences between these two product areas. Business software, in comparison to consumer software must be customizable for the specific needs of the company. The expenditure for adaptation and implementation of software products for business customers is typically in the same range as the price paid for the software or may even exceed it. Studies have shown that, for example, firms who employ ERP (Enterprise Resource Planning) software typically spend 30% of the total expenditure on the licensing of the software products and 70% on services for customization and implementation. Some software vendors perform this work for their customers themselves; others predominantly leave such activities to partner companies in the service sector. The advantages and disadvantages of the respective strategies will be more closely looked at in Chapter 4. In connection with this high investment in customization and implementation, the installation of more complex business software products typically lasts for months, while PC users are used to installing a product within a few minutes and immediately using it in a productive manner.

A further difference between business software and consumer software lies in the fact that consumer software is developed and marketed for millions of individual customers, while the number of customers for business software is clearly lower, but with significantly more complex installations on networked systems with a large number of users.

Business software and consumer software require significantly different prioritization of their most important product management tasks (see [HoRoPL00]). For consumer software, the marketing strategy is at the top of the list of priorities, followed by the partner strategy and the question of whether and how quickly a product will be offered on the international market. For business software, the partner strategy has the highest priority, followed by the service strategy, thus the question with which partners or resources the successful implementation of the product can be guaranteed to the customer. The marketing strategy is the next priority for business software, interestingly only in third place.

The influence of these characteristic attributes on software product management will be discussed in detail in Chapter 4.

Chapter 3
Software as a Business

The term "software", first coined in a 1958 article by John W. Tukey from AT&T's Bell Labs ([Tukey58]), has become an integral element of the English language and has been taken over into many other languages. In the beginning of the computer era, the computer was considered as a mere machine. Just like telling a motor to run faster by pressing the gas pedal, the computer was told by instructions what to do. Manufacturers sold the computer as a physical machine; the operating system and rudimentary software were added at no additional cost. Not before the early 60s was software considered as something independent and separate, and entrepreneurs started to see an opportunity for a software products business ([Cusuma04], p. 90).

At a NATO conference in Germany in 1968, the term "software engineering" was coined. It symbolized the decoupling of software programs from the machine which was triggered by several technical developments. In the beginning, the instruction sets were computer-specific, i.e. each processor had its individual assembler language. That is why programs were tied to the respective processor and could not be ported to any other processor. From the late 50s on, the first higher-level programming languages like FORTRAN and ALGOL were created that enabled programming on a more abstract logical level. Compilers which transformed high level source code into different assembler languages were offered for these languages which meant for a programmer that learning the higher-level language enabled him to develop programs for different processors. Porting a program from one processor to another came into reach, even though Java's slogan "Write Once, Run Everywhere" was still considered a vision in the mid-90s. IBM released the /360 processor series in the mid-60s that contained processors at a broad spectrum of performance points that could be programmed with the same assembler language. This development allowed the decoupling of software from the machine, the understanding of software as something independent, separate. Pressed by the US Department of Justice and facing forthcoming anti-trust law suits, IBM announced on June 23, 1969, that it would unbundle hardware and software in the future. This can be seen as the birth date of the software industry as we know it today. Within a few decades, it has developed into a software market with a volume that IDC estimates at 243 billion $ in 2007, and at 327 billion $ in 2010, i.e. a compound annual growth rate (CAGR) of 7.7%. The worldwide market of IT services is estimated by IDC at 486 billion $ in 2007, at 587 billion $ in 2010, i.e. a CAGR of 5.8%.

H.-B. Kittlaus and P.N. Clough, *Software Product Management and Pricing.*
© Springer-Verlag Berlin Heidelberg 2009

3.1   IT Doesn't Matter?

Since Nicholas Carr, then chief editor of the Harvard Business Review, published his infamous article "IT Doesn't Matter" ([Carr03]), there has been a lot of discussion about the contribution of information technology to business in a time when a growing part of the IT market is turning into a commodity market. Is there some truth behind this, or is it all hype?

Over the last 50 years, the world of business in the US and Europe, and increasingly in developing countries, has gone through change at a pace and extent of impact mankind has never experienced before. Over the last 15 years, the pace has increased even further. Most of this change is enabled if not driven by information technology. The fundamental drivers are:

- Moore's Law
  In 1965, Gordon Moore observed that the number of transistors that could be placed on an integrated circuit was doubling every two years. Since the mid-70s it has been doubling every 1.5 years. The same holds for the price/performance of processors. For storage, the price per storage unit has been going down by a factor of 2 per year. These exponential improvements have led to today's situation that people have more processing power and storage capacity in their home PCs than a mainframe computer in a computing center had 30 years ago. Processors and storage are embedded in all kinds of products like cars, cameras, or mobile phones. Due to the resulting shift from analog to digital, some industries have been totally transformed (see below).

- The Internet
  From its beginnings as the military communications network ARPAnet in the US in the late 60s, the internet has turned into the world's premier communications infrastructure that is used by hundreds of millions of people all over the world. It enables them to communicate via email. Since the introduction of HTML and the browser in the mid-90s, they have been able to access information at unprecedented ease and speed. The internet has given rise to totally new applications and business models. Examples are search engines like Google, online auctions like eBay, social networks like MySpace and Facebook, internet banking and brokerage, and retail platforms like Amazon.

There is no industry today that is not making extensive use of IT. Some industries are more fundamentally influenced and changed due to IT and in particular software than others:

- Banking and financial services
  The worldwide financial markets are totally dependent on IT, in terms of both size and speed. Prices and returns of many innovative financial products can only be calculated with the help of IT. In fact, some players in the industry consider themselves more as IT companies than banks.

- Music
  When the music industry switched from LP to CD, i.e. from analog to digital, in the early 80s, they did not foresee the consequences. In the digital domain, a copy is identical to the original whereas in the analog domain it is not. With the proliferation of PCs and the internet, making digital copies and distributing them has become as easy as a mouse click. The music industry has been helplessly watching its own decline. The pinnacle of humiliation was the success of Apple, an IT company, with iTunes, the music download platform that demonstrated how to be successful with music in the digital domain.

Given this significant impact of IT on the world of business and our lives in general, why is it that the seemingly ridiculous statement "IT Doesn't Matter" by Nicholas Carr ([Carr03]) keeps getting so much attention? At the core of the discussion is the question of whether IT continues to have significant impact on the competitiveness of enterprises, or if IT is becoming a commodity that is no more a differentiating factor in the market than electric power. Carr holds the latter position.

We think this discussion is misleading. The competitiveness of a company is certainly not influenced by replacing the old 15" tube screen of the receptionist by a super flat 21" screen. What does have an impact on competitiveness are the effectiveness and efficiency of the business processes of the company, the abilities of the employees and the design of the customer interface. It is a basic element of our economic system that these factors have been, are, and will be enabling differentiation in the market. So investments in IT that support these factors will be highly relevant for competitiveness in the future. Well known current examples of companies which are differentiating themselves in the market in exactly this way are Amazon, iTunes, and Dell whose success is primarily based on innovative processes and customer interfaces that could only be implemented with IT. Commodity products can be part of those solutions, but generally they alone will not result in competitive advantage. Of course, when commoditization leads to lower prices for both hardware and software and thereby higher performance per $, then innovative offerings become financially feasible that were not feasible before. Our view is supported by the results of Erik Brynjolfsson, Professor of the MIT Sloan School of Management ([Brynjo03]) who analyzed more than 1000 American companies and found a significant correlation between the intensity of IT usage and productivity. He stated: "Our statistical analysis found that IT is embedded in a "cluster" of related innovations, notably organizational changes outside the IT department. This cluster, which we call the digital organization, includes:

- Automation of numerous routine tasks.
- Highly skilled labor.
- More decentralized decision making.
- Improved information flow vertically and laterally.
- Strong performance-based incentives.
- Increased emphasis on training and recruitment.

On average, companies that successfully combine these elements produce more valuable output than competitors and achieve high levels of productivity. They also tend to have higher employee and customer satisfaction."

These findings do not irritate Carr. In his book "The Big Switch" ([Carr08]), he claims that the upcoming cloud computing will make corporate IT organizations obsolete and will lead to their disappearance. The term "cloud computing" came up in 2007 and is not yet too clearly defined. For this book, we will use the following definition:

Cloud Computing = An IT service provision model by which IT infrastructure is provided based on an architecture that ensures a high level of scalability and reliability, and accessed through the internet.

Cloud computing can be used for both data and applications which can be both software products offered by software vendors or company-specific applications. Early examples for these types of offers are Amazon's S3 (Simple Storage Service) and EC2 (Elastic Compute Cloud). Gartner predicts that by 2011, early technology adopters will purchase 40% of their IT infrastructures as a service ([Gartner08]). We agree with Carr that cloud computing can become the next step in the commoditization of IT products and offerings, but we do not agree with his conclusion. Corporate IT organizations that succeed in creating business value by focussing on their contributions to business processes and reducing cost by creatively integrating commodity products and offerings in their solution portfolios have an excellent chance to improve their position within the corporation.

Notice that cloud computing is not identical to the business model of Software as a Service (SaaS) since this is restricted to multi-customer software products. We define:

Software as a Service (SaaS) = business and delivery model that allows customers to use software over the internet without having to install it on their own computers.

A well known SaaS provider is Salesforce.com with its CRM application. Search engines like Google could also be interpreted as SaaS. This model means that the vendor does not sell a license to the customer, but a service. The vendor will install and run the software in his own or a subcontracted computing center and take care of the installation of any updates. The customer gets the right to access the software via the internet and use it according to its contractual terms which will have the character of a Service Level Agreement (SLA) (see section 4.6.6). The customer's data is typically stored on the vendor's system. SaaS, in combination with cloud computing, promises unprecedented levels of scalability for customers without any significant investments in their own infrastructure or operations. This may seem very appealing; however, TINSTAFFL ("there is no such thing as a free lunch") still applies. SaaS providers' real cost savings will be confined to the savings available from centralized management and infrastructure, which is what they will be able to pass on to their customers. Those savings may not be far in excess of those available from outsourcers today.

From a customer perspective, SaaS has several advantages:

- The customer does not have to deal with the operations aspects like installation, maintenance, data storage and backup etc.
- The software is automatically on the latest release level (which is hopefully compatible with the previous release level).
- The customer usually perceives the new pricing models as advantageous compared to the traditional license model.

The disadvantages are:

- The data is stored under the control of the vendor, so the customer needs to have sufficient trust in the vendor.
- The availability of the service is dependent on the availability of the internet which is typically neither controlled by the vendor nor the customer.

SaaS is a bit different from the ASP model (Application Service Provider) that came up in the 90s, but never gained significant momentum in the market. ASPs typically did not use the internet, but instead leased communication lines. The applications were usually customer-specific whereas SaaS offers standard software in a multi-user mode that the individual customer can only customize to a limited extent. The trend towards SaaS was predicted by [RusKan03] as early as 2003 when the authors still called it e-service. A summary on the current status of cloud computing and SaaS is provided in [Hayes08]. Given the advances in scalability and price/performance of grid computing and the low cost connection over the internet, SaaS's chances for success in some application areas are quite good if customers overcome their fear of allowing an external provider to access and control their business-critical data. Currently, a lot of software vendors are still in an experimentation phase to find out how to best design SaaS offerings. There are certainly limits in granularity and the number of different services that are combined into one application which are due to performance and reliability requirements. Trust in the vendors, both in terms of quality of the software, and reliability and longevity of the service. Amazon Web Services (AWS) demonstrate what is already possible. Gartner predicts that by 2012, at least one-third of business application software spending will be as service subscription instead of as product license ([Gartner08]).

In summary, we are convinced that IT and software in particular have, do and will continue to matter in spite of a constantly changing environment and an increasing market share of commodity products and services.

3.2 Specific Business Aspects of Software

A characterizing element of enterprise software products is that the fixed cost of development is almost the entire cost of production. The variable cost (like the cost of shipment media or paper documentation) for the single product instance is negligible. Only for low-price consumer software products like PC games or tools these cost need to be considered since they contribute a higher share of the total cost. In addition to this cost of production, there is the ongoing cost of maintenance that can be quite significant, but is often charged for separately.

In general the financial characteristics of software products are diametrically opposed to those of professional services that require low upfront investment, but high revenue-dependent variable cost. Of course, once a services team is hired the personnel costs can be considered as fixed unless one can immediately lay off when there is not work to keep the employees busy and rehire the same skill pool when there is more work. Software products are also different to typical investment or consumer goods whose variable production cost represents the dominant share of the total product cost. In contrast to professional services, the production cost per piece of produced goods can be significantly decreased by "economies of scale" effects with higher production volumes.

Given that for software products almost the total product cost are fixed cost, reaching a certain minimum revenue or minimum number of licenses is mandatory in order to reach the break-even point. In other words, there is no other product than software for which any additional dollar of revenue beyond the break-even point is almost pure profit. This means that there is a high incentive – or necessity – for software companies to offer their products internationally to increase volumes provided that the products address more than country-specific requirements of a national market. It usually requires that user interfaces and documentation are translated into the respective languages. The software market in general is international though there are some successful vendors for regional software solutions. This international orientation is an important element of the job of a product manager in software companies.

Compared to traditional industries that develop and produce physical goods, a software company needs relatively little capital and investments initially and over time. For software development "only" good know-how and a few PCs are required, and manufacturing basically means duplication of media and printing of brochures and hand books, or not even that in case of internet distribution. In reality, even in the software industry it can be a bit more complicated, but the famous garage start-ups are not just myth. Anyone can start a software company – but not necessarily make it succeed. As is true for all startups, the secret of success is good know-how and professional management, with the difficult transition of company leaders from entrepreneurs to businessmen.

This low capital investment means low market entry barriers. Somewhere in this world, new software companies are founded daily – and die daily. The significant asset of software companies – human know-how – is in the brains of the employees, i.e. highly mobile. The resulting high speed of innovation and adoption lowers the technical entry barriers, i.e. the software market is characterized by low market entry barriers and extremely high competition and fluctuation compared to other industries.

Nothing is a manufacturer of goods more afraid of than commoditization, i.e. the ability of his customers easily to replace his products with those of his competitors. The end user is not faced with big functional or economic barriers if he wants to change e.g. the brand of his car. Therefore manufacturers of commodity products invest heavily in brand and image marketing, as well as bells and whistles which attempt to differentiate the product or make it to some degree proprietary (though the latter may backfire). In the IT industry, the hardware manufacturers are in constant competition. With software, it is different. It requires considerably more effort and there is significant risk involved in switching from an installed software product to a competitive product than for any other element of the IT infrastructure. This statement is not only valid for enterprise software, but also increasingly for software on stand-alone PCs. The main reason is that software is never used in an isolated way, but always an integral part of the complete software landscape in a company including self-developed applications. Unless there is major improvement in a replacement product visible to the end user, the IT professional will correctly conclude that if he makes a decision to replace a working product, he will receive zero credit if he succeeds (no visible benefit) and the wrath of all his end users if the product fails. Another aspect is the high level of company-specific customization. The degree of interdependence of a product with the other components of the software landscape is extremely high and very often not properly documented. That is why software once installed and used is very difficult to replace. It also means that ongoing product development, maintenance of older releases, and compatibility of new to old releases and versions have high importance and are key success factors for software product management. We define:

Maintenance = product fixes, often including new releases

Support = help in getting the product to do what its specification says it is supposed to do.

Upgrade protection = similar to maintenance but sometimes offered discretely from maintenance, it offers only the right to upgrade to the next release(s); the number of upgrades may be limited.

Subscription = generally used to describe an offering which combines maintenance, support, and upgrade protection.

We will come back to these terms when we discuss their pricing in chapter 5.

3.3 The Financial Life-Cycle of a Software Product

As we just discussed, the start-up capital requirements for a software company are modest compared with those of a manufacturing company, for example. If one has a good idea, perhaps the beginnings of a demo or prototype, venture capital can be found which is sufficient to begin. Just as in almost any startup, there will be a great deal of expenditure before the first dollar of revenue is earned. Software is unique in that most of the capital outlay occurs during this period; from then on, excepting major enhancements, it's largely small variable cost and high marginal profit. Once sales begin, there will be pressure to show profits, certainly pressure to show dramatic year on year increases in revenues. In a periodic charge model with recurring charges there is no acceleration of revenue through initial sales, i.e. revenue is earned as the product is used over time rather than up front with the sale of an OTC perpetual license. Like someone who owns an apartment building and rents out the apartments, a software company with attractive products who licenses them using recurring charges may make a great deal of money in the long term, but that is not the way to show the most dramatic financial growth as one might want to do in a start-up, particularly if one were contemplating an IPO. This may influence the company to offer their licenses on a one time charge basis, relying on maintenance charges to provide a recurring stream of revenue following the initial sale.

As the product becomes established, the objective shifts to wanting to maintain price and preserve revenue stream with less regard for quick growth. Achieving this requires clarity of strategy, strength of will, and discipline in terms of discounting, periodic enhancements, continued marketing to increase share. As we said in the previous section, there is no fear so great as that of commoditization during this phase. Most software businesses will need the cash being generated by their successful products to finance the development of enhancements and new products, as well as potentially the acquisition of companies with interesting and innovative products. So the objective in the medium term is often to prolong product life as much as possible with modest expenditures to maximize profits, yet retain market leadership. As companies grow larger, they often choose to grow by acquisition, particularly if they have cash. One can see this clearly with IBM software, CA, Oracle, and others. IBM has been acquiring software companies at an average rate of a bit more than one per month for several years. Charlie Peters, chief financial officer of Red Hat Software, is quoted as saying "In many cases, it is easier to do an acquisition than to try to start something Greenfield" [Baseline07].

Eventually most products move into a sunset phase, replaced (hopefully) by a new product in the vendor's portfolio or perhaps by a competitor. However, for a variety of reasons covered in this chapter, once installed, a product may be devilishly difficult to replace if it is tightly integrated into a company's infrastructure. For these reasons, it behooves the vendor to provide an easy, effective, and financially attractive migration to his own replacement product. If the migration to the vendor's follow-on product is difficult or expensive, that will invite the customer to consider competitive alternatives. Failing a migration to his own product, the vendor is well advised to ensure that he is receiving a recurring revenue stream for the continued use of his now end-of-life product. This argues *against* conversion from recurring charges to one time charge, *against* paid up licenses or maintenance. Once someone has a perpetual license it is even harder to get them to migrate to a new product. Some IBM S/34 recurring charge software products continued to earn substantial revenue more than 10 years after they were withdrawn from marketing!

One final point before we move on: often it will be alleged that cost of maintenance of an old product is prohibitive for the vendor, that he cannot afford to tie up resources on old products, etc. We have never in our experience found a case where this was borne out by the facts. Usually, the truth is that almost no resource is devoted to the old product and that most bugs which are going to be found have been found by the time a product is withdrawn from marketing. Where a new bug is discovered, it often exists in the new version of the same product as well and fixing it in one place develops the basic fix for both. Legitimate counter-arguments may exist if the new version code base is entirely different, if the user population using the old version is so small that very little revenue is being generated by it, or if regression testing of the old version is very complex and therefore costly. For cases where a recurring charge is being paid for the license or where maintenance charges continue to be paid, the real cost of maintenance is usually a trivial amount compared to the revenues.

We will amplify on the subject of software pricing and financials in chapter 5.

3.4 The Software Ecosystem

Over the last ten years the term "software ecosystem" has found increasing usage. It is derived from biological ecosystems. The analogy expresses the interdependence of the players in business networks and was first drawn by James F. Moore in 1993 ([Moore93]). We define

Software Ecosystem = Informal network of (legally independent) units that have a positive influence on the economic success of a software product and benefit from it.

A most comprehensive discussion of business ecosystems can be found in [IanLev04]. Iansiti and Levien define three principle roles participants in a business ecosystem can play:

- Keystone
  A benevolent hub in the network that provides benefits to the ecosystem and its members. It usually takes a relatively small space in the network and reliably leaves sufficient room for the other members. The resulting distributed nature of the network makes it more flexible and less vulnerable to external disruptions. Examples are Sun, IBM, or eBay.

- Dominator
  A hub that aims at controlling as much space in the network as possible. It is not interested in sharing value, but tries to capture most of the value itself. An example is Apple.

- Niche players
  Most members of an ecosystem are niche players who do not try to compete with a keystone or dominator, but contribute to the ecosystem by covering a specialized area within it in a competent and reliable way. They operate as pilot fish to the shark, so to speak.

It is usually not part of the responsibilities of a software product manager to decide on the role his company wants to play in an ecosystem. This belongs into the realm of corporate strategy that is owned by executive management. However, once these decisions are made, they have significant impact on the work of the product manager, and he must conform to the role his company wishes to play in its ecosystem(s).

The software ecosystem not only consists of the sales-oriented partnerships described below, but also of more informal networks that emerge around important themes of the software industry, like leading products, system platforms or new technology trends. Examples are operating system platforms like Windows, Linux or zOS, development environments like Java or application software like SAP. Such themes are typically initiated by the corresponding vendors who act as keystones of the networks. Other market participants jump on the bandwagon and not only strengthen the trend, but also contribute to it. The participants of such an ecosystem can be partners with similar interests and competitors at the same time, it can be journalists, consultants, market research companies or specialized IT employees. An example is Java that competitors like SUN, IBM and BEA (now acquired by Oracle) add to. Once it has reached a certain degree of momentum that cannot be defined in absolute terms, a theme is established in the market and will not disappear quickly anymore. This is an emergent effect similar to a snowball system. The more market participants take up the theme and position their products and services in relation to it, the more it becomes a *de facto* standard. This can lead to the extremes of market dominance or monopoly. The best known example is Microsoft and the Windows operating system. Those trends can certainly be stopped or reversed. For example, the OS/2 operating system had been established in the market by IBM, but could not survive due to Microsoft's marketing power. Themes are not necessarily tied to their initiators, but can be hi-jacked by a competitor. An example is the company Visi-Calc that had developed and established Spreadsheet, but was pushed aside by Lotus 1-2-3 before Microsoft took over the market with Excel.

For software more than for other products, a well-oiled network machine of diverse partners is a significant prerequisite for long-term success in addition to the traditional direct sales channels. For a software company, there are several good reasons for establishing and managing a partner network as part of a software eco-system. Partners are needed in order to reach customers that could not be reached fast enough or at all with a direct sales force. To build up a sales organization is time and cost-intensive and requires significant revenue per person. A sales partner may be able to cover a sales area more easily and efficiently by combining products of several software companies and his own products and services. Moreover, many sales partners are already established in the market with customer contacts as value added resellers (VARs) or system integrators.

Customers of business software are usually not interested in a particular software product, but in a solution for their business problems and an implementation of their business processes as efficiently as possible. Because of the complexity and interdependence of business software, the desired solution is typically not achieved by a single software product and requires significant customizing and implementa-tion effort. Customers frequently rely on qualified consulting and service compa-nies that are contracted for the implementation and very often also for conception and design of the solution. This gives these companies a strong influence on the selection of software products, sometimes the decision is part of the contracted task. That is why partnering with these consulting companies can be more impor-tant for a software vendor than direct sales. This is valid for application software and especially for infrastructure software products.

In many cases, the decision for a certain software technology or a software prod-uct is not made by the customer, but by the vendor of an application software solu-tion who decides for a base technology, or by the system integrator who favors a technology or product and uses it as an integral part of his offer.

Last but not least, vendors whose products are not competitive, but cooperative, form technology alliances. These alliances have the purpose to bundle sales resources. This can happen as sales cooperation, or by preinstalling software prod-ucts on the hardware platform of another manufacturer. The advantage of preinstal-lation for the hardware manufacturer is that the additional software products make his product more attractive. The advantage for the software vendor is that this chan-nel allows easy access to many end users that would otherwise fail to be addressed in the usual sales process. In view of the high sales volume, the purchase commit-ment, the negligible amount of time and effort invested in sales and distribution, and perhaps even the money saved on media and documentation, the software ven-dor will offer to sell his software on very favorable conditions. Technology alli-ances also aim at offering integrated solutions that the market requires by combining products and services of several partners so that the customer can assume a proven level of integration. Often partners want to benefit from the image, the brand or the market position of other partners.

Roughly, we find the following categories of partners for software vendors:

- VADs (Value added distributors): for outsourcing of production and distribution activities, often for enrichment of products with solution components, for man-agement of smaller partners and a better market penetration.
- VARs (Value added resellers): as extended sales channel, for better market pen-etration, and sometimes for enrichment of products with solution components.
- ISVs (Independent software vendors): vendors of application software whose solutions are based on or favor a vendor's own products. ISVs play a special role as a sales and distribution channel insofar as they frequently install the other vendor's software in their own products and encapsulate the interfaces. This may make the software invisible and no longer capable of being used separately, or else the right to use is contractually limited to the ISV's solution. Therefore ISVs often take care of level 1 and level 2 support (see section 4.11).
- OEMs (original equipment manufacturers): manufacturers of branded products of their own who imbed vendor code into their product without vendor branding.

- SIs (System integrators): service companies that add solution components and take over the customer-specific installation and customizing up to the overall project responsibility.
- Technological alliances: as sales cooperation, for preinstallation, for completeness of solution offers and synergy in marketing.

An individual partner can often exist in more than one of these categories. In the end all partnering activities have one goal: faster growth and market leadership. A balance between growth and profitability needs to be found: The software vendor gives some part of the revenue and/or profit to its partners in order to grow faster and reach a leading position in the market. In order to do that, a software vendor establishes dedicated partner programs that specify:

- The prerequisites that a partner must fulfill for participation,
- What the software vendor contributes to the partnership,
- If a reseller arrangement, the differential between suggested retail price and selling price to the reseller so he may estimate his selling margin,
- If an agency arrangement, the fee or percentage of revenue the agent will receive and what activities are expected of him in return.
- When the partner gets a finder's fee for incremental revenues when the software vendor sells directly to the customer,
- What the rules are for joint marketing activities.

In order to manage its partner network, a software vendor usually has a partner management organization in parallel to its direct sales organization. We will come back to the options a corporation has to provide incentives and management across a spectrum of channels in support of the sales and marketing strategy and their pros and cons in chapters 4 and 5. Whatever the role of a company is with regard to software ecosystems, software product managers are well advised to participate in, contribute to and try to influence the ecosystems important for their products.

3.5   Law of Increasing Returns

As pointed out in [HoRoPL00], the software industry is governed by the law of increasing returns that was first described by the economist Brian Arthur ([Arthur96]).

This law says that a software product with a high market share will experience a further improvement of its market position just because of this high market share whereas a low market share leads to a further decrease. In other words, trends in market share intensify themselves. There are three main reasons for this phenomenon:

- The network effect:

  The network effect was described by Katz and Shapiro in [KatSha85]: "The utility that a given user derives from the good depends on the number of other users who are in the same network as he or she." There are direct effects like standardization of interfaces that allow users of the same software product to exchange data and user experience more easily – they speak the same language. With users in different companies this leads to a trend towards standardization of software products across companies. Indirect effects come from complementary products and services whose number increases when the base product is used by more customers (see [BuDiHe08], p. 21).

- Increasing cost of switching:

  The longer a user or a company has a certain software product in use (e.g. text processing software), the more effort a switch to a different product takes – because the data created with one program cannot necessarily be digested by the other program, and because the switch usually means significant education effort.

- Trust in the market leader:

  Consumers as well as big companies tend to rely on established brands and leading products. This gives investment security that the chosen product will not disappear from the market the next day. The market leading position is interpreted as a quality seal since a high percentage of customers has already decided for the product. The standardization of interfaces and data is also relevant in this context.

The influence of the law of increasing returns on the market position of a product and the importance of market share for software products is different dependent on the level of maturity of the market in which competition takes place. In an early technology phase there are typically a large number of young products with similar functionality and the customers are in an orientation phase. The first products are tested; some early adopters make product decisions and invest in installations. In this phase there is no market leader, but trends and camps emerge. The power and prestige of the respective camps will usually determine the market leader of the future. During the growth phase of a product market, two or at most three dominating products and vendors can be identified very quickly, i.e. within 12 to 18 months. In the maturity phase one can observe all three of the effects described above. This leads to consolidation and disappearance of the smaller vendors, and often a concentration on two or only one dominating product.

Because of this law, market leadership is more important for software products than for most other products. Of course, market leadership is an important competitive advantage for most products, be it for cost efficiency through economies of scale, be it as a marketing argument. But nowhere is market leadership so important for the future of a company in a market as in the software industry. That is why short term the goal of market leadership has priority against other company goals like revenue or profitability.

One note of caution on the law of increasing returns and the network effect in particular: it is insufficient in and of itself. If you reflect on times when Lotus dominated the spreadsheet market with "1-2-3," Netscape had a majority share of the browser market, or WordStar dominated the text editing market, it is easy to find example after example where a new technology emerged, a competitive bundle (often Microsoft bundling or selling with Windows) that broke the domination even though the market was mature and the product well established. This argues that, despite network effect, a vendor must be vigilant, particularly as new technologies are introduced (e.g. wysiwyg – what you see is what you get – substituting for markup language or PC software products available to replace dedicated hardware and software from companies like Wang). The best strategy appears to be continuous evolution and improvement and never resting on your laurels; an example might be Adobe's PDF or Photoshop, although Adobe's high price strategy creates a price umbrella for others to come in under and compete with compatible or similar products, which is happening today.

New software technologies develop and drive new markets for software products. These markets show fast, often drastic growth, during which a high number of competitors boil down into a few winners and lots of losers. Software technologies and their markets can be compared to layers of an onion. New layers are created continuously, and the old ones dry out and die. The art of running a software company is to leave the drying outer peels in time and jump onto a juicy inner peel, a new market in which there is a new fight for market leadership.

3.6   Business Models for Software Vendors

Software product management has been common practice for software vendors longer than for corporate IT organizations, but this does not mean that all software vendors manage their products explicitly. Often start-up companies are founded with the intention to go to market as software vendors, but lack the capital needed to develop the first release. If venture capital or bank credits are not available, an alternative is driving development through customer-specific projects that the customer pays for. Customers can often be found on the basis of sufficiently attractive prototypes. Experience suggests the following rule of thumb: the relation of the effort for a prototype versus a commercially usable piece of software is 1:3, of commercially usable software versus a software product that can be used by a higher number of customers again 1:3. An interested customer may be willing to pay for the way from the prototype to the commercially usable product that meets his specific requirements, but will be most watchful that his money is not "misused" for the way to the generally usable software product. That is why this approach does not succeed in most cases, and usually leads to separate code bases for each customer and not to a generally usable product. As long as further development and maintenance of these code bases is paid for by the respective customers according to effort, the model can work. But it is the business model of a service company, not of a software vendor. When company and customers switch to the software vendor model, the customers only pay standard maintenance fees that would be sufficient for maintaining a common product code base, but not separate customer-specific code bases. This approach frequently results in economic problems and customer dissatisfaction.

An example for this approach is NSE Software AG, a German company that developed front end software for sales in the finance industry. After the company had won a number of bigger customers in the 80s and 90s, it faced the flip side of the coin in the late 90s. A lot of solutions had been built that were totally customer-specific in terms of both the integration of mainframe legacy applications and the design of the front ends. The company experienced a life threatening situation and was finally taken over by Brainforce.

What can we conclude from this? The executive management of a company must be clear in what the company is supposed to be, i.e. which business model it intends to follow. Michael Cusumano, professor at MIT Sloan School of Management, writes in [Cusuma03]: "Regardless of the balance of products and services they choose, managers of software companies must understand what their primary business is, and recognize how the two differ—for selling products requires very different organizational capabilities than selling (professional) services." If a company is supposed to be a software vendor, the business model assumes standard software products that are suitable for a higher number of customers. Sales of these software products can be combined with product-related services that can be priced based on actual effort, or as a package with the software license, or as a subscription as is customary for product maintenance. Says Cusumano [Cusuma03]: "A general rule of thumb is that, over the lifetime of using a software product, enterprise customers pay between one and two dollars in service and maintenance fees per dollar of software license fees (the up-front product cost)." In particular when the economy is bad and product sales are down, the importance of this income for the survival of a software vendor becomes obvious. That is why maintenance fees and even more so the pricing model of Monthly License Charge (MLC) for mainframe software where there is no large up-front payment, but smaller monthly payments, have been a pleasant pillar for IBM for a long time since it results in a more balanced, smoother revenue stream (see chapter 5). The stock market deplores nothing so much as unpredictable earnings.

If a customer requires functions that are not part of the product, a decision has to be made if these requirements are implemented in the standard product, or if they are implemented as an individual paid service. In the first case, all customers will benefit from the additional functions, in the second case the functions do not become part of the standard product. Of course, customer situations are not always black-and-white; but basically these are the alternatives if the consistency of the standard product is to be maintained.

If there is an established development organization, usually it will retain product ownership of what it develops (unless so specialized for a single client as to be unmarketable elsewhere), i.e. the software product is owned by a company that develops and sells it, and this company formally owns the rights to the code. For bigger projects, this development team can be spread over different locations in different countries, and parts of development can be outsourced, but there is always a central project management and controlling. With the emergence of open-source-software like the Linux operating system an alternative to this paradigm has proven its feasibility. A growing community of developers contributes in a self-managed and parallel way to the development of a complex system that has gone through the metamorphosis from a cult object to a *de facto* industry standard. Through the internet, the Linux code is available to everybody at no cost whereas the packages of Linux distributors that add installation and implementation tools and documentation to the code have a price tag.

Given the success of the open-source-movement with software like Linux, Apache, the middleware JBOSS or the MySQL database, there is some speculation that over time all software may be free of charge. We think this extrapolation is misleading. If you look at the history of open source that started with free source-code-licenses for the UNIX operating system, motivations can be observed that are clearly rooted in specific characteristics of the programmer community of nerdy technocrats. There is a strong anarchic element that favors the elegance and beauty of a technical solution versus any economical considerations and tends to rebel against restrictions that companies put upon their employees or that the economic system puts on its market participants. A key factor of the open-source-community has always been resistance against companies dominating the market, in former times IBM, then Microsoft. In the community, recognition by peers, i.e. other acknowledged specialists, is more important than economic success, though many of these programmers use the recognition for getting well-paid jobs (see [LerTir05]). The movement is characterized by the contradiction between the economic interest of the individual whose work as programmer has to pay the bills and the anti-economic attitude of the community. Since this community consists exclusively of "techies", i.e. technically oriented programmers, it does not surprise that the primary focus has been on infrastructure software, i.e. operating systems and middleware. In recent years, there have been an increasing number of application-oriented open source projects, but none has reached market share comparable to the open source flagships like Linux or Apache. Applications can only be developed in cooperation with specialists from the application domain who typically do not share the anti-economic attitude of the open-source-community. Of course, commercial software can make use of open source code. Gartner predicts that by 2012, 80% or more of all commercial software will include elements of open-source technology ([Gartner08]).

Once a piece of open-source software has gained a certain market share, it becomes interesting for commercial software companies. Based on the open-source-code, software products can be sold with packaging and product-related services justifying the price tag. Examples are companies like Red Hat or Suse (acquired by Novell) in the Linux area. Established vendors have also embraced open source. Examples are Sun's acquisition of MySQL, or IBM that has jumped on the Linux bandwagon. What is the motivation behind this? The effort of a software company for the continuous development of a complex software product like an operating system is enormous. For this to make sense bottom-line, either the prices have to be high – an example is IBM's DB2 for z/OS – or the volume has to be high – as for Microsoft's Windows. If there is an operating system on the market that offers comparable function and quality at almost no cost, customers will be less and less willing to pay for a commercial product. This is what Microsoft has been experiencing in the public sector. There have been several reasons for IBM to embrace Linux:

- Destabilization of the Microsoft business model,
- Destabilization of the SUN business model that is based on Sun's UNIX derivative Solaris,
- Opening the door to the increasing number of applications based on Linux to run on zSeries hardware, after IBM had had the problem for many years that application software providers were not willing to develop their applications for the mainframe,
- Improvement of the company's image as an "open" vendor,
- As a way of offering an essentially "free" operating system on z systems without impacting existing mainframe software revenues,
- As a way of permitting distributed UNIX server consolidation on z hardware,
- Cost savings through participation in the new type of division of work in the open-source-community with the vendor taking responsibility for making the code run on his platforms in a robust and scalable way while other members of the community take care of functional extensions.

Besides open source, there are a lot of commercial products that do not cost anything or very little. They can usually be downloaded or used on the internet. Close examination shows that this is typically driven by commercial interests and marketing strategies that can differ:

- Freeware = product available at no charge
  Examples are viewer or player products like Adobe's Acrobat Reader and Flash Player or Real Audio's player. In these cases, the software vendor intends to make the usage and exchange of files in "his" format easy and at the same time to create demand for his costly full-function-product that is needed to create the files.
- Shareware = product available at a price, often downloadable from multiple sites, requires payment of a fee for continued use.
- Trialware = product available either from web download or sometimes media (CD or DVD) which offers a trial period after which it requires payment of a fee for continued use.
  Demo versions often have restrictions in functionality or capacity and/or become unusable after the trial period. This type of software does have the character of products, is part of a product family and is managed by the respective product management organization. Plans are needed in advance which functions are to be made available how long since this has to be implemented by Development.
- Upgradeware = product where a base version is made available at no charge but where the user is encouraged to upgrade to obtain additional function. The trial

versions range from full function products, where the upgrades offer additional
bells and whistles, to limited (or no) function programs that simply tell you what
they would do if they were fully functional.
- SaaS offerings financed through advertising
Examples are search engines like Google or Yahoo and Google Apps, the office
and collaboration suite that Google has launched. Google Apps can be seen as
Google's attempt to transfer its extremely successful search business model that
is based on advertising revenues to software market segments whose business
models have traditionally been based on license fees. Obviously, Microsoft considers this as a severe threat to its business model, and Microsoft's bid to acquire
Yahoo has to be seen as an attempt to buy a platform for this ad-based business
model. We will discuss the financial side of this model from a vendor perspective
in more detail in chapter 5. From a customer perspective, this offering is free with
regard to money, but there is a price to be paid in terms of being exposed to ads.

Both open source and SaaS offerings providing revenue through the support of paid
advertisements are examples of wikinomics at work. The term "wikinomics" was
coined by Don Tapscott and described in his book of the same name ([TapWil06]).
It stands for the emergence of new business models that are based on the network
effect enabled by the internet. We can expect to see more innovative business models over time in this context, in particular in connection with social and business
communities on the net, some of which will definitely impact software vendors.

As an alternative to the model of a software vendor, a company can follow the
business model of a professional service company. This means that the development of software is paid for, either based on effort or at a fixed price. The focus is
not on a software product, but on the employees who deliver the service. The goal
is to implement an application according to the requirements of the customer. It is
typically not designed for a broad and flexible spectrum of usage scenarios. The
cultural differences between software and service companies typically lead to failure whenever a service company tries to turn a piece of software into a standard
product that had been developed based on a service contract. One of the few counter
examples is the CAD software CATIA developed by Dassault in France that
became a very successful software product.

Cusumano lists basic questions that the executive management of a software
company needs to answer ([Cusuma04], p. 24):

- "Do you want to be mainly a products company or a (professional) services
company?
- Do you want to sell to individuals or enterprises, or to mass or niche markets?
- How horizontal (broad) or vertical (specialized) is your product or service?
- Can you generate a recurring revenue stream to endure in good times and
bad?"

In case of a software product company, the answers to these questions are a foundation for the work of a software product manager.

3.7 The Business Considerations for Corporate IT Organizations

Corporate IT organizations have traditionally not had the view that they developed, marketed and sold software products. Typically they saw themselves as the master and caretaker of an IT system that consisted of hardware and an application landscape that was difficult to comprehend and manage and most often not thoroughly documented. Where and when a new function was implemented was often more a case of arbitrary organizational responsibilities and informal relationships than of a forward-looking planning of individual applications or the complete landscape. This was typically accompanied by severe communication problems between IT and the business units. The increasing dissatisfaction of the internal contract givers with the price/performance of IT – whether justified or not – has led to initiatives over the last 20 years that have aimed at making the IT organizations more manageable. One area has been controlling where the former dissatisfying fixed cost allocation was replaced by a more cause-oriented cost allocation, often transaction-based. In addition there have been experiments to destroy the former monopoly of the IT organization by introducing competition. In some companies the business units were allowed to order hardware and software without coordinating with the IT organization. This succeeded in weakening the IT organization, but unfortunately it also weakened the whole company because the inexperience of the business units was taken advantage of by the vendors more often than not. This resulted in an unmanageable collection of badly integrated islands with increasing data redundancy and risk of data loss. The idea of introducing competition was also the main corporate motivator for outsourcing IT organizations into independent companies that were still fully owned by the parent corporation. The unfortunate executives of these companies were expected to achieve the square of the circle, i.e. stronger customer orientation, lower cost and new business as a service provider on the open market at the same time. It has hardly ever worked. Customer focus suffered because established communication paths were disrupted by the new organizational and often physical separation. The cost structures could only be improved long term. In Europe, the work councils made sure that short term no employee suffered due to the outsourcing. In the US, social pressures and potential loss of government incentives often had similar effects. And the new business did not materialize because selling on the open market was foreign to the company's culture and not realistic as any potential customer knew that he would always have second priority versus the parent corporation. Another issue was the lack of focus of the outsourcer on his client and in the welfare of the client's business. One can see this clearly in the press accounts of the relationship between EDS and GM.

The current trend is external outsourcing to big IT service providers that often take over a large number of employees, but put them under their own outsourcing management and new processes. Outsourcing a data center can really lead to significant cost savings if the vendor passes on the cost savings realized by consolidation.

For software development this is rare. Even if the service provider can do the development process more efficiently and at lower cost this is countered by its profit orientation and a very formal requirements management process that is usually not productive for cooperation and speed of reaction. Only if additional customers for the application landscape can be won significant cost advantages can be enjoyed. Successful examples are joint IT service providers of major German banking groups that provide services to a higher number of banking institutions, or service companies like First Data in the US that achieve significant economies of scale.

Some business executives in large corporations undoubtedly hope that Nicholas Carr's claim that cloud computing may eventually lead to the disappearance of corporate IT organizations (see above) comes true. But this is wishful thinking and might even be counterproductive. We have already discussed how dedicated, specialized IT can sometimes provide a competitive advantage. So far, all attempts to make internal IT more manageable have led to very mixed results. There is one positive outcome: The executives of the IT organizations – whether outsourced or not – have gained a much stronger entrepreneurial view of their organizations. Business units are considered more as customers than as solicitors. The willingness to understand and manage the offerings as products and services has increased. This has made these IT organizations and software vendors more similar so that software product management has started to be accepted as a useful concept by the corporate IT organizations as well. The core elements that are discussed in chapter 4 are basically the same for software vendors and corporate IT organizations, only the priorities may differ which will be covered in chapter 6.

3.8   The Changing Relationship between Software Product Management and Software Pricing

Software vendors are often organized so that Software Pricing is an independent organizational unit separated from Software Product Management, Marketing, or Sales. Often it is part of the Finance organization. The reasons for this separation stem from the objectives of Software Pricing that are in inherent conflict with or at least have different objectives from the other units, and that we will discuss in chapter 5. It has always been advisable for software product managers to stay in continuous contact with Software Pricing in order to make sure that there is agreement on the view on the market, business cases, and terms and conditions.

However, in the past decisions on pricing and delivery models usually did not result in significant product requirements. Pricing was – and still is – based on recurring charge, MLC (Monthly License Charge), or initial license fee plus recurring maintenance fee, OTC (One Time Charge). When the pricing models became more sophisticated and tried to incorporate usage or differentiate between, for example, concurrent and registered users, for the first time there were product requirements necessary to implement the measures the price was based on, like number of concurrent users, or percentage of machine capacity used.

When the PC entered the picture in the 80s, there were additional significant requirements due to the new retail delivery model, like foolproof installability and ease-of-use. Over time, additional requirements surfaced: copy protection, time bombs in trial code, the use of product keys, etc. designed to ensure payment for the product. But pricing per se did not change much, i.e. it was basically OTC. With the emergence of the internet in the 90s, these requirements were further refined for the download delivery model plus maintenance over the internet.

Now the emergence of SaaS as a new delivery model plus choice of paid versus ad-financed pricing models mean a revolutionary change. For the first time, there is choice regarding delivery and pricing models that has a fundamental impact on the technical architecture and design of the product. SaaS offerings require multi-client capability and a degree of scalability that a traditional standard software product is not built for. An ad-financed SaaS offering needs to integrate ads in its front-end in a way that allows sufficient monetarization. That means that the decisions regarding this choice cannot be made two weeks before launch date, but have to be made very early before development actually starts. So Software Product Management has to involve Software Pricing much earlier and closer than ever before. We will come back to this need for cooperation in the following chapters. We also see this as a strong argument for combining the topics of software product management and software pricing, as we have done in this book.

For corporate IT organizations pricing is relatively easy as long as it is cost-based. The more a corporate IT organization acts as a profit center, the more its pricing must come closer to the pricing of software vendors. There are even examples of corporate IT organizations whose offerings can be interpreted as predecessors of SaaS. In Germany, there are joint-use IT centers in banking organizations that have provided central mainframe-based IT services to their member banks for decades based on applications that have been multi-client-capable.

With this chapter, we have described the major pillars and trends of the software business. This is the environment in which both software product managers and software pricing managers have to operate. The elements of their work are described in chapters 4 and 5, respectively.

Chapter 4
The Elements of Software Product Management

This chapter describes in detail the tasks that we have designated as pertaining to software product management. These tasks remain the same regardless of whether or not software product management is a separate organizational unit within an organization (see chapter 6). They arise whenever a company or a business unit develops and markets software products (as defined in chapter 2). How the various tasks are weighted will depend on the type of company concerned and on its software products. This is shown in section 6.4 which can also serve as a roadmap to chapter 4 for readers who only want to read the sections directly relevant to them. After discussing the objectives and the role of a software product manager, we will introduce our Software Product Management Framework in section 4.3 that provides the structure for the rest of the chapter.

4.1 Objectives

Although the term business enterprise is applied to various manifestations in our economic system, ranging from non-profit companies for tax write-off purposes to companies whose only purpose it is to keep employees for a limited period of time who are no longer needed by their parent companies, most companies continue to aim at ensuring their long-term existence on the basis of continuous economic success. This means that sustainability should be a corporate management objective, even if investors have been demanding ever more short-term success in the past 20 years. Sustainability should be included in the corporate vision statement and strategy (see section 4.6.1) and become part of a lasting business model. For instance, an IT consulting firm cannot suddenly become a software vendor company and vice versa. Such changes are basically feasible, but would take several years. An example is the German company Softlab (now called Cirquent), which over several years was transformed from a software vendor company into a consulting firm.

Successful products are not automatically sustainable. In the music business, for example, concert tickets are seasonal articles that lose any value when the concert is over. Companies who promote or arrange concerts can have a sustainable business model and a sustainable product family, but their individual products are not sustainable. Furthermore, a music group can serve as a brand name, so to speak, and thus be sustainable.

This means that even if a company has an inherently sustainable business approach, its individual products will not necessarily be sustainable, but its product families and business model may be. Sustainability is thus found in a company's assets, i.e. in the company's true values, that need to be protected and developed, because they will determine the company's sustainability. The precise purpose of product management is to manage systematically such product-related assets on a long-term and sustainable basis, regardless of whether this involves single products, product families or product platforms.

In the case of software products, the single product itself is usually sustainable, at least for a time. An exception to this are low-priced consumer products, such as computer games, where the individual product may enjoy a burst of popularity and then fade away, while the product family or platform is characterized by sustainability and should be managed accordingly. Software product management refers to the management of a software product (or product family or platform) over its entire life cycle in accordance with corporate level objectives.

When corporate management presses strongly for short-term success, i.e. routinely assigns higher priority to exigencies than to essentials, this needs caretakers whose job it is to ensure that all urgent major and minor demands in the company are pursued and attended to. In our opinion, such caretaker tasks are best organized in a staff function like a "management assistant," for example, who could deal with them across the organization. If, on the other hand, corporate management is geared more to a sustainability concept, it will need people with managerial skills to manage the corporate assets according to the strategies and objectives already laid out. It is the software product manager's task to manage these assets insofar as software products (or product families or platforms) are involved.

In reality, of course, a company is never quite as black-and-white. The emphasis on sustainability does not imply that a company need not quickly and actively take care of urgent customer problems, for instance. Nevertheless, we find such an exaggerated comparison useful for defining software product management objectives and job descriptions. If corporate management institutes software product management with the aim of having its software products managed as sustainable company assets, this approach will only be successful if the person responsible for the job is not also burdened with endless day-to-day tasks. Otherwise, management would only create another caretaker function with a new name. Such a function can be useful and important for the company, but it would not be software product management as defined in this book.

In our view, the primary objective of software product management is to achieve sustainable success over the life cycle of the software product (or product family or platform). This generally refers to economic success, which is ultimately reflected by the profits generated. Since profits lag behind investments, i.e., an investment phase involving losses will be followed by an extended highly profitable phase, customer satisfaction is often considered as a significant measure of software product management success. This is based on the hypothesis that there is a strong correlation between customer satisfaction and customer loyalty to the product and the producer. According to recent publications and based on our own experience, this is only partly true (see [Reichh96]). Of course, an extremely dissatisfied customer is likely to switch to a different product and producer. Conversely, a high degree of customer satisfaction will not guarantee that a customer will not switch to a different product or producer. However, only if functionality of a replacement product is much better (e.g. technology leapfrog) or one is very dissatisfied with the current product is it worth the risk of changing. So there is value in customer satisfaction, and it is definitely an important factor to be taken into consideration. However, measurement is challenging as we will outline in section 4.5.

In certain situations and with some products, software product management does not focus primarily on profits attributable to a single product. For example, it could be in the interest of the company to achieve a maximum number of installations of a particular product platform as a prerequisite for selling other profitable products. One example of this is the pre-installation of the Microsoft Windows operating system on new computers, for which the computer manufacturers pay Microsoft a relatively small license fee. By doing this, Microsoft ensures the continued dominance of its Windows operating system, which in turn serves as a platform for a large number of profitable software products sold by Microsoft and other vendors. In this case, market share is a better measure than profits. However, it needs to be taken into account that no one ever made much money from high market share at low or negative profit.

Two things become apparent in this discussion. First of all, a conflict exists between software product management which, by definition, has a rather long-term focus and the desire to define objectives and variables that can be linked to business periods and thus evaluated annually. The conflict continues as development cycles or product success may not fit neatly into those same business cycles while management will want to check whether product management is on the right course and, if necessary, to make corrections. And there is the need to set individual objectives for each staff member and meet with them once a year to discuss performance and a salary increase. Unfortunately, this conflict is usually resolved in favor of more short-term objectives and measurements. Furthermore, the sentence that a high-ranking American manager had hanging up as a poster in his office saying "Measurement Systems Do Work!" is true. So, if a company uses measurement systems to evaluate the performance of its employees and perhaps even makes bonuses and increases dependent on the results of such an evaluation, then it must assume that the employees will try to optimize those measurements. This means that unless the measuring system uses measures that reflect exactly what is intended, the employees will be optimizing the wrong things. Since measurement systems are supposed to be simple so as to minimize the amount of time and effort necessary for evaluation, it is the normal case in our observation that the wrong things are optimized, which often has absurd consequences. Sometimes software licenses are unnecessarily given away in order to achieve certain target values with respect to the number of licenses installed. More work is sometimes invested in the manipulation of figures than in actual business activities.

We do not have any easy solution regarding the topics of "objectives and variable elements of compensation". In the end, the only possible solution is for software product managers and their superiors to talk about the problems we have described and reach an agreement together. This agreement should include important, period-linked objectives regarding actual individual employee tasks, yet at the same time ensure that the product manager will still be able and willing to pursue the objective of sustainable product success. There are some available levers: milestone payments, employee rankings, longer term quotas and evaluations, career enhancement (many levels in a professional position). Richard Campione, SAP's Senior Vice President of Suite Solution Management, confirms this: "The core concern is that the measurable KPIs (key performance indicators) tend to be significantly lagging indicators, and so while good for communicating intentions, and useful for long term, they frequently are inadequate for the short term. Here one needs to blend the solid quantifiable KPIs with softer measurements and people's judgement." He uses criteria like product usage, deliverables, market responses to product, and 360-degree evaluations involving responsible counterparts in the other units of the company like Sales, Marketing, Development, etc.

4.2   The Role of the Software Product Manager

If software product management is implemented as a unit in the company organization (see chapter 6), corporate management must not only define the purpose and objective of this role and communicate it throughout the company, but also ensure that all those concerned find the job description acceptable. Regardless of how a company is organized, responsibilities will always be incompletely defined, i.e., some issues and problems will always be neglected because no one feels responsible. Product management is therefore often misunderstood as being a universal caretaker responsible for all such issues and problems. We will discuss how to handle this in a moment, but corporate management must deal with this problem by defining and delimiting the scope of all relevant tasks, provided that the software product management function has been instituted with a genuine focus on sustainability.

The software product manager is supposed to be the person chiefly responsible for all relevant aspects concerning his product. Management skills are individual, personal qualities, but they can also be backed up organizationally. A management position tends to be easier to fulfill when it has managerial authority. This is frequently not the case with product managers (see chapter 6). The following sections of this chapter detail the broad spectrum of issues and tasks that a software product manager is responsible for. Irrespective of the scope of his managerial authority, the software product manager has a cross-organizational role, requiring a high degree of communication and coordination between all functional, organizational units. This challenging task is described in detail in [Condon02].

Focusing on essentials instead of exigencies is made easier for software product management if the company organization includes a full-time "caretaker function," for example a "management assistant". Alternatively, the software product management function can be staffed with enough personnel so that employees can be assigned to individual tasks, with caretakers, branding and requirements management specialists all cooperating. Various company organization models are discussed in detail in chapter 6. In any case, software product managers, as defined here, and caretakers must work closely together.

A job description should include the skills required for this position, i.e. the knowledge and experience needed to perform the tasks associated with the job. It will reflect the scope of responsibility of the software product manager's position as discussed in this chapter. This approach to the software product manager position is problematic, since the scope of responsibility is so extensive that it will hardly be possible to find a candidate who can meet all the qualifications. This does not mean that a "software product manager" position should not be established and filled. Such a position should rather be created with the understanding that a candidate cannot be equally experienced and knowledgeable in all aspects of the job. It is a management position for which it is more important to work in cooperation with specialists from all relevant organizational units, ask the right questions and be able to draw conclusions. Provided a candidate possesses basic managerial skills, more extensive knowledge and experience in two of the relevant subject areas and is otherwise capable of seeing things in a broader perspective, this will usually be an adequate basis for performing the job. Software vendors always find it difficult to fill product management positions, since there is no specific training for the job. This typically leads to a mixture of very experienced people in such positions who have worked in completely different areas of the company or industry during their career on the one hand, and specialists who can competently assume responsibility for a certain subtask due to their training and career, e.g. branding, on the other. This is even more so if a software product management function is staffed with enough personnel to allow a certain degree of specialization by skills. In any case, career entrants are seldom seen here.

Appendix A presents a sample job description for a software product manager. Corporations use various titles for the software product manager's position, such as product manager, program manager, brand manager, and so on. Essentially, most of these names refer to the software product manager described in this book, although minor differences often exist.

4.3 Framework

The previous chapters and sections have already indicated the broad spectrum of topics and tasks that a software product manager is concerned with. Software product management is not primarily focused on a single development project or on a single marketing action, such as a product launch. These are "merely" steps taken in the pursuit of long-term sustainable objectives. Software product management, viewed collectively as a combination of all the tasks described in this chapter, can therefore be conceived neither as a project which by definition would have a beginning and an end nor as a process which by definition would consist of a well-defined sequence of process steps. Only subtasks can be interpreted or organized in this manner. Requirements management, for instance, can be described as a process with respect to individual requirements (see section 4.7.3), whereas the development of a new product release is normally considered to be a project.

In conformance with the sustainability of the software product (or product family or platform), software product management viewed collectively as a combination of tasks is an ongoing activity. This fact is rather unpopular at a time when most people believe that they can measure the efficiency of an organization by the share of its project work. This idea stems from a vague feeling that unproductive colleagues might just comfortably while away their time performing ongoing tasks, whereas strictly organized project work would force everyone to be productive. In over twenty years of experience in the software business, we have not found any reason to support such views. We have experienced many unproductive projects and highly productive employees performing ongoing jobs. Furthermore, when ongoing tasks that do inherently exist, such as market analysis or personnel development, are neglected, this tends to create enormous problems in the medium term for the company as a whole. Our observations showed that good corporate management and a good working atmosphere help significantly to influence productivity. Software product management in particular is a good example of an ongoing task that is one of the most challenging jobs in a company. It requires a high degree of personal commitment and diligence for the product manager to be successful in the medium and long term.

So even when we cannot organize the tasks of a software product manager as a process or project, some kind of structure would certainly be helpful. In the literature, there are hardly any attempts to provide structure. An exception is the Reference Framework for Software Product Management developed by Inge van de Weerd, Sjaak Brinkkemper e.a. at the University of Utrecht, Netherlands ([WBNVB06]) (see fig. 4.1).

This reference framework was developed by studying SMEs (Small and mid-size enterprises) and is focused on the core activities of a software product manager in the areas of portfolio management, product roadmapping, requirements management and release planning. It is based on the concept that a product manager is concerned with a hierarchy of entities (called artifacts in [WBNVB06]):

1. portfolio
2. product
3. release
4. requirement

These entities are reflected in the core activities. When interpreted as a process, the framework shows the core of what some software vendors call their product lifecycle management (PLM) process which is an iterative process for software repeated for every release. We consider this framework as very helpful and shall come back to it when we discuss the individual activities. However, as pointed out in chapter 3, we see sustainable economic success as the main objective of a software product manager. The economic aspects are only indirectly reflected in this framework when the business case is mentioned with one of the connectors. In our view, the business aspects must play a much more prominent role in a software product management framework.

Inspired by the Pragmatic Marketing® Framework ([PragMark08]), we have developed our own Software Product Management Framework (fig. 4.2) (see also [Kittlaus08]). The columns show the major functions with which a software product

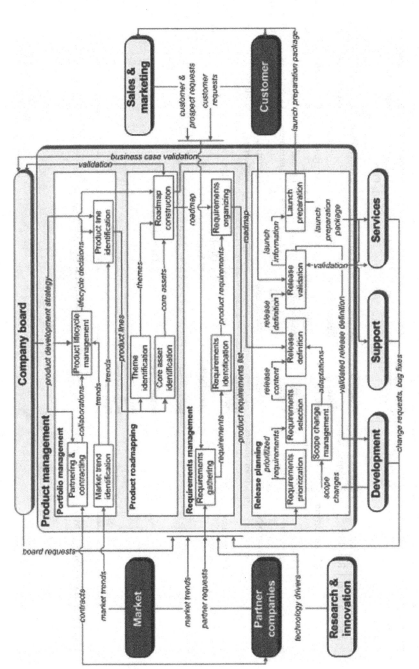

Fig. 4.1 Reference Framework for Software Product Management (© I. van de Weerd, S. Brinkkemper e.a.)

	Market Analysis	Product Analysis	Product Strategy	Product Planning	Development	Marketing	Sales and Distribution	Support and Services
Often on corporate level			Portfolio Management	Resource Allocation	Resource Allocation	Marketing Strategy and Plan	Sales Strategy and Plan	
Product (family) level	Market Research Market Sizing Market Problems Technology Assessment Competitive Analysis	Product Performance Customer Satisfaction Win/loss Analysis Opportunities	Positioning Delivery Model Pricing Model Pricing Business Case Make or buy Ecosystem Legal Terms Protection of Intellectual Property	Roadmap Release Plan Requirements Management Functional Specification	Project Plan Technical Specification Project Requirements Management Implementation Quality Assurance Technology Innovation	Launch Plan Customer Analysis Partner Management Operational Marketing Material	Channel Preparation Operational Sales Operational Distribution Material	Customer Support Technical Support Marketing Support Sales Support Services Preparation Operational Services Provision

Fig. 4.2 Software Product Management Framework (Core Product Management, Core Pricing, Tasks to participate in or to orchestrate)

manager is involved. Market and product analysis provide quantitative and qualitative data regarding the market and the product which is the basis for the product manager's work. Product strategy and planning contain the core activities of product management as shown in fig. 4.1 plus the more business-oriented tasks like business case, pricing, and legal aspects. Development, Marketing, Sales and Distribution, and Support and Services are functions within the company that often do not report into the product manager, but need to be orchestrated by him since they have significant influence on the success of the product.

We differentiate between activities that are performed on the level of a product or product family, and those on the corporate level. The columns provide the structure for the rest of this chapter.

4.4 Market Analysis

A software product manager will continuously assess the market and its development on the basis of input received from a number of different sources:

- Colleagues in Marketing, Sales, Support, Services, and Development,
- Direct contacts with members of the ecosystem and other market participants,
- Internal Market Research or Competitive Analysis unit (usually only in larger software vendor companies),
- External market researchers.

While a product manager who maintains an extended network inside and outside of his company tends to have a good feeling for the market and its development, a more systematic input comes from the specialists in Competitive Analysis and Market Research. If there is an internal unit, their output is typically based on external market research results enriched by some research of their own.

There are a lot of smaller market research boutiques that are specialized in certain geographic or functional segments. The worldwide leaders conduct qualitative and quantitative analyses on a larger scale, such as IDC (www.idc.com), Gartner (www.gartner.com), and Forrester Research (www.forrester.com). IDC specializes in quantitative market analysis and Forrester in new technologies. What they all have in common is the relatively high prices that they charge for the use of their research results. They are all very eager to stress their independence though, in fact, they are forced to cooperate with the software vendors in order to obtain the information they need. Moreover, the analyst companies have in the course of time expanded their business models to include consulting, a service regularly used by vendors and corporate IT organizations alike which can easily lead to a conflict of interests.

The results provided by the market research companies are nevertheless a useful source of information, even if you should not rely on them unquestioningly. It should always be remembered in particular that market research companies do not consider it their job to merely penetrate the vendors' marketing hype and conduct serious analyses, but that they also like to produce their own hype to promote their business. In the end, a product manager has to use his own sense of judgment and make business assessments and decisions in consultation with colleagues and superiors. It can be very useful to have a competent market research department in the company, as some large corporations do. Above all, it can conduct specific analyses of competing products, the results of which can be of interest to both product management and marketing as well as development. The results of market research can serve as a source of information for ongoing requirements management (see section 4.7.3).

The fact that market research results are not only input for product management, but can be useful for marketing too, was shown by CRM software producer Siebel (in the meantime acquired by Oracle) in the spring of 2003 when it published the results of a CRM market analysis conducted by Gartner in full-page advertisements worldwide. The advertisement displayed, among other things, the "Magic Quadrant," a Gartner evaluation of companies and their products based on a system of coordinates with a "completeness of vision" axis and an "ability to execute" axis. There is no better advertisement for a vendor than to be located in the leaders quadrant, as Siebel was in the majority of the analyzed CRM segments in the above example. In the meantime, Gartner has changed their publication policy and does not allow the use of Magic Quadrant graphics in vendor's advertisements anymore.

Figure 4.3 shows the Magic Quadrant's skeleton, in which companies are positioned. Gartner describes in [Hawkins08] how a magic quadrant is to be read. The axis "Ability to Execute" summarizes factors such as the vendor's financial viability, market responsiveness, product development, sales channels and customer base. The axis "Completeness of Vision" reflects the vendor's innovation, whether the vendor drives or follows the market, and if the vendor's view of how the market will develop matches Gartner's perspective. The quadrants are interpreted as indicated in Fig. 4.3.

The Gartner Hype Cycle describes the response to new technologies. Gartner defines the terms used as follows (see [Fenn08]):

- **Technology trigger:** A breakthrough, a public demonstration, a product launch or some other event generates significant press or industry interest.
- **Peak of inflated expectations:** During this phase of overenthusiasm and unrealistic projections, a flurry of well-publicized activity by technology leaders results in some successes, but more failures, as the technology is pushed to its limits. The only companies making money are conference organizers and magazine publishers.
- **Trough of Disillusionment:** Because the technology does not live up to its overinflated expectations, it rapidly becomes unfashionable. Media interest wanes, except for a few cautionary tales.
- **Slope of Enlightenment:** Focused experimentation and solid hard work by an increasingly diverse range of organizations lead to a true understanding of the technology's applicability, risks and benefits. Commercial off-the-shelf methodologies and tools ease the development process.

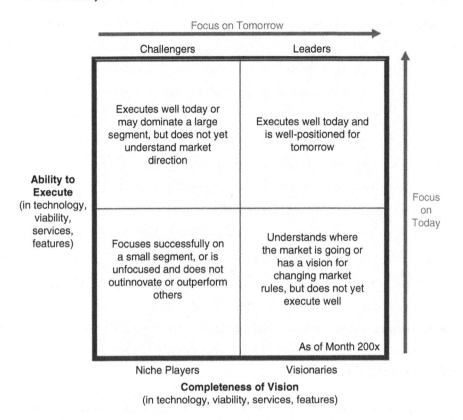

Fig. 4.3 Gartner Magic Quadrant (© Gartner, Inc. 2008)

- **Plateau of Productivity:** The real-world benefits of the technology are demonstrated and accepted. Growing numbers of organizations feel comfortable with the reduced levels of risk, and the rapid growth phase of adoption begins.

New technologies positioned on the Hype Cycle do not move at a uniform speed through the cycle. A software product manager must be able to assess this speed in his business planning.

If a product or product family covers an ever larger functional field, the market will become increasingly difficult to define. The rather vague term enterprise resource planning (ERP) market was coined for SAP, for example. SAP now, however, also sells a data warehouse, called business warehouse, and a CRM solution, and includes middleware which is opened to the outside under the name NetWeaver. The classical, functional market segmentation approach is unsatisfactory for such wide-ranging, highly integrated product families.

The market research companies also provide quantitative analysis on the size of market segments and the market share of players within a segment. It is more difficult to obtain information on the pricing of a particular competitor in the B2B market since prices are usually negotiated individually (see chapter 5).

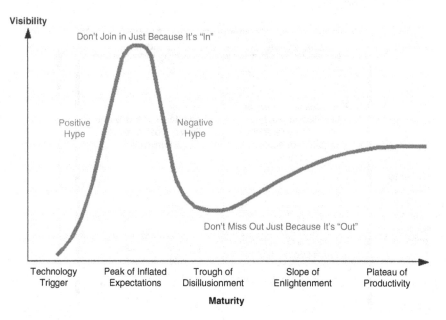

Fig. 4.4 Gartner Hype Cycle (© Gartner, Inc. 2008)

4.5   Product Analysis

Once a product is launched, the software product manager needs to know at any time how his product performs from a business perspective. There are hard measures that are usually provided by the Controller or Controlling unit within the Finance organization, and there are soft measures.

These units can provide numbers on the financial performance and product indicators like:

- Revenue (per version, per time period)
- Cost (development/maintenance/support/ marketing/sales, per version, per time period)
- Profit (per version, per time period)
- Number of licenses (sold/installed, total/new, per version, per time period, per customer)
- Defect rate (per version, per time period)

The software product manager needs to ensure that he gets these numbers frequently and that they are current and correct which can be a challenge in a lot of companies. He then needs to analyze the numbers regularly in comparison to the product plans and report on his findings. Any significant deviation requires action. In a negative case, this typically means that the product manager puts pressure on the responsible unit to come up with plans for corrective action. If all this does not help, forecasts, outlooks and plans need to be adapted. In a positive case, i.e. the actuals exceed the plan, the product manager has to ensure that resulting resource requirements (e.g. adequate service personnel) are addressed. Again, forecasts, outlooks and plans need to be adapted.

Soft measures are weaker indicators, but can often point to problems much earlier than the hard measures. The software product manager needs to analyze information from different sources (for more details see section 4.7.3), for example:

- customer satisfaction,
- feedback from market analysts,
- trade press articles,
- individual customer feedback,
- information from the sales channels (like win/loss analysis or opportunities),
- information from the support and service functions.

Customer satisfaction is difficult to quantify. It is generally not determined on the basis of a single factor, but rather as a group of up to 20 variables regarding a range of topics, such as reliability, documentation, usability, service quality, sales coverage, etc. An example is shown in Fig. 4.5.

Fig. 4.5 shows the results of a customer satisfaction survey for a single product, but for two different user groups: data processing (DP) and end users (EU). Overall satisfaction with the product and the satisfaction index with respect to several quality factors were assessed. In addition, the significance attached to each factor by the customer (whether DP or EU) was determined. The results of the survey clearly indicate where customer satisfaction is insufficient and product management should plan to make improvements.

It is obvious that the product is evaluated differently by the different user groups, also with respect to the significance of each factor; IT experts evaluate most of the criteria more critically than end users. An overall satisfaction rate of about 80% can be considered as good; however, documentation, compatibility, support and functionality – especially at the end user level – show room for improvement.

IBM initially attempted to interview customers directly, which often led sales staff members to fill out the questionnaires for the customers. The figures obtained this way were fantastic, but they did not really reflect what they were meant to measure. This is why third parties were subsequently commissioned to conduct the interviews, which were sometimes done anonymously, sometimes under IBM's logo. The number of responses was disappointing, especially when the interview was done anonymously, and the results were frequently exceedingly negative due to the fact that angry customers were much more likely to answer the questions than satisfied customers, since this gave them the opportunity to voice their complaints. After these surveys had been carried out regularly over a longer period of time, the customer satisfaction figures were found to correlate with events that had occurred just prior to the interview instead of with actual product changes. For instance, a price increase shortly before the interview had a negative impact on code quality satisfaction, whereas a customer event that had taken place in pleasant surroundings prior to the interview caused all of the customer satisfaction figures to climb. Customer expectations were then added to the survey as a correction factor. This

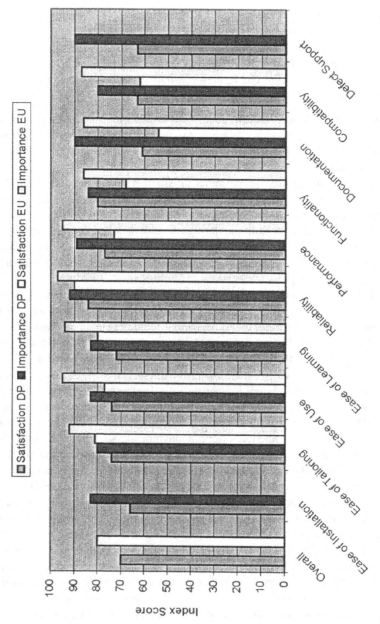

Fig. 4.5 Results of a customer satisfaction survey

made customers give more thought to their answers and also made the question-naires easier to evaluate. These experiences must not lead to the conclusion that customer satisfaction should generally not be quantified. Evaluating customer sat-isfaction is definitely useful if done over an extended period of time so that the effect of single events is statistically recognizable. Another way to do this is to sample 1/12th of the base (or sample population) every month. On average the data is never more than 6 months old, workload is spread, trends show up but single events don't slant the overall results in any particular direction. It offers the benefits and pitfalls of any rolling average. One has to be wary of the statistics for any small group. One of the authors was able to effect a 15% improvement in overall cus-tomer satisfaction in an IBM branch with roughly 60 large customers, simply by calling on and catering to 8 customers who had been declared *"non grata"* because they had chosen competitive mainframes. While it appeared the results were very favorable, 8 customers were happier and 52 loyal customers of equal or greater business importance were treading water. This type of evaluation is not suited as a period-linked target value or measurement for software product management. There is a lot of literature available on the evaluation of customer satisfaction for all industries. We find [JohGus00] und [Myers00] quite useful.

4.6 Product Strategy

The pace of technological development in the past several decades has been faster in the IT industry, specifically in the software sector, than in any other industry. This makes it necessary for the organizations concerned, both software vendors and cor-porate IT organizations, regularly to make far-reaching decisions that have consid-erable financial and even survival consequences. Yet, in spite of the fast pace of change, it is clear that companies with a clear strategic view are the ones that prove to be successful in the long term. Microsoft, IBM, and SAP are excellent examples. This does not mean that at these companies all product ideas lead to successful products or that every product strategy produces the desired results. However, it does mean that these companies routinely manage to reach agreement on and con-sistency in their corporate vision, corporate strategy, product strategies (or product platform and family strategies) and more short-term implementation plans by means of iterative processes that sometimes require a great deal of time and effort.

The software product manager is responsible for defining the strategy for his product (or platform or family) and to support and update it using a standard proc-ess over time (also refer to chapter 6). What does such a product (or platform or family) strategy consist of? Normally a strategy covers a time span of about one to five years in the future. The strategy should include the development or evolution of each of the items in the list below during this time span:

- Product scope, i.e. the approximate functional scope of the product,
- Target market, possibly segments,

- Product delivery model
- Product positioning
- Business expectations, i.e. development of market share, sales, etc.,
- Budget and resources planning,
- Roadmap planning.

These items are, of course, very interdependent. If, for example, the available budget is smaller than originally assumed, it will only be possible to expand the product scope to a lesser extent or more slowly. If new segments are to be added to the target market within the strategic time frame, the product scope may have to be expanded. Dependency on other products can also have considerable consequences, e.g., if certain functionalities or enabling code must be available in several products at the same time. In addition, the aggregate resource planning for all products needs to be coordinated with the resource planning for the company as a whole. As a rule, the larger a company is and the more dependencies of this type exist within a company, the more difficult, complex and time-consuming the entire planning process will be. Budget, resource and roadmap planning will be covered in the Product Planning section 4.7.

In this section we will look in more detail at the product manager's participation in the company's development of vision and strategy and portfolio management which are usually done on the corporate level (see fig. 4.2). We will discuss some fundamental decisions like the delivery and pricing models and make or buy decisions. The positioning of a product in the market is subject of section 4.6.3. Then we will focus on the business view that includes the business case and the link to Pricing which is covered in detail in Chapter 5. In 4.6.5 we discuss the management of the increasingly important software ecosystem. Then in 4.6.6 and 7, we look at the legal side, i.e. the legal terms of a product and the protection of intellectual property.

4.6.1 Corporate Vision, Strategy, and Portfolio Management

It is not the objective of this book to provide a handbook on executive management. This is covered by a huge spectrum of publications. However, since a software product manager has the responsibility for his product(s) and thereby a partial responsibility for the success of the whole company, he is very directly involved in some aspects of executive management. At this point we want to go into these elements and the role that the product manager plays in them.

A primary task of executive management is the definition, communication and implementation of corporate vision and strategy. These need to have a certain stability over time so that the employees of the company are reliably guided by them. At the same time they must not be written in stone so that the company can adapt to changes in the market, in technology and in society in time. This balancing act demonstrates the quality of executive management. Whether a software product manager is allowed to contribute to the definition of vision and strategy depends on his reputation in the company. In any case, corporate strategy and vision will be the foundation for the definition of his product strategy.

McGrath (see [McGrat01]) coined the term "Core Strategic Vision" (CSV): "A CSV is the answer to three absolutely basic questions: Where do we want to go? How will we get there? And why do we think we will be successful?" ([McGrat01], p. 1). On the stability of a CSV says McGrath: "Sticking to an obsolete vision for too long is almost always the reason that once-successful companies fail." ([McGrat01], p. 16). The next step in the implementation of a vision is the alignment with the corporate strategy that according to McGrath ([McGrat01], p. 36) is expressed in

- Core competencies (value chain)
- Financial plan (economic model)
- Business charter
- Technology trends / strategy
- Product strategy
- Market trends / competitive strategy

The corporate strategy describes how a vision can be implemented. This is supported by the concept of product or project portfolio management. Portfolio management is a term that is well known in the financial services industry. An investor or a fund manager invests the available capital in a diversified way, i.e. in different stocks, securities, real estate etc. The total collection of these investments is called a portfolio. Portfolio management is the management of these investments over time following profit and risk criteria. This same approach can be applied to an enterprise. It can make sense to consider current and future products as a portfolio and base investment decisions on this approach. Industry leaders like SAP have established corporate portfolio management teams at the Board level. Graphical presentations can help in positioning products in relation to size and growth rate of their respective markets, their budget requirements and their risks. Some examples are shown in fig. 4.6 and 4.7.

Fig. 4.6 shows a portfolio of existing products A to H. The axes stand for growth of the market segment and market share in the segment. The size of the respective product circle symbolizes the investment planned for the current year, the colour shows product families. The quadrants have the following meanings (see [Cooper00], p. 200):

- **Pearls:** These are the star products with a high market share in a strongly growing market. Most businesses desire more of these. In the example, only product C is in this quadrant.
- **Oysters:** These are the hopefuls with a still small share of a strongly growing market.
- **Bread and Butter:** These are the products that pay the bills, i.e. generate stable revenues with a high market share in slowly growing markets.
- **White Elephants:** Products with a low market share in slowly growing markets that a company should not have too many of.

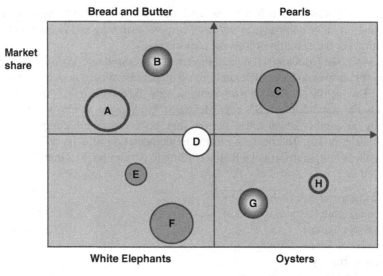

Fig. 4.6 Product Portfolio

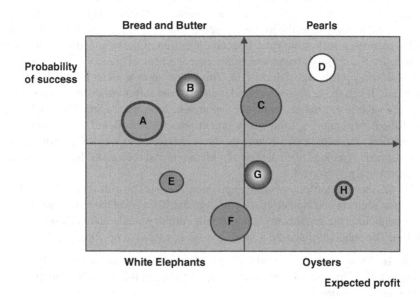

Fig. 4.7 New Product Development

Fig. 4.7 shows a portfolio of new products A to H whose development has or will be started. The axes stand for the expected profit of a product and the probability of success of development. The size of the respective product circle symbolizes the investment planned for the current year, the colour shows product families.

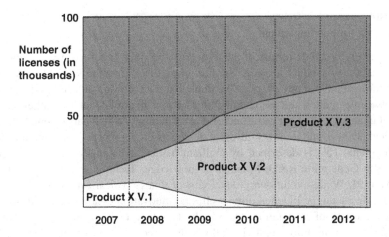

Fig. 4.8 License Distribution

Analogous to the examples in fig. 4.6 and 4.7, there are numerous possibilities how to visualize the product portfolio using relevant criteria (see [Cooper00], p. 199).

An important aspect when analyzing a product portfolio is the product life cycle. This concept is not software-specific, but needs some special considerations for software. For simple consumer products the number of sold products per time period is analyzed. For software the long term commitment of the vendor for support of the product needs to be taken into consideration. Graphically the software product life cycle can better be represented by the number of product licenses in use over time. New versions and follow-on products need to be added. An example is shown in fig. 4.8.

A number of measures are connected to the position of a product in its life cycle. Typically there is a high investment in development and marketing in the startup phase of a product whereas during the later maturity phase the investment volume is reduced. The resulting increased profits can then be invested in new products. Maintenance is also influenced by the life cycle position. A vendor will always try not to have too many versions of a product in maintenance in parallel since this produces portfolio and organizational complexity. Therefore the maintenance of older versions is frequently decommitted with some lead time in order to motivate customers to migrate to newer versions. This is often a point of conflict between vendor and customers that vendors try to mitigate by offering discounted upgrade prices.

In [Cooper00] Cooper uses the portfolio management approach for projects of new product development. As helpful graphical presentations he lists

- Risk vs. reward
- Technical vs. market newness
- Technical feasibility vs. market attractiveness
- Competitive position vs. attractiveness

- Cost vs. reward
- Cost vs. time to implement

He has a very broad definition of the term "new product," i.e. for software any new release is a new product for him. Similarly non-discriminatingly, he also uses the term "innovation" for any change. We think that for software we need to differentiate between evolution and innovation. "Innovation" in our lexicon is a rather radical type of change, e.g. a change of underlying technology, which carries much bigger risks and chances and requires different management approaches than evolutionary development. This is described by William Miller and Langdon Morris in their book "4th Generation R&D: Managing Knowledge, Technology, and Innovation" [MilMor99]. While evolutionary development that is typical for established software products can be planned quite well, real innovation escapes planning simply because the risk of total failure is so high. This type of innovation blooms in an atmosphere that nurtures creativity, allows the freedom to pursue it, supporting it even to the brink of business insanity. That is why management and controlling methods that are helpful and common for evolutionary development are deadly for real innovation, because they strangle innovative ideas early due to the inherent uncontrollable risk. This is also why contrary to the image that big leading technology companies like to portray the really disruptive innovations usually come from smaller companies or from developers in big companies who work on them under the covers and enter them into the company processes when the innovation has already reached a level of stability that makes the risk look manageable. An example for the second case is the porting of Linux onto /390 mainframes that was done by a few developers in IBM's development lab in Boeblingen, Germany. After the port was successful, a company-wide controversial discussion started that led to a new IBM product. In some corporations which have venture capital of their own, a number of these projects are allowed to go forward, on the theory that many may fail but that one or two may become pearls.

So in portfolio management, not all projects should be put in one single portfolio even though they all compete for the same resources. It makes more sense to build separate portfolios with different criteria for analysis and decision. It is a proven approach to look at project portfolios for development of existing products (evolution with low risk), for new product development based on known technology (evolution with medium risk), and for targeted research (innovation with high risk) separately. In the preceding process, a designated part of the company resources needs to be assigned to each of the portfolios.

Projects in the third portfolio, the research category, are typically started at a point in time when the shape of a potentially resulting product cannot yet be foreseen, and when there is not yet a software product manager assigned. Nevertheless it is prudent and reasonable to involve marketing and product management early to avoid spending large sums of money on technologically brilliant ideas that afterwards nobody wants nor needs. At the latest when a research project has produced a result that seems sufficiently stable, an explicit product management should be established that analyzes the market potential systematically, participates in the definition of products based on the research results, and manages market positioning and introduction.

In [Cooper00] Cooper addresses only the top management and leaves out the human factors that play an important role in go/no go decisions and in portfolio management in general. The importance of this human factor is convincingly described in the book "The Smart Organization: Creating Value through Smart R&D" [MatMat98] that contains some good examples. Typically a software product manager has to represent his products and the projects needed for its development in the portfolio management processes of the company. In companies where the individual career is strongly dependent on getting as many resources as possible for one's products and projects, portfolio management will not lead to the intended optimal allocation. In fact, results may reflect more the strength of the individual product managers than of the products they represent or their worth to the company.

Some consultants advocate for a project portfolio management approach even in companies that use the term project in very fine granularity. While in the discussion above the term "project" was used to refer to the development of a complete version or release of a product, some companies define the implementation of a single requirement as a project when the estimated effort is above a certain threshold. In those cases, we consider the portfolio management approach as inappropriate since its purpose is the coarse-grained allocation of capital. The fine-grained decision on the implementation of an individual requirement should be subject of the requirements management process as described in section 4.7.3.

4.6.2   Some Fundamental Decisions

When a decision has been made to offer a new software product, we recommend assigning a product manager as early as possible. Before significant investment has gone into development, some fundamental decisions have to be made that are best driven by the product manager.

The first decision concerns the delivery model. Historically, the standard delivery model for software vendors has been that when a customer buys a license for a software product, the software is transported to the customer on a medium like tape or CD, the customer installs the software on his computer hardware (possibly with the help of the vendor) and runs it on his own. Depending on the type of contract, the customer may be entitled to maintenance updates that he can install on his computer over time. Over the last few years, a new delivery model has emerged called Software as a Service (SaaS) (see chapter 3) that often comes with new pricing models like usage-based pricing or funding through advertisements.

The reason why we discuss these delivery and pricing models here is that they can have significant impact on the specification and implementation of the new software product. If SaaS is chosen as the delivery model it means that the software must be highly scalable and multi-client-capable. These are requirements that most standard software today does not fulfill. The same is true for the new pricing models. Usage-based pricing or the integrated display of ads cannot easily be implemented on top of an existing piece of software, but need to be considered as requirements early on in the initial design.

Another decision that needs to be made early is the make-or-buy decision. When the decision has been made for a new software offering, it may be economically better not to develop the new software from scratch, but to buy or license an existing product on the market that matches the requirements sufficiently. Reasons can be faster time to market, skills shortage, or resource shortage. The product manager should not leave this decision to development since developers always want to make and not buy. In case of a buy decision, it is of utmost importance to negotiate the contract with the partner that provides the software such that the dependence on the partner does not lead to a disaster like losing the right to use the software on short notice, or facing extreme price increases. There should also be consideration of what could happen in the longer term. Because IBM was not sure of the future of the PC, they refused to pay Microsoft for PC DOS and insisted on a royalty arrangement. The cash flow generated by that decision enabled the emergence of one of IBM's strongest competitors.

4.6.3   Positioning and Value Definition

A major issue in software product management is the positioning of a product in its market. This requires a number of questions to be answered:

- Which market is of relevance? How is it going to develop? (definition, volume, competitors and their market shares, customer segments, geography and/or functionality)
- Where does the product play a role? Where should it play a role? (scope, segments, market share)

Determining the relevant market for software is by no means trivial as we already briefly discussed in section 4.4. The most comprehensive definition of the market is the overall software market, which the software product manager can certainly use as a basis. However, as a whole, it is so huge and inhomogeneous that it is not really useful for product positioning. The smallest conceivable market consists only of one product. This definition is not absurd if this product creates a new market without any competitors. In between these two extremes, of course, there are practically unlimited numbers of ways to define the market that intelligent people play with in practice. If you like to point out the enormous sales potential of a planned product, for example, you select a broadly defined market segment with a correspondingly high volume. If you want to demonstrate what a large market share your product has, you choose a narrower definition of a market segment. Unfortunately, there are no fixed rules for deciding which market definition is the best for a product. Market research companies that analyze software markets often divide the overall market into multi-layered market segments by functions, geographic regions and customer groups (see section 4.4).

There is a close connection between the market definition and the definition of the product scope, which the product manager must deal with iteratively. On the one hand, the analysis of the market, market development and competition will influence the definition of the functional product scope. On the other hand, the product scope will determine in which segment of the market the product can successfully compete. What is needed, ultimately, is a time-related close correspondence between product scope, target market and business prospects. Planning the further development of such a correspondence over time requires coordination with the corporate vision statement and strategy and constitutes an essential aspect of product strategy (see section 4.6.1).

The scope of requirements ensuing from the definition of the target market should not be underestimated. If the target market is the consumer market, the product must meet different requirements with respect to usability, packaging, pricing (see section 5.6), sales channels, support structure, etc. than a B2B (business-to-business) product. Some market segments are so special that they even require different approaches to development and requirements management. For games for example, development is often based on a story line rather than a technical specification, and developers typically have more freedom in the graphical design as part of an iterative prototyping approach (see [Waldo08]).

The requirements for a product to be marketed internationally are significant, both in terms of product requirements (see section 4.7.3) and in the marketing and support structure. The resulting expenses will be offset by higher sales expectations. This correlation is discussed in detail in [McGrat01], pp. 235–255.

Concise, understandable positioning is a key product success factor. It makes it easier for sales and marketing to address the right customer groups with the right messages. It also helps internal cooperation, since it serves as a good basis for all product-related decisions.

Once the market for the product is defined, the positioning must focus on describing the value of the product. Again this has to be considered over time since the value of the product will hopefully increase with each new version or release. The value definition needs to be approached from a customer perspective, e.g. what is the business value that the customer will get from using the product? For example, if the use of a web portal product will add $10M in revenues and $5M in profit, arguably that product is providing $5M in value to the customer. This approach provides a solid base for pricing, but no one should conclude that an appropriate price for this customer is $5M! (see chapter 5).

One of the important aspects of positioning is the question how a product differentiates itself in the market. For proprietary products, the typical differentiating arguments have been better functionality, higher level of integration, performance etc. However, over the last decade standardization has become more and more important. But how can a product differentiate itself if it only implements a public standard? The vendors found this answer in the 1970's and still apply it: They implement the standard so that they can claim standard-conformance, and then they add useful proprietary features. Once a customer makes use of these features, he is tied to the vendor's product. So the features not only provide differentiation, but also the glue that makes a product more difficult to replace.

4.6.4   The Business View

As pointed out earlier we see tracking and managing the business aspects of a software product as an important part of product management. This is not limited to the product manager keeping track of the revenue numbers. It means a much more active role in shaping the parameters that are paramount for the economic success of a product or product family.

One business aspect that a product manager is responsible for is the business case. We define

Business Case = Comparison of the costs associated with a product or project to the quantified economic benefits or value to be derived from it.

Depending on company rules, a business case may be required for each requirement within the requirements management process (see section 4.7.3). At the minimum, a business case is required for any new release of a product: if 300,000 lines of new code are proposed for a release, at a cost of $3M, there had better be a forecast of additional revenue from new customers or increased product usage which is several times as large over the vendor's ROI (return on investment) period. The calculation of the cost side bears some risk, but is typically easier than the value side; for one thing, the costs all occur within the developing company's control. On the value side the challenge is threefold: often benefits and value are of a qualitative nature that is difficult to convert into actual earnings or savings; the monetary benefits may (and usually do) vary from customer to customer; and the benefits/value may be realized over an extended time period after the release is made available. So an estimate comes with a high level of uncertainty. That is why some people in the software industry claim that any business case is more a pseudo-scientific quantification of the gut feelings of the decision makers than a valid prediction. But even if this were true, we think it would have some value.

The next important business aspect is the pricing of the product. When a company has a separate Pricing organization, the product manager is advised to cooperate with his pricing manager early, continuously, and closely. When there is no separate Pricing organization, pricing is often part of the product manager's responsibilities. In any case the pricing considerations that we will describe in great detail in chapter 5 have a significant influence on the success of a product. Most of the time, the product manager and the pricing manager are natural allies since both have the objective of sustainable economic success. However, there can be conflicts when the pricing manager focuses on consistency across platforms or families whereas the product manager is only interested in his own product.

Another most interesting business aspect is the bundling of products. We define

Product Bundle = Set of products that is sold as one product with its own price.

There are different types of product bundles:

- **Pure:** The products are only sold as part of the bundle, not individually.

- **Mixed:** The products are sold as part of the bundle and at least some of them also individually.

Bundling may have several different motivations:

1. The bundle makes it easier for the customer to buy a complete solution and signals that the vendor has already taken care of a tight integration of the involved products. The vendor hopes for increased revenue and profit.
2. The bundle is less expensive than the sum of the individual products and thus gives the customer the impression that he saves money by buying the bundle. Again the vendor hopes for increased revenue and profit since a percentage of the customers would not have bought all products in the bundle individually.
3. The bundle combines market-leading products with products that are new or have strong competition. The vendor hopes for increased market share of the new or weaker products because for customers who buy the market-leading products anyway the bundled new or weaker products look like zero-cost add-ons.

Case 3 is a frequent cause for legal action if the vendor has a dominating position with his market-leading products. An example is RealAudio's fight against Microsoft for bundling the MediaPlayer with the Windows operating system.

In case 2, the price motivation has been analyzed scientifically (see [Biering04]), but unfortunately the results are often only applicable in special situations. We will also discuss the price aspect of bundling in section 5.4.

One must exercise care with the implementation of bundles; the reaction of some customers when IBM offered a tightly integrated VM bundle in the early 1980s was negative, even though it offered a complete solution and there were integration elements they liked. Their view was that IBM did not have the leading products in each area of the bundle and that they would not switch from what they were using to the IBM products simply because they were part of a bundle. In fact, they resented having to engage in technical gymnastics to remove or disable parts of the bundle and wanted tools which would help them integrate products from multiple sources into an in-house "bundle" of their own, much the way an enterprise might build its own standard desktop or laptop suite today.

Despite the cautions, there may be cases where bundling (or even the incorporation of functions once external into a core product as Microsoft has done with Windows) is effective. If a product manager is responsible for a product family, he may consider bundling within his family, but in most cases bundling means that several product managers have to cooperate.

4.6.5   The Ecosystem

We have discussed software ecosystems from a business perspective in chapter 3. Depending on the role that a company wants to play in a particular ecosystem, the company needs to be visible as an active member of the ecosystem and influence and support it. This work is typically split between Product Management and Marketing. SAP is an example for a company that has an exceptionally strong focus on partner management with a partner management unit reporting directly to the CEO. Marketing is responsible for sales-oriented partner management (see section 4.9). Here Product Management is involved in dealing with the partner's product requirements. Product Management takes care of product-related in-depth discussions with market research companies and journalists, the overall positioning within the ecosystem, and the selection of product-specific partners.

4.6.6 The Legal Terms

"Software" products are first and foremost intellectual property and their special nature, already discussed in chapter 3, becomes particularly evident as we examine the legal characteristics of the agreements between software vendors and software customers. We will discuss first the licensing of software between vendor and external customer; then the special cases of 1) the corporate IT organization providing software for other business units within the corporation and 2) providing software functionality under SaaS.

The contract by which software is "acquired," the so-called "terms and conditions," usually comprise a license (in case of SaaS a service agreement), possibly a second document describing product-specific terms, and last a transaction document which contains conditions specific to the sale and may modify either of the first two.

License Agreement between the Vendor and the Customer

Depending on the nature and complexity of the software offering, one may find only a license document, all three of the documents described above, or sometimes even more, usually with a hierarchical reference structure. We will discuss each of these in turn, but let us focus first on areas of potential conflict between licensor and licensee, which may help explain the necessity for some of the various terms.

Conflicts between vendor and customer generally arise in one of four areas:

1. whether the product is doing what the vendor claimed it would do and if not whose fault it is that it is not performing;
2. the quantity of product in use compared to what the vendor authorized;
3. the way in which the product is being used compared to what the vendor authorized; and
4. unused quantities of the product which the customer paid for but which he is not using, which is referred to as "shelfware" (sometimes a derivative of "1").

The license attempts to deal with most of these items; what it doesn't cover, the other documents will. In a moment we will examine each "usual" term in turn, but first a bit more about potential conflicts and license complexity.

Re-examining the list of potential conflicts between vendor and customer, one can conclude that most of them arise because a software "purchase" typically does not mean that ownership or any proprietary rights are transferred as they usually are in the case of material products. Only a right to use is granted by the vendor, subject to various restrictions and often priced based on the scope of use or projected use. This circumstance gives rise to a legal complexity that results in similarly complex licensing terms and conditions, the details of which frequently differ from one country to the next, since the local legal requirements must always be taken into account.

Contrast the acquisition of software with that of a tangible widget: if you buy a shovel, you can use it one day to dig a trench, lend it to a friend the next day to mix cement, and your wife may use it to plant roses the third day. In fact, if one discovered that he had purchased too many shovels, he could try to sell his extras. Not so with software which will probably have restrictions on the purpose for which it may be used, the number and nature of the people who may use it, and possibly on where and how it may be used and/or resold. The wording of the terms and conditions of the license and related documents has by now become so creative that in some states in the USA, e.g. California, initiatives have been undertaken calling for a law to regulate standard software license agreements, as the terms and conditions of license agreements now used by vendors can often no longer be understood by either retail or corporate customers nor on occasion by the vendors themselves.

The software product manager dealing with licenses and other contractual matters always requires the assistance of attorneys specialized in this subject area. Nevertheless, he should at least be familiar with the basic provisions of his company's license agreements and transaction documents, which we describe below. Even within a single company, there may be multiple license types to cover different sorts of products: the most obvious categories are "rental" products where a fee is paid for use and right to use terminates if the fee is no longer paid; perpetual right to use; and services. For definitions of the most common charging alternatives see section 5.5.

Within each of these categories there will be some terms which are set by corporate management and which are rarely if ever variable by product (e.g. a limitations of liability clause) and others which have more scope for variability (e.g. the metric by which a product is priced, for example registered vs. concurrent users). The product manager will need to know the first set of license terms to ensure that he does not undermine them with any product-specific terms; he then may choose amongst variable license terms for any specifically needed by his product(s). While he will have benefit of counsel to advise him, their concern will be the macroeconomic legal consequences of certain terms while the product manager will need to understand the microeconomic implications of his options and use them within allowable constraints to optimize terms for his specific product.

It is in everyone's interest to keep variation to a minimum: the customer will perceive less complexity; the sales force (or channel) will have fewer variations to remember and explain; legal, pricing, and administrative functions will have less work to do to handle the full portfolio of products which the company sells. When a customer asserts that he requires a special term, consider whether it is a term that you as a vendor wish to offer to all customers. If not, consider if granting it is wise: what are the economic consequences, will it proliferate, how will you justify granting it to some and not others? We will consider these topics at length in section 5.6.

Licensing is also relevant to open source software. There is a so-called general public license (GPL) and several variants of it that regulate copyright issues. A current hot topic for customers of products which include open source content is protection by the vendor against lawsuits for copyright or other infringement of code imbedded in the open source and used by the vendor in his product.

Service Level Agreement (SLA)

If the software is not installed by the customer, but rather provided as a service by the vendor, a so-called service level agreement is concluded to define the relationship between the customer and the provider. In this case the customer generally has neither a license nor a maintenance agreement. We will discuss SLAs below.

4.6.6.1 License Structure

"General" Terms

These will include most of the following:

1. Some form of acceptance of the contract, e.g. "By opening this package or by downloading this program you accept..."
2. Definition of specific terms used in the contract
3. The entitlement or **scope** of the license: the content of the license agreement, i.e. the scope of software, documentation, any hardware included (e.g. user backups) must be defined. Vendor services (e.g. for custom modifications, initial migration work and for user training) and further services such as additional copies of the documentation are usually defined in a separate services agreement.

    It is worthwhile here to explain an accounting principle which will be important to the vendor (and which may explain certain vendor behaviors to the customer): in most countries, revenue for OTC software is generally bookable upon delivery of usable product and invoice to the customer. However, if there are services to be performed or an acceptance test following modifications or there is a right of the customer to cancel, then the revenue will not be bookable until all of the contingency conditions have been performed and are accepted. In today's frenetic scramble for more and earlier revenue, such contingencies will be very hard for a vendor to accept.

4. **Money back Guarantee, Warranty, Maintenance, and Customer Remedies**.

    One of the peculiarities of software is that inherent in most licenses and contracts there is an assumption by both the vendor and the customer that the software contains errors (bugs). That is why the terms and conditions of the license must define how such bugs and any necessary modifications are to be dealt with:

- **Guarantee:** the only true "guarantee" with most software is a money-back provision if the customer is not satisfied; this generally takes the form of a trial period after which you must pay or you will no longer be able to use some or all of the functionality or a "pay now and we will refund your money within xx days if you are not satisfied". The "xx" usually ranges between 30 and 90, seldom longer. Both of these approaches, while helpful to the customer raise revenue recognition issues for the vendor.
- **Warranty:** a period during which the vendor agrees to make the product perform as promised in specifications, advertising, or sales presentations. The warranty period is typically one year, unless specifically stipulated otherwise. Assistance with debugging and provision of fixes are usually free of charge during the warranty period, i.e. included in the license price. This situation may continue longer if maintenance is paid for the license.
- In this area the definition of a "bug" is always a critical item. A frequent matter of customer/vendor dispute is determination of the severity of a bug and whether or not it really is a bug or rather a request for product enhancement. IBM says that if the code does not do what the product specification says it does, that is a bug. However, on occasion, when a bug cannot be fixed, the specification is changed rather than the code. It may be impossible to achieve a legal definition that is absolutely airtight.

5. **Transferability** provisions (if any)
   The license agreement takes effect after it has been legally signed, or in the case of shrink-wrapped software after the package has been opened, downloaded from the web, installed for the first time, or used for the first time depending on the legal situation. Software downloaded from the internet typically requires the licensee to agree explicitly to the terms and conditions of the license. Among other things, it must be stipulated:

   - whether or not the licensee may transfer the license to a third party,
   - whether or not the licensee may transfer the license to another physical computer,
   - how to proceed within a local area network,
   - how copies of the code are to be handled.

If a larger company wants to use a greater quantity of one or more of the vendor's workstation software products, a corporate license agreement including maintenance is often purchased covering deployment and maintenance for a specified period of time. This allows the company to install and use any number of or up to the defined number of products included in the agreement. Software license management may thus be somewhat simplified, though generally there is a vendor requirement that the customer keep track of what has been deployed or is in use (these numbers will in any event be required when the customer extends the contract or seeks to purchase maintenance for what is deployed).

Such corporate licenses are always negotiated on an individual basis. Company-wide licensing requires not only the price to be stipulated, but also, among other things,

- whether or not subsidiaries are also included, and if so, what parent company ownership percentage is required,
- whether or not the number of installations is unlimited, even if the company grows to a significant extent (e.g. through mergers),
- how to proceed if parts of the company are sold,
- whether or not the company may also use the software as an application service provider (ASP) or for hosting,
- whether or not home offices are included.

6. **Type of charges and what they cover:** not the specific price but possibly how the product is charged in terms of metrics. This is also a candidate for a product-specific addendum to the generic vendor license.
7. **Limitations of liability** clause which usually prevents claims resulting from consequential damages (e.g. a database program renders your customer database inoperable, costing you $10 M in lost sales). In fact, most vendors try to limit liability to the price of the products.
8. **Maintenance provisions:** Usually if a customer wants to continue to use the debugging service described under "Warranty" and have access to fixes past the end of the warranty period, he must acquire a maintenance contract. The provisions for such a contract may be imbedded in license or may, once again, be a separate document. In the maintenance agreement the vendor will define the entitlements being conveyed, charging and duration, and termination provisions. The vendor may also define a support escalation process which brings more resource to bear depending on the severity of the bugs. But see also under "Warranty" what a fix may entail. Some vendors also include upgrades to new product versions in their maintenance agreements. Various other aspects of the maintenance services may also differ from vendor to vendor.

   In general, a vendor reserves the right in the terms and conditions of the license to terminate maintenance for a software product or product version, the common practice being to give notice of this in advance. The vendor does this with the aim of reducing maintenance costs and motivating customers still using older product versions to migrate to new ones. The announcement that maintenance services are to be discontinued is usually not received very well by the customers involved. This regularly gives rise to fierce protests that are then settled by reaching a compromise.

   Different geographies will have different views on this. Different product sets may attract different reactions. In Japan there is a tendency to stick with a product for a very long time, to the extent of being willing to pay extra for product "n" maintenance in order not to have to move to "n+1". This is an extension of the adage "if it ain't broke, don't fix it." But this can also delay introduction of new technology. When IBM withdrew VS1 from sales and support in the early 1980s, there were only about two hundred customers still using VS1 and there was essentially no pushback from those customers, most of whom moved to MVS (or off the platform). But when, a few years later, it was announced that IBM intended to stabilize VSE and withdraw it from marketing in 10 years time, there was an uproar. Of course, there were multiple thousands of customers using VSE and the difficulty of conversion was much greater.

9. **Legal provisions and limitations**, e.g. definition of the period during which one can make claims, governing law, and which courts will be used in case of dispute. Other legal provisions to be included pertain to the mutual handling of confidential information as well as to the rights and responsibilities entailed in terminating the license agreement, legal remedies and issues of compensation for damages and liability. A corporate customer in doubt about a producer's soundness may insist on a source code escrow (escrow service). This allows the corporate customer to access the source code in the event that the producer declares bankruptcy, thereby ensuring that maintenance can be continued. While customers sometimes ask for this, it is usually more a bargaining chip in negotiation than a practical request. The source code of an operating system, for example, would not be helpful for a customer. Some vendors like IBM even have large chunks of code in proprietary languages for which compilers are not commercially available. And where would the customer find the resource and talent to work on such code? Often customers lose interest in such a request when confronted by the cost of having an escrow agent keep a copy of the code.

10. **Any country unique provisions:** this might include, for example, the use of Brazilian courts for disputes involving licenses installed in Brazil.

4.6.6.2   Product-Specific Provisions

Terms specific to an individual product or family of products which differ from the standard license may be part of the same license document or the license may be structured so that it covers the terms common across all the vendor's products and refers to separate product-unique documents for the special terms for specific products. The latter structure has the advantage of consistent terms at the license level with uniqueness only as required by specific products. The division we have made in this section between general and specific terms are somewhat arbitrary but do reflect the structures in place with some vendors. These specific terms may cover a variety of product-specific provisions:

1. **Special metrics for charging**, e.g. a database product charged based on quantity of data managed
2. **Unique service terms (if any)**
3. **Restrictions of use**, e.g. this program may not be exported outside the European Union without permission from... .
4. **Where the program may be installed and used**, e.g. on a desktop and laptop provided only one copy is in use at any one time.

5. **Product-specific modifications** to any of the general terms; e.g. "this product is supplied on an 'as-is' basis and warranty terms do not apply."
6. **Availability of Source Code and Modification Rights:** Most software products are delivered with the object code only, and are subject to the provision included in the terms and conditions of the license that reverse engineering, i.e. a recreation of the source code is prohibited. The purpose of this is to protect the producer's intellectual property, although the legal enforcement of such stipulations is controversial (see [Samuel03] for the US). Some products are delivered as hybrids (executables, installation procedures, online documentation, samples, i.e. source code), but source code components must be recompiled when they are integrated into the customer's environment. Many application solutions also have an "inalterable" kernel (delivered only as an object code) and a shell (for which the source code is also provided), which allows customization. In contrast open source products usually provide the entire source code as available and alterable. Although open source products are by definition available for use without any license fees having to be paid, these products are also subject to licensing terms and conditions in which at the least copyrights are laid down.

If custom modifications are to be made, significant additional detail needs to be added to the contract (usually not the license):

- The precise nature of the modifications (perhaps by referencing a separate specifications document)
- The changes which may be requested to those specifications and what the implications of changes will be in terms of cost and time
- Delivery date of the code and any penalties for late delivery or bonuses for early delivery
- Definition of an acceptance test and the consequences and remedies if the code does not pass
- If appropriate, performance criteria for the modifications and explicitly who will own the code and the rights to use such modifications. It must also be stipulated whether or not anyone apart from the corporate customer's personnel may have access to the code, e.g. external consultants for modifications and customization or an outsourcing company providing data processing services. Any vendor-performed code modifications or installation support, e.g. hardware customization, will require a services contract, often with an annual maintenance supplement if the support of the modifications is ongoing.

4.6.6.3   Transaction Document

The transaction document is a key component of the contract between vendor and customer. It often takes the form of an invoice, though it may be a full-fledged contract. It may incorporate by reference terms from a customer purchase order and will usually, if a contract, make reference to all the documents we discuss in this section. It may also contain terms and conditions, the most typical being payment terms. But there may be other terms included by both vendor and customer: terms can be attached to a purchase order as easily as to an invoice. These might comprise specified discounts for subsequent additional purchases, maintenance, might limit transferability based on terms of acquisition etc.

The following would not be in a license, but would be in any contract (or covered in a transaction document):

1. **Definition of enterprise:** defines the scope of the organization who is the purchaser of the software and across which corporate entity the code may be used as well as their specific entitlements.

   For example, if General Motors were to acquire licenses there would probably be no restrictions on using them in either GMC or Chevrolet divisions. However, there probably would be limitations on their ability to give or sell those licenses to Ford.

   We will discuss this again in the section on pricing for corporate customers; for our purposes here, let us simply say that such contracts usually are discounted and the enterprise definition is critical to limit the discount to the intended party and prevent "buying clubs" in which a number of customers could pool their demand and insist on a discount.

2. **Terms of payment:** This might be anything from due when presented to a financed contract over five years. It could also stipulate conditions which define the limits of use and price for exceeding those limits.

3. **Contract duration and renewal; situation at end of contract:** Often today vendors are eager to sign "overlay" or "relationship" contracts providing additional benefits in exchange for larger sales, ongoing purchases, and broader acquisitions within the portfolio. Examples are IBM's ELA (Enterprise License Agreement), Microsoft's Select program, and IBM's Passport Advantage offering for distributed software. Because these offerings continue for a period which may transcend the specific purchase at a moment in time, there is often need to say what happens when/if the contract ends and/or what provisions exist while it is in force.

4. **Remedies for contract non-compliance:** Simply how disputes will be resolved – from either side.

5. **Termination:** For a contract which is ongoing for a period of time, under what provisions it may be terminated by either party and what the consequences of such termination might be. For example, if $2 M of distributed software is acquired and financed over three years and then the customer decides he wishes to terminate the contract, clearly settlement charges will be due at the very least to repay the unpaid borrowed principal.

6. **Audit clause:** In the ever more complex world of IP (intellectual property) licensing with ever more complex ways of pricing and measuring software usage, differences sometimes arise between the vendor's and the customer's view of the amount of software deployed, in use, whose use has been measured, etc. In order to protect their intellectual property and to provide a neutral view of disputed situations, vendors are insisting more and more to have the right to audit if there is a dispute. This is often unpopular with customers; however, it

should be viewed as a motivator to keep good records and as a safeguard as much against vendor overcharging as a protection for the vendor.

4.6.6.4 Relationship between a Corporate IT Organization and Other Units of the Corporation

A corporate IT organization acts as a service provider for the company's other business units. The services provided include further development and operation of the software and hardware used to support the business processes of the other departments. Whereas in the past the relationship between the in-house IT department and other departments was often informal, it has lately become common practice to use formal service level agreements (SLAs) to define this relationship, especially if the IT organization has been restructured as a legal self-contained corporate entity, almost like an outsourcer.

SLAs stipulate which services a customer can expect to receive from a provider. In particular, this includes the:

- functional scope,
- availability as an average as well as the maximum length of downtime,
- quality in terms of absolute errors per time period according to degree of severity and maximum time for debugging according to degree of severity,
- performance guarantee, e.g. response time behavior or load values,
- scope and quality of user support, e.g. hotline, and maximum reaction time to operational demands, e.g. special evaluation of data on hand,
- reaction time to new functional demands,
- test options for new releases and versions including the scope of support and maximum debugging time according to degree of severity (we have used IBM terminology where a release is part of the product and considered to be at no additional charge whether OTC or MLC. A new version is a new product for which there is no inherent entitlement in the old product license, though there may be transition offerings).
- backup frequency and maximum restore time,
- disaster recovery measures.

The SLAs not only define a price and a price structure, but, at least for contracting parties that do not belong to the same corporation, also the penalties that must be paid in the event of a breach of the warranty terms or the contractual performance stipulated by the service provider. The purpose of this is to motivate the provider and compensate for damage incurred by the customer in the event of a system failure.

4.6.6.5 SaaS Agreement between the Vendor and the Customer

In case of SaaS, the customer does not acquire a license, but a service. So here the relationship between the customer and the vendor is very similar to the one between a business unit and a corporate IT organization. This similarity suggests that a similar type of formal agreement would be used. However, so far SaaS providers have mostly avoided SLA-type commitments as described above. The typical argument is that the vendor/provider cannot take responsibility for the reliability and performance of the internet connection between his server and the customer's site.

We predict that this will change over time. For business-critical applications customers cannot rely on vendors/providers that refuse such commitments. There are service providers which have strong market positions both in networking and in running big (offshore) computing centers offering combined services to software vendors for running their SaaS business. On this basis, tight SLAs including the network connection will be feasible. Also some SaaS providers add offline components to their SaaS offerings thus enabling customers to continue their work during downtimes of the communication network or the SaaS server, but this will not be practical for all types of applications.

4.6.7 Protection of Intellectual Property

In section 4.6.1 we discussed the fundamental difference between evolutionary development and groundbreaking innovation. The software product manager normally deals with evolution. The task of bringing products to market that are based on real innovation will be the exception. In such a case, the software product manager will typically not be involved until the innovation has reached a stage at which it can be included in the normal development process. Regardless of whether it is a question of evolution or innovation, the results can lead to a significant market differentiation and to major competitive advantages. The software product manager will then be responsible for finding a way to turn these competitive advantages into market success and safeguarding the competitive edge as long as possible.

There are a number of different legal constructs for the protection of intellectual property the details of which have been and will continue to be a subject of discussion. From a macro-economic view, protection leads to more innovation since it increases the return on investments in innovation. On the downside the use of the innovative idea by others is delayed or made more expensive, since it cannot be directly copied. An example is a pharmaceutical company that develops a new drug and keeps the price high, thereby limiting its use. On the micro-economic level, if a company seeks legal protection it needs to make a description of what it wants to protect public which makes it easier for competitors to understand it and duplicate it legally (and sometimes illegally). Since this can be difficult to prove with software, smaller companies sometimes avoid publishing their innovations, whereas larger corporations mostly prefer it. The advantages are the protection of competitive advantage, possibly an extra income through license fees, negotiating leverage in case of conflicts with other patent-holding companies, and the marketing aspect of an innovative corporate image. Of course, there is no automatic correlation between the innovative capability of a company and the number of patents it holds, since the acceptance of a patent does not signify that the content is useful. So far, the general public does not seem to have realized this.

So how can intellectual property be protected? Here are the basic alternatives:

- **Trademark:** Protection for the names of brands.
- **Trade Secret:** Protection of company-internal knowledge (primarily against employees). This protection is exercised by restricting knowledge to a very small number of people; a frequently quoted example of this is the formula for Coca-Cola.
- **Copyright:** Protection against copying of information or algorithms or specific expressions of an idea or way of doing something.
- **Patent:** Protection of the specific technical implementation of a concept or idea. For software it can often not be separated from the idea.

Traditionally, text has been subject to copyright law, technology to patent law. Since software became an issue, legal authorities and software developers, seeking protection for their intellectual property, have sought to choose existing recognized forms of protection under the law and have tried to press software into these existing alternatives (see [Klemens06]) not accepting the fact that it does not really fit. This has led to continuous controversial discussions and country-specific regulations that are not aligned internationally, not even within the European Union.

In the US up until 1980, patent rights were hardware-oriented, i.e. it was hardly possible to have software patented. In response to pressure from software vendors, a Supreme Court decision changed the rules. Suddenly almost everything was patentable, even business processes. This resulted in a glut of patent applications, some of which seem rather useless or even ridiculous (see [Klemens06], p. 1 ff.). In order to extend copyright law, the Digital Millenium Copyright Act was introduced in the US in 1998 which forbids the ownership of tools that can be used to circumvent copy protection.

As long as software patents refer to implementation details, they can be circumvented by implementing the functionality in some other way. This becomes more difficult if user interface elements that implicitly describe a business process are patented (see the Amazon example below).

Over recent years conflicts have increasingly arisen regarding open source software and patents, as companies have introduced patented elements into open source processes and subsequently requested license fees. All open source groups have refused to accept this, arguing that using patents this way prevents progress. In 2002, open source guru Richard Stallman said that U.S. patent logic would have forced Beethoven to pay Mozart for the right to create a new symphony.

The monetary judgments that have been sought and sometimes granted in patent infringement cases in the US are increasingly seen as life-threatening for participants in the US software market.

The way that patent offices review software patents is also being criticized more and more. Officially, an application may not be accepted as a patent if its content already constitutes public property, i.e., whatever is already generally being used may not be patented. Unfortunately, there are good examples showing that patent offices were not capable of judging this. In [Besaha03] Besaha proposes measures for improving the patent process. In two ground-breaking rulings in April 2007, the US Supreme Court decided to lower the requirements regarding the non-obvious-ness test (Teleflex vs. KSR International) and restricted the applicability of US pat-ent law to US territory (AT&T vs. Microsoft).

Amazon is a widely discussed example of how patents can be used to safeguard the competitive edge of a product platform. Amazon had its one-click technology patented, making the ordering process extremely easy for registered customers. This discussion revolves around the issue of patentability. Opponents argue that, ever since the invention of the mouse, a click has always been used to effect a transaction. In their opinion, this technology is therefore not patentable. Proponents say that this special type of one-click technology used in connection with the online commercial transaction process for which Amazon has submitted a patent application did not previously exist in this form and can therefore be patented. Pamela Samuelson pro-vides a good summary of the discussion of patentability in [Samuel08].

This subject is being heatedly discussed in Europe, too. In compliance with the current European patent agreements, neither a computer program nor a business method can be patented as such. However, since it is not clear how a computer pro-gram differs from an invention that includes a computer program as one component among others, the European patent office has accepted software-related patents in the past few years. The European Commission started a legislative process in order to establish more explicit common regulations that would be valid for all of Europe, but failed to come to an agreement. The urgency for Europe is obvious since the heterogeneous legal situation within the European Union means costs for patent applications are higher than in the US by a factor of 10.

Changes in the legal situation in both the USA and Europe regarding the granting of software patents can be expected on an ongoing basis given the discussions described above. Yet, regardless of how the legal situation develops, the software product manager will still be responsible for considering a patent application as a means of protecting intellectual propoerty and safeguarding competitive advantages.

There are additional ways and means to do this. A key factor is assuring that val-uable technical employees continue to be committed to the company. Studies show that typically less than 10% of the development staff actually possess the essential product- or technology-related skills. These are the employees that the company definitely wants to retain. This requires company-wide personnel retention pro-grams that are generally not within the software product manager's scope of respon-sibility or authority. However, the software product manager needs to ensure that the employees relevant to his product are included in these programs. The competitive advantage can also be maintained by continuing to expand the differentiating ele-ments through further product development. SAP, for example, continued to increase the scope of SAP component integration faster than any competitor.

A major problem for all vendors selling software licenses is software piracy. IDC conducted a new study for the Business Software Alliance (BSA) ([BSAIDC08]) on global software piracy. According to this study 38% of all PC software installations worldwide are not properly licensed leading to a total revenue loss of 48 billion $. The piracy rate ranges from 93% in Armenia to 20% in the US. Even if these numbers are a bit inflated there is no doubt that there is a significant problem and only slow progress. Many large software vendors now insist on the contractual right to audit customers as one way of curbing losses. That of course offers no protection for software usable by single clients, pirated versions of which are often available in Russia, China, and elsewhere for a fraction of the normal cost. Microsoft now checks routinely whether the requestor has a legitimate license before allowing downloads of maintenance and upgrades. One of the attractive features of SaaS for vendors is that it eliminates the piracy risk.

4.7 Product Planning

A Software Product Manager spends a lot of his time with the rather unproductive, but necessary task to represent his product (or family or platform) in the internal planning processes of his company. This includes the marketing and sales plans and the budget and resource planning. The underlying question is which resources will be dedicated to the product short, medium and long term. This decision is based on market and revenue forecasts, the positioning of the product in its life cycle, the dependencies with other products (in particular with families and platforms), etc. From these elements the product manager puts his "story" together that he uses to "sell" his product within the planning processes.

The company's culture influences how these planning processes work and what is expected from the product manager. Ideally all involved parties should have the common goal to get to a joint result that is optimal for the company. Often, however, these processes degenerate into a competition that the players try to use for their personal advancement. The "winner" is the one who gets the most resources for his product. Only the executive management can prevent this degeneration. The individual product manager will have to play his role according to the company's culture, good or bad.

Typically, the corporate planning process is a mix of bottom-up and top-down planning; bottom-up in the sense that each product manager develops a plan from his product perspective; top-down because Corporate, typically under the lead of Finance, looks at the aggregated bottom-up plans and cuts them down to what seems affordable. Since the assigned budget and resources have their consequences on the revenue side, this process is iterated until an agreement is reached. So this process serves as a synchronization point at which the plans on all levels and of all products are in sync. The schedule for this process is usually defined by Corporate. IBM for example goes through two cycles per year, the spring and the fall plan.

Product planning belongs to the core activities of a software product manager as described in the Software Product Management Framework (see section 4.3). In the narrow definition of van de Weert, Brinkkemper e.a. [WBNVB06], software product management is basically defined by these planning processes plus portfolio management. The main elements of product planning are the roadmap definition, release planning, and requirements management which for application software leads to the functional specification. These elements are discussed in detail in the following sections in a top-down sequence. From an execution perspective, requirements management is a continuous activity while roadmaps and release plans are only revised at discrete points in time. So these revisions can always be based on the knowledge that has been accumulated in requirements management and is most current. In that sense requirements management precedes release planning.

4.7.1 Roadmap

In the software business, a product roadmap gives an overview how a product is going to develop over the strategic timeframe of up to 5 years in terms of new releases or versions, their schedules and major themes. Usually important dependencies on other products or platform technology are shown. In some companies, the roadmap includes a rough financial picture, i.e. expected revenues and costs. While the roadmap can be rather detailed and precise for the short-term timeframe, the more it looks into the future, the less precise it tends to be.

The main purpose of a roadmap is to give direction internally and externally. Internally it shows the relationship between product plans and financial forecasts and the major themes and requirements governing the plan. It indicates if the product will provide continuing career opportunities for employees who work on it, be they developers, sales, or support specialists. Externally the roadmap plays an important role in demonstrating the viability of a product as well. Often bigger potential customers are willing to sign non-disclosure agreements in order to see a product roadmap before they make a significant investment decision. Similarly, market analysts mostly base their judgement on a convincing story about a product's future expressed in the roadmap.

In reality, only the first one to two years in a roadmap are more or less reliable, and even those are often impacted by slippages caused by development. The outer years can usually not be considered as more than a formal way of saying that the vendor has a long-term commitment to the product. In several decades in the business, we have never seen the contents of a roadmap for the outer years become reality without significant change. Nevertheless, the roadmap is important for a product manager in order to reach agreement within his company regarding the longer-term direction and priorities, and for the roadmap's useful effects described above. The roadmap is usually updated as part of the corporate planning cycle.

4.7.2 Release Planning

Release planning is concerned with two questions: when and what. The academic world has done some interesting work on this subject by considering it as an optimization problem (see for example [SalRuh07]). Major factors to be taken into account are the value and effort estimated for individual requirements, marketing themes attached to new releases or versions, and dependencies between requirements and on other products or outside events like trade fairs, and sometimes even customer commitments. Some of these, like value and effort or dependencies between requirements can be dealt with in formal optimization approaches, others cannot. That is why Ruhe and Saliu have entitled one of their articles "The Art and Science of Software Release Management" ([RuhSal05]), and it is one reason why scientific solutions are not yet broadly used by product managers.

The ideal, of course, is a well-balanced release that contains all mandatory requirements, all important customer requirements plus some strategic initiatives, quality improvements for an increase of customer satisfaction, functional and non-functional requirements, and is perfectly timed (see also section 4.7.3). This ideal will rarely be achieved in practice. Usually focus areas have to be defined for a release like a quality release or a migration release that supports a new database system. There are often disputes whether smaller releases with higher frequency or bigger releases with lower frequency are a better choice:

- Smaller releases with less effort can be implemented faster and allow a more flexible reaction to customer situations and changes in the competitive landscape. On the other hand, due to the high fixed cost per release for product and project management, regression test, cost of packaging and distribution and sales and marketing, they are comparatively more costly. More variants in use usually means higher support complexity. This has often been a reason for withdrawal of support.
- Bigger releases are more economical, and sometimes unavoidable due to requirements whose implementation can only be done with higher effort and duration. In any case, the release cycle must not be too long in order not to risk changes in the market.

Customers are usually more hesitant when they are faced with installing a bigger release. They prefer to follow the guideline "Never change a running system" unless there are strong reasons for the change like attractive new functionality or unavoidable support of new infrastructure, i.e. hardware or software. With smaller releases, they see less risk.

A lot of software companies combine frequent smaller releases with infrequent bigger releases. A typical structure today is the issuing of critical fixes as they are developed followed by an entire release dedicated to maintenance and rolling up the fixes with perhaps some more necessary changes that cannot be implemented except in conjunction with all the critical fixes. An example is Windows XP, then SP1, then SP2, and SP3 with critical fixes all along the way. The product manager must keep an eye on upward and downward compatibility between releases and versions as descibed in chapter 2.

Release planning becomes a complex multi-dimensional problem when product families, lines, or platforms are involved (see section 4.7.3). When there is not only the time-oriented versioning as described above, but also horizontal versioning like the same product in different languages or on multiple platforms, or vertical versioning like different variants of a product with reduced functionality and different price points, this also adds to complexity. When a product comprises a bundle of separate products with individual release plans where a particular release of one product has functional dependencies on a particular release of another product, release planning and execution for the bundled product can become a nightmare. This operational complexity needs to be taken into account when bundling alternatives are considered.

Release plans are frequently revised outside of the corporate planning cycles since these revisions are often triggered by schedules not met, be it the product's own schedules or schedules of products it is dependent on. In those cases the next corporate planning cycle provides the next formal synchronization point.

4.7.3 Requirements Management and Specification

One of any product manager's core tasks is requirements management. Given the special importance of this topic, we will deal with it in some detail. In our opinion, the best and most comprehensive book on the subject of requirements management was written by Bruno Schienmann [Schien02]. We have therefore adopted his approach of considering three dimensions of requirements management, namely customer, product, and project requirements management, and we will describe the processes associated with each of these dimensions. Other good sources of information about requirements management are the books by Suzanne and James Robertson [RobRob06] and Chris Rupp [Rupp07].

A software product manager is focused on the product dimension for which he uses requirements from different sources as input. Product requirements are typically implemented as part of a project, i.e. they are included in the management of project requirements. Studies on the reasons for the success and failure of products and projects like the Standish Chaos Report ([Stand06]) confirm again and again that the most frequent cause of project failure is the lack of or insufficient requirements management. This includes the identification, exact specification, prioritization, and documentation of requirements and, above all, the way in which requirement changes are handled during product development. On the other hand, when we examine successful projects, the most important success factor is usually rigorous requirements management. Standish Group studies based on more than 50,000 projects up to now show that in the majority of cases project failure is directly linked to requirements management.

The product manager can use various sources of information to define the requirements – depending on the type of product, the sales and distribution channels used and the available infrastructure. This section lists and assesses these sources. Later, it discusses how requirements can be categorized and evaluated according to various criteria. This can then be used as a basis for prioritizing and bundling or packaging the requirements for releases. This is all based on the assumption that each requirement is thoroughly documented and analyzed.

In reality, during the development of essentially every product there will be the need to change existing requirements or include completely new ones. Such changes pose a high risk for most projects and possess a high potential for conflict between Sales and Marketing, Development, and Product Management, which the product manager will need to resolve. It is important in this context to understand how requirements management and the development process are interconnected, since different development methods also differ in how "enthusiastically" they react to requirement changes and to the frequency of such changes.

Very often, products do not stand alone but are part of a larger group of products, brand, platform, or offering. Finally then, we address the issue of how requirements management for individual products can be embedded in the product management of product families or platforms; and we examine the resulting interdependencies as well as the possibilities of achieving synergies.

Sources for Requirements

The project manager can and should consult various sources to gather requirements for a new product or release he is to manage. These sources can be external (i.e. outside of one's own company and organization) as well as internal.

Each of the groups or sources mentioned below has its own view of the product to be developed and of its requirements. The more possibilities the product manager has to access different sources, the more assured he can be that he has gathered a balanced mixture of requirements to use as a basis for his own prioritization, that he has not completely forgotten or neglected any group, and that he has thus minimized the risk of planning and developing a product that fails to meet the market requirements completely.

Product Positioning

As described in section 4.6.3, the initial positioning of a product or changes to the positioning during the product life cycle frequently result in significant requirements. One example is the decision to sell a product internationally. The resulting requirement for different languages may be the most apparent, but While far from the only characteristic distinguishing an international product from a purely domestic one, different languages are the most apparent, so let us look at the language requirements first.

If a product is first released in local language and subsequently translated into another language and made available in another country, retrofitting the second or nth language is often very time consuming if NLS (national language support) enabling was not taken into account in the product specifications and design. Such an approach requires language-dependent parts of the product (user interface/screen masks) as well as messages, help functions and online documentation, etc. to be separated from the logical code, for instance, a potentially herculean task if not provided for in the original design.

In addition to the language requirements, there are usually legal regulations (e.g. tax laws, social insurance contributions), standards or certificates and permits (e.g. GAAP certificate or FASB criteria for financial applications) that need to be observed, met or obtained, respectively, for each specific country. There may be cultural issues to consider or local usage: consider the trivial example of the use in the U.S. of the period as a decimal separator and the comma as a thousands separator, while in Europe and much of the world, the roles of those punctuation marks is reversed. Getting such points right may be crucial to the success of products in specific countries. Years ago, one of our French IBM colleagues, frustrated by the decommitment of NLS in a VM release, drove home his point by delivering his formal sales position on release to sales of VM/SP 5 entirely in French to a stunned audience of US developers and executives. After a while he paused and asked, "Now do you understand the importance of national language support?"

Even in the case of purely functional requirements different countries have different priorities, often due to cultural differences. As all these cases show, an internationally oriented and synchronized product management that takes these various aspects into consideration and prioritizes them properly is particularly important to successful international development and sales.

Market Research/Market Studies

Market research was covered in section 4.4. Knowledgeable market analysts can provide helpful feedback on product weaknesses and strengths. Information on technological and market developments can also result in product-specific requirements.

User Groups or Associations

User groups are associations of standard software users (usually corporate customers). These groups focus on exchanging information with other members of the group and, above all, also with the software vendor, in particular for the purpose of directly influencing the vendor's product development.

This is an excellent tool for the product manager to obtain first-hand feedback from many customers on the strengths and weaknesses of his products. Requirements for future products/future releases are usually defined in great detail and based on technical competence, allowing the product manager to critically evaluate them. The members of the user associations hope they will be able to exert greater influence or even pressure on the vendor than they could if each individual customer contacted the vendor directly. On the whole, both parties profit, however, since the product manager can hardly find a more efficient way of maintaining direct contact with the customers of his products and thus obtaining relevant, unfiltered information. Most major software vendors have user groups and conferences on an international scale, e.g. SAP with its SAPphire conferences and its country user groups which cooperate in SUGEN (SAP User Group Executive Network) on a worldwide level.

For consumer market software products, a good source of customer feedback on both one's own products and competing products are the pertinent Web logs, or so-called blogs.

No matter the source of inputs, the product manager must always view customer input in an overall context. He must know how representative the requirements suggested by a select circle of users are for all customers. The requirements that are presented most vehemently are not always the most important or the ones that will in the medium and long term help to promote or secure the product and its market position. Given finite resource to develop, he will need to be sanguine in choosing those requirements which, if implemented, will result in additional sales.

Customer Input

Customer satisfaction surveys usually do not result in detailed requirements, but can provide valuable pointers to product-related areas that need improvement (see section 4.5).

Events held for individual customers, whether in the form of a systematic interview or a workshop, are a suitable instrument for generating, critically evaluating, and detailing product requirements. Interviews should be well prepared and proceed systematically (questionnaires) in order to obtain comparable results in case several events are held, but should also give the customer enough leeway for discussions and suggestions.

Depending on the customer contact person concerned, it seems sensible for the product manager to engage members of the sales and marketing staff (head of sales and marketing, account manager) and have them attend the events. However, a vendor must be careful to have consistent marketing messages to the customer representatives. Otherwise the enthusiasm of a lab developer for the next release can easily leave the distinct impression that the current release has numerous problems and that any implementation ought to be delayed, the opposite of what sales would like the customers to take away from the session. The developer point of view can easily be delivered in a slightly different way, "The product is excellent now, and we are continuing to invest to make it even better. By installing now, you reap rewards from the function it provides today and all the benefits from future development as a plus." As opposed to what one of the authors heard from a developer at his first customer meeting, "Well, yes there are a number of problems now but those can all be avoided by installing the new microcode release when it's available next year."

Workshops are suited for detailed technical discussions of individual requirements and problems as well as for presentations of prototypes or potential solutions by the vendor. There are cases when the customer himself has developed a product "add-on" for a requirement that the vendor is interested in because it could be integrated into the standard product. In such cases, it is advisable for the product manager to meet with the customer together with a development manager or a system architect. Another proven forum is a "customer advisory council" of carefully selected and representational users to review plans and critique them before new functions are invested in. However, this only works if the customers are representative of the target market and insightful about where the technology or requirements for the specific product set are headed.

Retailers/Partners/VARs

Software products that are sold and distributed by other than direct sales (retailers, partners, value-added resellers) are often particularly difficult for the product manager to "grasp." If the product is sold and distributed by third parties only – which is frequently the case with consumer products – the in-house sales department does not have any direct customer contact and thus cannot obtain any pertinent information.

In this case, the retailers and partners are an important source of information for obtaining suggestions for new products or feedback on existing products. In any case, since such business partnerships can only work if both parties benefit from them, a retailer or partner must be positive about the vendor's products – regardless of whether he makes money out of the license or product consulting and implementation services. The reseller will be as keen to remove inhibitors to sales as the vendor and is a good source of such information. The notion that the vendor takes this input seriously will be key to his faith in the vendor's commitment to the product.

So this is an important target group for the product manager, and he should ensure two-way communication. Retailer and partner events organized in cooperation with the partners' sales department are – like the user meetings discussed above – a good forum for the exchange of ideas.

Consultants/Professional Services

Consultants can also be a valuable source for gathering new requirements, especially for commercial software products that require a great deal of consultation, customization and implementation services. Here advantages are that they are independent, are often familiar with the products in various customer environments, and have usually already worked with similar competing products. This also applies – with certain restrictions – to in-house professional services organizations, if existent.

Research

There are few companies that only produce software and conduct their own basic research. As an alternative, software vendors may work with universities. In any case, this source needs to be taken in consideration, since researchers can give a product manager important ideas and directon, especially for product strategy and further technological development. Even if a lot of research ideas cannot be directly converted into products, it is of key importance for the product manager to keep a long-term perspective, to recognize new developments to be expected within the next three to five years, and to think about how current products can be positioned accordingly early enough.

Furthermore, many innovations can be implemented in a better way if they are initially tested in a research environment, where they are not subject to the constraints of product development, and are not given to the development department until sufficient experience has been collected using them (see chapter 6).

Development

The development function is always a good source for new requirements. No other unit has a deeper understanding of the technical details or needs to develop such an understanding when a new product is to be developed. This also poses a certain risk, however, as every software developer would like to develop something that is technically interesting – and in some sense perfect. That is why sometimes not enough attention is given to actual market and customer requirements. Moreover, a simple technical solution to a problem that is available in a timely fashion is usually better and above all financially more promising than the famous "gold-plated" version that the development team might like to present. One of the most difficult phenomena to manage in this context is the tendency of executives and development managers to match or just slightly outdo the competitor of the moment. This can be referred to as "shooting behind the duck," because it fails utterly to take into account that the competitor (duck as target) will move whilst development takes place on those features to match him. In order to be successful, a product manager must anticipate what customers want beyond what current competition offers and get there before competition while at the same time matching what competition has today that appeals to customers.

There are also numerous requirements, however, that are due to technical necessity and must be implemented – some of which the customer does not even notice. An example is changing over to a new operating system or database release as a necessary prerequisite. This can become necessary because maintenance for the old version is being terminated or because the new version delivers functions that offer advantages for one's own product and should therefore be utilized (such as improved performance).

Sales and Distribution

At any company the sales and distribution team has the most – and hopefully the best – customer contacts. This is reason enough for it to be an important source for gathering requirements. Due to their broad scope of responsibility, however, many sales people have trouble precisely defining requirements for a single product – unless the person concerned is a product sales specialist.

The requirements obtained from the sales and distribution staff are therefore often only vaguely defined or simply express customer opinion in general. Yet, this information is also important for the product manager to have and should be taken very seriously, particularly as an "early warning system". The sales and distribution channel is most often the first to be contacted by a customer who is unsatisfied with a product or product service. In this event, it is not too late for the product manager to react and take appropriate measures before the customer switches to a comparable competing product. Meeting with the customer together with a development representative or organizing a requirements workshop often works wonders. The effect of this is that the customer is more satisfied – feeling that the vendor has taken his problems seriously – and that the sales specialist feels upbeat, having been able to define his fuzzy requirements more precisely together with the customer.

Caution must be exercised when developers meet with customers, however. The very act of bringing a developer in to talk to a customer will allow the customer to infer an expectation that his requirement will be addressed, where it may not be appropriate for the vendor to undertake at all or it may be low priority. So it should be made clear it is information gathering only unless of course there is existing functionality within the product which could help the customer. One must also guard against an excess of candor if it takes the form of "That's the silliest requirement I ever heard!"

With all the varied inputs, the product manager must develop a good instinct for identifying the real problems. Every member or head of the sales and distribution team – with minds focused in particular on the next sale – has a tendency to present his customer's requirements as the most important of all. This will often create a conflict for the product manager. On the one hand, he should always work in close collaboration with the sales unit, and on the other, he must prevent the sales and distribution staff from sidestepping him and submitting requirements directly to Development.

Marketing

The marketing team can also provide valuable inspiration for the design of a software product. Marketing is less likely to supply detailed technical requirements, but rather information about what the product must be able to do so that it can be marketed successfully in the separate channels and which features could make the product more attractive. The way in which a product is presented on the internet or is packaged for sale or advertised certainly play a major role as far as consumer products are concerned. The marketing staff can, in addition, be consulted for information regarding licensing terms and conditions, pricing, etc.

Support

The support team can be a very helpful source of information for requirements management – especially concerning consumer products not managed by a separate sales and marketing organization. The support department probably knows best which problems customers have – no other function receives as many customer complaints – so it is worthwhile for the product manager to monitor and evaluate the problem database.

Moreover, the costs generated by support are generally not negligible. Numerous call center studies have shown that 80% of all calls concern the same 5 to 10 problems. In many cases, these problems involve installation, documentation errors or ambiguities, or workflow. Improving the installation procedure, documentation, help functions or user interface can drastically reduce support costs as well as increase customer satisfaction.

Evaluation

The discussion about the various sources for requirements has illuminated the many different options available to the product manager – but also the many challenges and causes for conflict that he faces. Not all of the sources mentioned above are available or useful in every situation or for every product. It is up to the product manager to decide on the appropriate combination of sources to use. The evaluation matrix below can therefore not be considered universally applicable, but should rather be used to help in decision-making and as a trend indicator.

Source	New Product	Subsequent Product	Single Customer	B2B Product	Consumer Product
Market Research/ Market Studies	++	o	–	+	+
User Groups	– –	++	– –	++	o
Customer Interview/ Workshops	+	++	++	++	o
Customer Satisfaction Surveys	– –	+	– –	++	++
Retailers/ Partners/ VARs	–	+	– –	+	++
Consultants	o	+	++	+	–
Competitive Analysis	++	+	–	+	+
Research	++	o	o	+	+
Development	+	++	++	++	++
Sales and Distribution	+	o	++	+	o
Marketing	+	+	o	+	++
Support	–	+	o	+	++

– – not relevant; – less important; o should be taken into consideration; + important; ++ very important

Perspectives on and Categories of Requirements

Not only the diverse sources of requirements, but also the different activities, processes and interfaces suggest three supplementary perspectives on requirements management ([Schien02], p. 16 ff):

- Customer orientation: customers have requirements in order to get solutions to their problems. These requirements do not necessarily refer to particular products or projects.
- Product orientation: products provide solutions to these customer problems and the corresponding requirements. Product requirements are specified based on requirements from customers and other sources and implemented in projects.
- Project orientation: new releases of products are developed in software development projects with well-defined contents and schedules addressing product requirements.

From these three perspectives, Schienmann defines three central areas and processes of requirements management:

- Customer requirements management (customer RM): ensures that customer requirements are recognized and implemented in products.
- Product requirements management (product RM): ensures sustainability and profitability of product development by defining and prioritizing product requirements from diverse sources and mapping them to product releases.
- Project requirements management (project RM): analyzes and details product requirements and ensures implementation within the project boundaries.

Common to the three areas of requirements management are the following tasks:

- Collection of requirements from the diverse sources.
- Functional analysis that includes clarification, more detailed description, comparison with existing requirements and estimation of value.
- Documentation of the results of the functional analysis as a base for development.
- Technical analysis that includes the If and How of implementation and estimation of effort and cost.
- Go/no go decision according to the company-specific decision processes.
- Implementation according to the company-specific development and release process, i.e. outside of requirements management.
- Quality assurance, if possible through an independent QA organization, that verifies and checks if the implementation is consistent and complete compared to the original requirement.

The following tasks complement and guide the full requirements management process:

- Implementation management: ensures tracing of the individual requirements, i.e. documents where and how each requirement from the diverse sources is implemented and can be used for customer feedback.

- Change management: documents the history of accepting new requirements and changing or dropping existing requirements.

For the development of a product, it is of key importance that exactly the right requirements are implemented. This can only happen if the requirements are comprehensibly documented and categorization and evaluation help the selection process. Requirements can be grouped following different criteria. Most important are:

- Mandatory requirements
  A requirement is mandatory if not implementing it would automatically result in a loss of customers and revenue and potentially drastic consequences for the company. Examples are contractual obligations with a customer, or legal requirements, e.g. TurboTax for US taxes which must react to annual changes in tax law.

- Optional requirements
  These are all other requirements that have a lesser degree of urgency. Of course, they can be further differentiated by urgency. Over time, an optional requirement can turn into a mandatory one.

From a product perspective, the differentiation in functional and non-functional requirements is common practice. Functional requirements deal with the functional behavior of a system:

- An online account must show the revenues of the last 6 months.
- When a new customer is entered into the system, his mobile phone number must be automatically activated.

Non-functional requirements typically describe quantitative aspects of a system or of parts of it, or the quality of certain functions:

- When an account is queried, the response time must be below 3 seconds.
- Each new customer can use his mobile phone within 30 minutes after his data was enterd into the system.

Non-functional requirements usually have a significant impact on customer satisfaction. The following criteria are typically considered:

- Reliability
  Reliability means the degree to which a software product is able to deliver correct results repeatedly. Robustness is a part of reliability and means the ability of a system to react adequately to erroneous inputs and user actions without error situations.

- Security
  Security – in particular of business-critical data or customer data – is one of the most important requirements. It includes the management of the access to data and functions based on user authorizations.

- Availability
Many critical applications require an availability above 99%. (This may seem like a high standard but reflect that 1% downtime is roughly 8 hours per month. You can think of it in terms of entirely lost business day or, perhaps more disruptively as 32 quarter hour outages during a 4.5 week period). This can frequently only be achieved by utilizing adequate hardware and software architecture (like redundancy and hot stand-by, clustering of application components etc.). These have to be implemented on the system and application level. Equally important are fast restart/recovery in error situations and disaster recovery mechanisms and backup computing centers.

- Performance
This includes the response time behavior and throughput (for batch processes). The definition of performance requirements based on realistic assumptions about volumes is one of the most difficult and most important topics before development is started. Hardly anything has such a strong influence on the architecture and the design of a software solution as the performance requirements. They must be considered and validated in all phases of the development process since the correction of performance problems is more difficult and more expensive the later they are detected.

- Usability
Usability is a key success factor for essentially all products with direct human interfaces. This includes being easy to learn, consistent design of the user interface, understandable error messages, searchable, indexed help functions and documentation.

- (Un-)Installability
For consumer software, the user expects a smooth installation within a very short time, i.e. minutes. Not meeting this expectation means frustration and dissatisfaction. For enterprise software and customer-specific software, the requirements are typically different, but also important for customer satisfaction.

- Documentation
Even though most users of consumer products do not read product documentation anymore and expect to be able to install and use a product intuitively, in the commercial area product documentation that addresses its target audiences continues to be a signifcant quality aspect.

- Maintainability
Maintainability is primarily an internal objective for a software company. It can be achieved by a thorough and current documentation of the results of development, i.e. architecture, high and low level design and code plus the conformance to development standards like naming conventions, coding standards, in-code-comments and interface descriptions.

- Portability
  Portability means that a piece of software can run on different hardware/software platforms without any significant migration effort. This is desirable for software companies who want to sell into more market segments as well as for customers who want to be more independent from platform vendors. In general, it has become easier over time to achieve higher degrees of portability by using new languages and development environments like Java.

The categorization of requirements is followed by the most difficult task of the product manager: the evaluation and prioritization of requirements and the packaging into releases (see section 4.7.2). This requires experience and creativity, since there are always more requirements than can be implemented with the given resources and budget. In addition time restrictions need to be considered, e.g. fairs or announcements of competitive products. Conflicts are inevitable. In some companies, a business evaluation of the individual requirements is to be done. That means that a business case is calculated that considers the cost side - in cooperation with development for the estimation of effort – and the value or benefits that an implementation of the requirement would bring (see also section 4.6.3). Other aspects to be considered are dependencies between requirements, i.e. they can only be implemented in combination, or groups of requirements that need changes in the same code modules so that a combined implementation means less effort or less cost.

Based on this evaluation, the product manager needs to make a decision what is to be done given the resources, budget and time restrictions (see section 4.7.2).

Documentation of Requirements

Requirements management is a documentation-intensive task. Each requirement must be individually documented. Then all requirements from all the diverse sources are combined into a one document, the high-level specification of a product (release). This is the main working document of product requirements management. From this the technical specification document is derived. In the following, recommendations for the structure of these documents are given:

For the documentation of individual requirements, Schienmann ([Schien02]) suggests this template:

Customer requirement no.:

---

1. Source of the requirement
2. Classification
   2.1 Product relation (if available)
   2.2 Type of requirement
3. Motivation
   3.1 Description of the problem
   3.2 Objective
4. Description of the customer requirement

---

5. Environment and constraints
6. Evaluation
   6.1 Value (qualitative/quantitative)
   6.2 Importance
   6.3 Urgency
7. Cost/effort
8. Other aspects (Criteria for acceptance, stability, risk)

When requirements management has documented the requirements in this way, and the product manager has categorized, evaluated and packaged them into a release, he will combine the release requirements in a high-level specification for which Balzert ([Balzert00]) suggests the following structure:

1. Objectives
The objectives describe the reasons why a customer would use the product.

2. Product usage
Product usage is a description of the target application areas and groups for which the product is intended.

3. Product overview
The overview gives a (graphical) presentation of the product environment.

4. Product functions
Product functions describe the main functions of the product release on a high level of abstraction from a customer perspective. This means that the typical business processes that the product is intended to support are listed. The functionality can be systematically described by use cases and actors or with interfaces and data flows.

5. Product data
The main data entities that are to be stored and their volumes are listed from a user perspective.

6. Product performance
This section lists the product performance requirements.

7. Quality requirements
Quality requirements like reliability, usability etc. are defined.

8. Miscellaneous
This category is used to describe special requirements, e.g. the user interface.

This high-level specification for a product (release) is the basis for development and for the technical specification which has a technical perspective compared to the customer perspective of the high-level specification.

These documents need to be subject of quality assurance checking

- correctness
- completeness
- clarity
- consistency
- validity
- prioritization
- verification

The described documents aim at a common understanding of all parties involved. This must not result in a process that is too inflexible. The project requirements management must allow changes during the development process in a tightly managed manner.

Management of dependencies on other products

In most cases, there are some requirements which originate not from customers or internal units, but from dependencies on other products. The product manager needs to keep an eye on these requirements since they can easily turn into major problems. Dependencies can exist on products from other companies (external dependencies) or within the same company (internal dependencies). External dependencies usually involve software products that are prerequisites:

- operating systems (Windows, Linux, zOS etc.)
- database systems (Oracle, DB2, MySQL etc.)
- middleware (transaction, messaging, queuing systems)
- other application systems that the product has interfaces with

Typical situations in which dependencies require some kind of action are:

- The vendor of a prerequisite product replaces the product with a new one or decommits maintenance of an older release. Therefore the dependent product needs to be migrated to the new product or release. In the best case, this only means a regression test. In the worst case, significant effort has to be spent on data migration and/or changes of interfaces. Most software vendors try to be upward compatible in order to protect the investments of their customers, but there are no guarantees. In any case, the requirement to support the new product or release becomes mandatory when support for the old product is no longer available.
- The prerequisite product offers new functions and improvements that would be beneficial for the dependent product. These can be both functional and non-functional changes. In the best case, this can be addressed by a simple recompile and regression test of the dependent product. In the worst case, APIs (Application Program Interfaces) may have changed that lead to a large number of changes in the dependent product. Here it is usually the decision of the product manager if he wants to implement this or not and in what timeframe.

The same situations can come up with products from the same company, in particular when the products belong to the same product family or platform. A prominent example is Microsoft's original Office 2007 product in which at first Powerpoint could not open Excel 2007 files. In contrast to the external dependencies, these internal dependencies should be easier to manage since the product managers can communicate more openly, synchronize schedules, detect cross-functional dependencies early and manage requirements accordingly. Nevertheless, bundles of products frequently lead to complex situations that result in a lot of effort and sometimes drastic solutions like shipping down-level code of a product because the current code level does not work with all elements of the bundle.

The product manager is well advised to keep a complete list of external and internal dependencies and make sure that he is up-to-date on any news regarding those products. Important deadlines and other timing aspects are part of the list.

Requirements Management for Product Families, Platforms, and Lines

The terms "product family," "product platform," and "product line" were defined in chapter 2. A key success factor for establishing a family, platform, or line is cross-product requirements management.

For a product family this means that product management has to ensure continuously that the marketing statement that the family is based on is justified by the contents of the products. If the marketing statement aims at the similarity of the products belonging to the family (e.g. IBM's DB2), a cross-product family requirements management must ensure that this similarity is at least maintained and, better, increased over time. This may manifest itself in the same interpretation of standards, the same (or very similar) functions, implementations and interfaces in all products of the family. Ideally, these implementations become available at the same time, but that is rarely achieved in practice.

If the marketing statement aims at the synergy of the products in solving a problem or task (like Microsoft Office), family requirements management must ensure that the integration of the products is improved, there are no redundant functions, the look-and-feel of the products is similar etc. A special challenge is the integration of software bought from other companies into a family. One source of early customer feedback on the release content of families is the customer advisory councils mentioned above.

Whenever a product family is established, the question arises which products within the family are sold as stand-alone products, and which ones are sold only as parts of family bundles. In general this is subject of product portfolio management. As long as owners of stand-alone products are measured not only on the success of the family, but also on the success of their individual products, there is a high potential for conflict between family requirements management and the requirements management of the individual products. Experience shows that this leads to frequent escalations that can best be addressed by making the individual product owners report to the family owner.

Even more complexity comes with the establishment of a product platform or line. For any functional requirement, a decision is needed if it is implemented (partly) in the platform or base product or in individual products. Again a reporting structure is recommended that keeps decision processes manageable.

Typically a product platform is of significant importance not only for the success of the individual products, but of the company as a whole. Changes to the platform have to be evaluated from a customer perspective with regard to investment protection, growth paths and migration efforts. Therefore executive management is often involved in these discussions.

Success Factors of Requirements Management

Like all business processes that are cross-organizational and require the cooperation of different organizational units, the requirements management process is a big problem in a lot of companies. The establishment of a process owner who is measured on how well the end-to-end process works has proven to be a key success factor. Measurements can be defined that reflect how fast and thoroughly requirements are worked on, e.g. the average time from the initiation of a requirement to the point of decision on implementation and to the availability of the product release that contains the implementation. For this process to work properly, in addition to the clear definition of the sequence of process steps and of roles and responsibilities, the process owner needs to monitor continuously that the flow of requirements through the process is not stopped at some point. The role of the process owner is not always pleasant, but necessary. The management board needs to support him and give escalation rights to him. A good assignment of process ownership is shown here:

Requirements management process for	Process ownership with
Customer requirements	Customer Management
Product requirements	Software Product Management
Project requirements	Development

Customer requirements management can be more tightly connected with product requirements management. Project requirements management, however, is closely connected to the project management and development processes so that the connection to customer and product requirements management is usually looser.

4.8 Development

Software Product Management may be positioned in several different places in the corporate structure (see chapter 6). Our suggestion, regardless of structure, is to give the role of (internal) contract giver for all development activities to Product Management as part of its product responsibility. This includes responsibility for budgets, contents and acceptance of the results of the development activities. Budgeting needs to be ensured in the planning processes of the company (see section 4.7). The content is managed through the release planning and requirements management processes (see section 4.7). Acceptance of development results is typically based on reviews and tests that are part of the development process. The Software Product Manager has to rely on qualified internal or external reviewers and testers, e.g. a Quality Assurance department, who provide a reliable basis for his acceptance decision.

The establishment of such a strict separation of contract giver and taker for development is usually somewhat difficult to start since the developers tend to see this more as annoying control than as help whereas people on the business side often feel forced into sharing responsibility for the results of development. If these initial difficulties can be overcome, the separation usually turns out to be helpful because it makes the role definitions more precise and, in the best case, leads to better cooperation. This does not prevent conflicts between Product Management and Development, but the rules of conflict resolution are clearer.

Changes to requirements during the development process are a frequent source of conflict (see section 4.7.3). From a development perspective, it would be ideal if all requirements were completely and precisely defined at the beginning of a project without any subsequent changes during the project. From a business perspective, however, changes in the market, in customer situations or on the legal side can lead to changes of project requirements at any time. In these situations, it is the task of Development's project requirements management to ensure timely decisions. The additional efforts in development that are caused by such changes depend to a certain degree on the type of development process employed. Since the good old waterfall model that assumes a strictly sequential process cannot cope well with late changes, newer approaches like incremental models or Extreme Programming that assume iterations are better suited to handling change. Their disadvantage is that it is more difficult for the software product manager as contract giver to evaluate the status of a project than with the waterfall model. Prototype-oriented models provide early indicators for project success with regard to customer acceptance of the results. They allow customers or representatives of the business side in a relatively early phase of the project to get hands-on experience with a prototype that already shows the main elements of the usage interface. A detailed comparison of the different types of development processes can be found in [Balzert08].

The theoretical ideal of Software Engineering is expressed in the Capability Maturity Model (CMM) of Carnegie Mellon University stating that the "perfect" software development organization can work with all types of development processes in the same reliable and masterful way and selects the optimal type at the beginning of each project following certain criteria. We do not know any existing development organization that is perfect in that sense. Most are glad when they master one process type in a reliable way. That is why selection is very limited in practice. The Software Product Manager as contract giver is not recommended to enforce a certain process type that the development team does not master since this would increase the probability of project failure significantly even when the selected process type is theoretically optimal. In the long run, the product manager ought to motivate Development to adopt more flexible process types dependent on the type of software. For example, the development process for software games is highly prototype-oriented and seems to be closer to the production of a Hollywood movie than to traditional commercial software development (see [Waldo08]).

In general the software product manager is dependent on being able to predict reliably if Development can meet the plan in terms of time and quality. Once Development has written the project plan, the product manager is advised to follow the progress of the project in comparison to this project plan closely whereas he does not need to be involved in the technical specification and implementation. He has to ensure marketing and sales activities for the launch of a new product or the availability of a new product release. Mistakes in the prediction can result in significant additional cost, bad press and revenue loss. Since these mistakes happen frequently within most software organizations, a lot of software companies do not publish fixed dates anymore, but start with limited availability for pre-selected customers before the product becomes generally available. Internal IT organizations can follow this model by introducing new applications for a small number of users first, but this is often impractical for applications that are company-wide without building extensive interface code – e.g. payroll.

4.9   Marketing

In this book we assume that software product management and marketing are two separate tasks that are assigned to two separate units within a company. However, in cases when a company does not have a separate Marketing unit, the software product manager often has to take care of some or all of the marketing responsibilities and may get the title "Product Marketing Manager" or similar. That is why we describe these marketing responsibilities in some detail.

It is always the software product manager's responsibility to make a product available in its target market at the right time, with the right functionality, and at the right price. One of the most important tasks that the software product manager thus has is to ensure that his product is well positioned in the sales and marketing strategy, and that executive management supports the product in the sales and marketing channels utilizing the marketing instruments. This must be done with the understanding that the sales and marketing strategy for a product is a part of the overall corporate sales and marketing strategy and must be consistent with this overall strategy.

As a rule, the software product manager is not directly in charge of the sales and marketing activities for his product which will be performed by the responsible sales and marketing units in the corporate organization (see chapter 6). The software product manager will, nevertheless, influence these activities within the framework of a matrix organization and should know the structures and motivators according to which they function and are organized.

Marketing is a top priority in the software industry. Software is a highly technical product, but, even given very good products, the success of a software product or a software company depends to a significant degree on its sales and marketing. Successful software companies spend a comparatively high percentage of their total revenue for sales and marketing – on the average twice as much as for research and development of new products. There are several reasons for this:

- First of all, software is an intangible commodity that is not easy to describe. This makes it all the more important and time-consuming to give the customer an "idea" of the product by way of marketing measures.
- Due to low variable costs, gross software sales margins are very high. These high margins can be used to pay for expensive marketing measures, boost sales numbers, and thus create a yet higher profit margin, even after marketing expenses have been deducted.
- The law of increasing returns in the software industry challenges every vendor to have his products achieve market leadership. Sales numbers and market share are therefore crucial figures for every software company.

Determining the target market for a software product is a fundamental prerequisite for defining the sales and marketing strategy. As described in section 4.6, this definition is decisive for market success. The definition of the target market is inseparably linked to the definition of the scope of functions and characteristics – each has an effect on the other. Of course, to be really successful, considerable demand for a product with specific functions must either already exist in the designated target market or else it must be possible to create such a demand by means of appropriate marketing measures. This requires the product manager's sound judgment to beware of delusional demand or "demand" created by passionate developers who survey a potential market with questionnaires that contain questions to which no one could say "no".

All of these components – target market, functionality and product characteristics – are key factors influencing both the marketing strategy and the sales strategy of a company.

Defining the Marketing Strategy

The marketing strategy defines how a company wishes to position and present itself or one of its products in the market. The primary objective of the marketing strategy is to establish a brand that is easy to recognize and has positive associations. The marketing strategy for a product will be based on the marketing strategy for the company as a whole – the two must not be contradictory, but rather complement and reinforce each other. The software product manager has the task of understanding the implications and consequences of the corporate marketing strategy, influencing it if necessary, and helping to define a product marketing strategy that is in line with the corporate marketing strategy and supports the defined product objectives.

A prerequisite for successfully establishing a brand with positive associations is company-specific competence which not only means technological know-how within the company, but also knowing what customers want, being customer-friendly and having a special sensitivity for the communication with customers. Time and effort must be invested in all of these competencies on a consistent and ongoing basis, since they establish a competitive edge in knowledge. Company-specific competence manifests itself not only in the company's products, but also in the performance of its personnel and corporate management. No marketing strategy can ever replace such competence; but the right marketing strategy will reinforce this competence in a positive way and be useful for establishing a brand.

A sales and marketing strategy must, in addition to the actual customers, target the complete ecosystem (see chapter 3), i.e. partners and other important market players who play a central role in product decision-making. Today, no customer can avoid being influenced by third parties when making product decisions, and many customers consciously do not want to rely solely on their own judgment. Product tests, analyst opinions, market trends and other users' experiences play a major role in product decisions and must definitely be taken into consideration when defining the marketing strategy.

Particularly when decisions are made to purchase middleware products, the preferences of system integrators or solution providers play a very important role, since the customer does not request or experience the product's functionality as directly as with other products. When choosing application software, customers will often rely on the recommendations of consultants, too. This can lead to the case, in which both the technology and the product are selected by the consultant or system integrator.

Brand Marketing vs. Product Marketing

A source of continuous dispute at every multi-product company is the conflict between brand marketing and product marketing. The software product manager will always tend to encourage more product-specific marketing for his product. This certainly can be useful for marketing measures geared to a target group or designed to boost sales. If marketing is aimed at establishing a brand, however, it must always be taken into account that a successful brand requires a strong publicly visible profile and that every company only has limited resources for establishing and maintaining such a profile.

Especially in the software market, the creation of a powerful brand is essential for successful market recognition, as the product itself is very difficult to describe. In the software industry, the marketing expenses in relation to revenue are significantly higher than in the other IT market segments. As a general rule, it can be stated that a software vendor spends 5–6% of its total revenue for external marketing programs. This does not even include personnel expenditures and other internal expenses.

A brand is frequently the most valuable asset that a company has, and a product marketed under this brand name will generally benefit from the brand recognition. Oracle, for example, consistently markets all of its products using the corporate name. This brand name is consistently used for its diversification strategy and to market both Oracle database products and other products, such as financial applications or application servers.

A company such as IBM, on the other hand, would have difficulty marketing all of its products using the corporate brand name IBM, since it offers such a wide range of products and services. The brand is extremely powerful in this case, but because of its breadth it fails to evoke the associations desired for specific software products. Particularly in the software market – where IBM is traditionally not recognized as a major player – powerful brands need to be differentiated. IBM therefore deliberately continued to use the brand names "Lotus," "Tivoli," and "Rational" after the acquisition of these companies in order to achieve better recognition in the respective market segments and to prevent losing the intrinsic value of these brands. On the other hand, immediately after acquiring Informix or Sybase, IBM merged these brand names with its own IBM DB2, which never attained the same brand status as Oracle. What we can see here is the area of conflict between the corporate brand and the individual brand names for products or product families, reflecting the conflict of interests between corporate marketing and product marketing. IBM has never succeeded in establishing "IBM Software" as a distinct brand in spite of attempts to do so, perhaps because these attempts were not consistently pursued or implemented.

Characteristics of Successful Brands

There are various qualities that characterize a successful brand, which a software product manager must be aware of:

- A brand is based on an identity that has gradually developed, namely the corporate identity, which consists of company-specific competence coupled with the experience and culture of the company.
- The core values of a brand should be outlined as clearly as possible, and easy to understand. Focusing on only a few dimensions constitutes a key success factor.
- A powerful brand develops its own "ecosystem" as described in chapter 3. Such an ecosystem is also decisive in determining how a brand and a company develop, thus having a restrictive character. This type of system does not permit arbitrary diversification attempts, as these could be detrimental to the brand.
- Powerful brands require publicly visible profiles. These can be created more easily on the basis of technological leadership or on the fringes of a niche market than in a mainstream market.
- Powerful brands above all owe their existence to a convincing core element, namely the company-specific competence, or alternatively to their fascinating aura. Adding emotional desire to the core creates the ideal situation. In the IT market, Apple is a good example for generating such an aura.
- Especially in difficult times or in saturated markets full of cut-throat competition, powerful brands have a clear advantage and tend to improve their market position relative to weaker competitors.

Positioning with Regard to Competitors

Apart from the brand name, positioning in relation to direct competitors is important to achieve market recognition. A software company will always try to position itself and its products as the technology leader. A company that has launched a new technology on the market or addressed a new issue relevant to the industry will initially be recognized as a technology leader. Examples are Sun with Java, or Siebel with CRM. These examples also show how difficult it is to maintain this association over time, and how this position is undermined by other companies. In these cases, other companies adopt a new technology position themselves as runners-up. They are pursuing the "second best" strategy, presenting themselves as responsible for perfecting the technology to maturity and increasing its usability in their products. A variant of this strategy is placing more emphasis on a specific financial benefit for the customer. In the example of the mouse-activated user interface, the original inventor Xerox is no longer associated with the technology, but Apple and Microsoft are.

Another cogent marketing argument is market leadership, preferably in conjunction with technology leadership. In the software market, customers also observe the law of increasing returns (the larger the vendor's share, the more likely the customer is to buy from him), which makes market leadership an even stronger argument in the software industry than in other markets. Software companies have their market shares "calculated" by market research companies, such as Gartner, IDC, etc. Of course, every company tries to select a market segment that can be analyzed to its own advantage (also refer to section 4.4). However, this only works if the market segment selected is of relevance to and recognizable by the customer. One often hears, for example, "nine out of ten banks have this product" even when the product has no greater applicability to banks than to retailers. The truth may be that manufacturing and distribution are entirely penetrated by a competitor, but by redefining the segment the product sounds more successful.

If a company is not successful in positioning itself as a technology or market leader, the only position left for it is to be a "me too" vendor. This position is especially problematic and unrewarding in the software industry. Due to low variable expenses, high price flexibility, and risk factors customers associate with change, it is hard for a software company to position itself as a price leader in order to undermine the technology leader's dominant position. Examples of this are the various attempts made by Oracle to diversify its product range beyond the database sector which have led to increased revenue, but very uneven profit distribution.

Obviously there should not be too much of a gap between positioning and reality, or customer perception. However, clever marketing can certainly affect perceptions, and after all, how a company is perceived in the market is the marketing reality.

Another interesting aspect of positioning is the question whether a software company wants to focus on specific issues or present itself as a vendor of a broad range of products and services. Whereas a company such as IDS Scheer has a primary focus on Business Process Management, a company such as IBM with its broad range of diverse products focuses mainly on the advantages of "one-stop solutions". These two positions – the "best-of-breed" approach vs. the "single vendor" – also reflect different customer preferences. In general, a vendor with a clearly defined focus is more likely to be perceived as a technology leader. Being perceived as a best-of-breed vendor also depends a great deal on the aura surrounding a software company's brand name in the market. Companies are usually not successful when they try to be perceived as both best-of-breed supplier and single vendor.

A software company interested in expanding its range of products and focusing on new items previously provided by companies perceived as best-of-breed vendors will have tremendous difficulty repositioning itself as a single vendor. Larry Ellison (Oracle CEO and best-of-breed database vendor) made an interesting comment on this subject: "Best of breed is dead except for dog races!"

In this context, careful consideration must also be given to the question whether a software product is to be marketed more on the basis of its technology, i.e. targeted at software developers and IT specialists, or its financial benefits, i.e. targeted at department heads and business managers. The marketing messages and channels will be completely different depending on how this question is answered. This is also known as the dual market problem: does the vendor sell to the independent users and risk the wrath of the IT structure or to the IT department which may not have the buy-in of the users?

Marketing Strategy and Partners

Effective partner sales require marketing to address two different partner characteristics: First of all, partner companies are a marketing target group like customers. It is important to awaken their interest in the company and in certain products. The software vendor's "value proposition" for partners, however, has to demonstrate how cooperation with the software vendor will result in added value for the partner in terms of "more sales" or "more profits".

Furthermore, joint marketing is a very important element of cooperation among partners. Co-marketing activities enable both companies to profit from each other's market power and market image. Co-marketing allows companies to bundle their resources, reach a larger target group and make a more complex, more comprehensive and more solution-oriented marketing statement. This means, though, that the marketing message will be less focused and pointed.

An important aspect of co-marketing activities is the frequently desired independence of each partner. Consulting firms and system integrators, in particular, must first present themselves to customers as being independent and objective, even though their customers will eventually expect them to explicitly recommend a technology or a specific product. These partners therefore do not want to be associated with a particular software product or vendor. Joint marketing activities are rather the exception here.

Solution providers and technology partners, on the other hand, like to use each other's brand image to multiply their own market recognition. It needs to be taken into account that this type of partnership will have the desired positive effect only if the partner's multiplication factor is large enough (this means >1 in terms of the mathematical analogy), otherwise it is more likely to have the contrary effect.

To the extent that the price of a product in a bundle may be much less than standalone, the sales amplification must be measured in positive revenue and profit, not just product placements.

A key component of every marketing strategy for software companies consists of positioning the product or the company in an ecosystem with respect to major software topics. The initiators of a topic are interested in articulating the topic and establishing it in the market as quickly as possible. Adaptors, in contrast, are interested in documenting that they are leading participants in the debate and hope to profit from the popularity of the topic. Whoever is not perceived as being a major participant in the discussion of key topics does not get any attention and is squeezed out.

All marketing measures aimed at positioning within an ecosystem – e.g., advertising, public relations, technology conferences – serve the purpose of "mind sharing" in the market, which is a necessary, though insufficient, prerequisite for attaining a significant market share.

Significance of a Marketing Strategy for Corporate IT Organizations

It is certainly advisable for corporate IT organizations to likewise develop an appropriate marketing strategy. The objective of such a strategy in this case is not to establish a brand, but to position the software products and services within the company itself. The target market comprises the internal customers in the company and the objective for the internal IT service providers is to establish themselves as "preferred suppliers". This status is an essential prerequisite for the business success of a corporate IT organization, but it should definitely not be taken for granted. Many IT organizations in many large companies are struggling with the bad image of their products and services. Quite often this is not justified. Apart from an assortment of possible explanations, such as a lack of customer orientation and poor product quality, which can affect any vendor or service provider, a major factor for the lack of acceptance of a corporate IT organization can be a flawed or poorly implemented IT strategy. The required cost efficiency as a target of every IT strategy can only be attained by standardizing the IT infrastructure to achieve cost benefits in purchasing, development and business operations. This automatically results in conflicts and requires support by executive management. Another situation to be avoided: at times a business unit may be told that their project cannot be implemented because of limited resource, even if the business unit is willing to supply the budget. This is usually the by-product of separate measurements being placed on IT and the business units it supports, which in such a case clearly suboptimizes for the corporation. An added difficulty is that the corporate IT organizations do usually not have marketing means that are comparable to those of the software vendors and service providers.

Even the best marketing strategy cannot compensate for deficiencies in corporate IT strategy or be a substitute for a powerful CIO, but it can help make a good IT strategy be even more successful. The marketing strategy will include not only the company's own software products and services, but also the selected vendor's products.

Thus, the corporate IT organization's and vendor's marketing strategies will have similar objectives, at least in part, and definitely be able to complement each other.

Marketing Communication (MarCom) Plan

The marketing communication plan for a product evolves from the marketing strategy and defines the objectives for the individual marketing measures. Besides advertising, other important software marketing measures include public relations, telemarketing and sales support. A special case in the MarCom plan is the launch of new products or new versions or major releases of existing products. Usually a launch plan for each case is developed and implemented that has to be integrated in the overall MarCom plan. The significance of launch activities depends on the type of product. Typically the launch focused on a release date is more important in the consumer market. In the enterprise market the focus on a hard release date is no longer the rule for the reasons given in section 4.8. Also adoption of new products or versions takes a lot longer with enterprise customers than in the consumer market. Therefore launch activities are spread over longer periods of time. There is a lot of literature on the subject of product launches like [Lawley07] or [Cooper00].

A combination of the various marketing components is generally used for integrated marketing in the software industry. The MarCom Plan describes media planning as well as the campaign's creative strategy for advertising and public relations. Marketing communication determines whether a company's marketing messages are positive or negative, strong or weak, or consistent or inconsistent.

Public relations have top priority in marketing communication for software companies. Leaders of successful software companies spend more time discussing market trends, corporate visions and strategies with both the technical and business press as well as with analysts than in other industries.

User conferences are another important forum for software companies. These conferences are either organized by the company itself for its own products (e.g. SAP's SAPphire) or aimed at certain industries (e.g. the European Banking & Insurance Forum, EBIF, JAVAWorld, etc.) or specific issues. A software company will generally recruit not only its corporate management to champion such conferences and target groups, but also chief architects and other technology community leaders.

Marketing Activities Management

As part of operational marketing, various activities need to be carried out to implement the marketing strategy and the marketing communication plan, such as:

- advertising (press, radio, TV, Internet),
- events and trade fairs,
- public relations (press and analysts),
- direct mail to customers,

- customer-specific marketing,
- database marketing,
- internet marketing,
- membership in associations.

In planning these activities, the objective of each individual action must be clearly defined and the success of the action evaluated accordingly. This requires a realistic assessment of the objectives that can actually be achieved with each action, for example:

- enhance the brand or image,
- establish new customer contacts for potential business opportunities,
- support sales and marketing.

Another major marketing activity in addition to marketing communication is market research. This includes the analysis of one's own market position and of competitors' positions, early detection and evaluation of all measures taken by competitors as well as the analysis and early identification of trends in customer behavior (also see section 4.4).

So-called in-house fairs or IT workshops are very effective instruments for corporate IT organizations to present themselves and their services to internal customers in connection with selected vendors. The software vendors will usually pay for most of the expenses in connection with such co-marketing activities, since it gives them the opportunity to position themselves as selected partners in the internal corporate IT strategy.

Assessing the effectiveness of each individual marketing activity is always an indispensable element in successful marketing management. It is more difficult to measure effectiveness in marketing than in sales, since sales volumes are easy to use as objective measures. Nevertheless, there are parameters that are useful in quantifying marketing activities, including:

- number of new customer contacts,
- number of new business opportunities,
- satisfaction of participants in an activity,
- number of overall and positive references in the media,
- number of sales contracts associated with a marketing activity.

If the software product manager is not responsible for marketing himself he will still be involved in some of these activities. In particular, he will represent his product at conferences and customer events.

4.10   Sales and Distribution

The selection of appropriate sales and distribution channels depends on the definition of the target market and the product characteristics. A sales and distribution strategy must be developed for the channels selected. This sales and distribution strategy, like the marketing strategy, cannot be derived from the needs of a single product, of course, but must be consistent with overall corporate strategy. The software product manager is responsible for understanding the corporate sales and distribution strategy and organizational structure in order to develop an appropriate sales and distribution strategy for his product in cooperation with the sales and distribution manager. An important question that needs to be answered in this respect is whether or not it is reasonable and feasible to establish sales and distribution structures and management systems dedicated to one product or one group of products.

Sales and distribution play a very important role in the software market, similar to marketing. The level at which a greater expenditure for sales and marketing no longer generates an overall higher profit margin based on increased sales numbers or volume is significantly higher in the software market than for most other products due to the economic considerations described in chapter 3 and the marketing leverage described earlier in this chapter. An important question to be answered is whether the objective is to maximize sales volume and market share as measured by sales volume or to maximize the number of licenses placed in the market. This ultimately depends on whether the main objective of the strategy is growth or profitability.

Whereas appropriate marketing measures create the necessary "pull" in the market stimulating demand, sales activities provide the supplemental "push," so that products are actually purchased and contracts signed. Sales success determines the "top line," i.e. total corporate revenue and market growth. The organization of the distribution channels depends on the sales and distribution strategy. The typical sales and distribution organization in a software company consists of direct sales including telesales and internet sales, and partner sales.

The software product manager is typically only involved in aspects like positioning his product in the Sales Strategy and Plan. On the operational side, his involvement is typically limited to pre-sales meetings with major customers or partners. In most companies, the relationship between Software Product Management and Sales is conflict-laden. While a product manager wants reliable commitments regarding the sales volumes of his product, Sales is typically only willing to commit numbers for larger product groups, but not for individual products. So the product manager often complains that Sales is not sufficiently focused on his product, while Sales will claim that the product does not fulfill the current market requirements. Those conflicts can only be overcome if both parties are forced to commitments early in the development cycle of a product version. This can only be achieved if executive management enforces it.

Direct Sales

Direct Sales encompasses any kind of sales activities of a vendor that aims at selling software to a customer without an external intermediary. This includes the traditional "blue suit" sales force of representatives that have in-person contact to their customers, as well as telesales and internet sales. In the enterprise market, the standard sales and distribution system for IT products and thus for software products as well involves selling directly to major clients. This is the type of sales and service system that large companies continue to expect their suppliers to provide. Key account managers attend to existing key customers, ensure that the products and licenses purchased by these customers are deployed as smoothly as possible, assist in licensing management and maintain customer contacts. At the same time, the key account manager will attempt to sell additional licenses and boost sales by "cross-selling," i.e. selling supplementary products to the company, or "up-selling," i.e. increasing the number of installations of products already sold by having them installed in other company divisions.

In addition, direct sales personnel are assigned to the task of acquiring new customers. Potential customers must, of course, be recruited from the defined product target market. Apart from this, these customers can be selected as the opportunity presents itself, although customer acquisition is generally more successful when it is done systematically based on data obtained in advance. This includes the use of information acquired by telemarketing resources. A basic criterion for selecting new customers is company size (measured by the number of employees or revenue). Depending on the industry, this is a decisive factor that directly determines the size of the IT budget, which in turn allows the potential sales volume that a customer can generate to be estimated. Direct sales personnel can then focus on those key clients presenting the greatest potential for the respective products.

Maintaining contact with existing customers is extremely important, since satisfied customers are a reliable source of future revenue, especially in the software industry. In comparison, winning new customers requires far more time and effort, but it is a process that is essential for further growth. As products and markets mature and continue to develop over the life cycle of a product, software companies must adapt to new target markets for their products and acquire new customers in these markets. For business software, for example, this entails a transition from the large-market capitalization (large-cap) sector initially targeted during the launch of a new technology to the market sector of small- and medium-size companies (small-caps and mid-caps). This is what SAP is trying to achieve. The most difficult and time-consuming customers to win are those already using competing products.

The sales responsibility and activities of an account manager for existing customers are completely different from those required for new customer acquisition. The terms "farmer" and "hunter" can be used to describe these two different types of account manager. Depending on the size of the company and on the product, it can make sense to assign different persons to each of these two tasks or even to establish special sales units for new customers.

A vertical sales structure organized by industries has become increasingly popular and proven successful for both existing customer service and new customer acquisition. Today, practically every IT product vendor – and most of the larger consulting and service companies – has such a vertical structure, if the company size and critical mass of the sales organization permit this. The reason for this lies in market expectations: Customers no longer seek information technology as such, but rather IT solutions to improve their business processes. Therefore, IT providers must be able to describe the advantages of IT and its positive effects on the business processes of an industry or a single customer.

Customers do not expect the sales person to be an expert in their industry, but rather an IT specialist for the vendor's products who knows enough about the industry, however, to be able to explain how IT advantages can be converted into financial benefits. The winning market player will be the one whose sales structures and processes can most convincingly communicate this type of conversion.

The disadvantage of such a vertical structure is that it does not allow comprehensive, regional customer service. In increasingly specialized IT markets, the advantages of focusing on an industry clearly outweigh the disadvantages of not being able to provide regional service. In some companies the vertical sales organization even takes precedence over and has a more binding character than individual country or territorial organizations.

In an ever more globalized world it is no longer possible to provide regional service to key customers anyway. It is increasingly becoming a major competitive advantage to have a sales organization operating on a global scale that is available to global customers. Many large IT vendors have therefore implemented concepts such as "global account management" in order to provide one-stop service to global clients and also to conceal internal conflicts between individual sales units from the customer.

Sales Structure in Companies Selling Diverse Products

Vendors offering a very wide range of products also need to decide whether to institute a product sales organization dedicated to product groups in addition to having an organizational structure based on industry specialization. The advantage of and need for a product sales organization is that it alone allows complex and specialized products to be successfully positioned with the customer relative to competing products. Having a sales organization dedicated to one product in addition to a vertical organization based on industries results in a two-tiered, overlapping sales structure and matrix organization, which can create problems, such as duplicate pricing and conflicting objectives. In view of the broad range of diverse IT products and services it offers, IBM ultimately decided to use a 3-dimensional matrix for its direct software sales:

- Customer contacts are maintained by industry-specific account managers who are responsible for all IBM business relations with the customer.
- A software account manager is responsible for all IBM Software Group business relations with this customer.
- There is one direct sales unit dedicated to each of the four software product groups (database, middleware, collaboration and system management).

In addition to this, there is also a sales staff in charge of hardware servers, services and other product areas. It is easy to imagine how difficult it is to coordinate these vast sales resources and how many different people a customer will come into contact with. Nevertheless, experience has shown that increased focusing leads to greater sales success.

The pre-sales personnel often called system engineers (SEs) or similar plays a central role in every direct sales organization. They provide sales support, know the products far better than the sales persons, give technical lectures and demonstrations. Although they are members of the sales staff, they are not directly responsible for sales. Customers therefore often consider them to be more "objective" and credible persons to talk to.

The direct sales force as the classical type of sales system for key clients is practical only if the sales volume per customer exceeds a certain minimum, since the service capacity of sales personnel is limited.

Telesales

Telesales, also called inside sales, is done by a team that performs sales or sales support tasks exclusively by telephone. These activities can include answering customer questions and taking orders, as well as actively dealing with customers, cold calling potential customers and qualifying new markets. Obviously telesales very quickly reaches the limits of its sales potential, particularly with respect to software products and business software which require a lot of explanation. However, it is an excellent and efficient instrument for very quickly contacting large numbers of customers individually or for dealing with large customer organizations with numerous contact persons.

Internet Sales

Over the last ten years, the internet has turned into a major channel. On the internet marketing and sales are mostly intertwined. Advertisements usually include a direct link to a web page on which a software product can be bought and downloaded. The ads can be much better targeted than in most other media by making use of the context and/or prior knowledge about a user. Examples are Google's algorithms for matching ads with search results or Amazon's product recommendations based on a customer's previous purchases. This channel works extremely well for consumer products. The more complex a product is structured or the licensing terms are in the enterprise market, the less appropriate this channel is for immediate sales, but it can still be used for advertising that creates leads. The types of software products that can be best sold over the internet are listed in chapter 3.

Partner Strategy as Part of the Sales Strategy

As already pointed out in chapter 3, the role played by partner companies is a significant factor in selecting sales and distribution channels and in defining the sales and distribution strategy and the marketing strategy. Each partner can have a completely different type of role to play. One role is that of the product reseller, or distributor. Another major role is played by partners who directly influence customers' purchasing decisions in connection with their own activities.

It is important to realize that in the software industry, product and technology networks are extremely complex and that these partnerships can thus never be exclusive. A sales and distribution partner may market one company's product in a particular customer situation, and then some other company's product in another customer situation involving different requirements. A technology partner may recommend a specific product in a certain situation and at the same time compete with this vendor with regard to other technology issues. This type of behavior is not a sign of disloyalty, but due to the complexity of the multilayered software infra-structure. The software industry has coined the term "coopetition" for this behavior. It means that the respective partners are independent companies acting in their own financial interests, and both cooperating and competing with one another.

With the increasing relevance of outsourcing and SaaS, companies that provide outsourcing and hosting services become important partners as well. The business models in this area, in particular for SaaS, are still evolving, but it is clear that these providers need to be considered in a partner strategy.

Sales and Distribution by Resellers

The lower the expected sales volume per customer is, the more important it is to have partners as a sales and distribution channel. Descriptions of the different categories of partners may be found in chapter 3. From a structural point of view these partnerships can be considered as a type of sales and distribution outsourcing managed by a dedicated partner sales and distribution organization. If this partner organization works well, the software vendor increases the performance – as meas-ured by the number of potential customer contacts – of the sales resources used significantly. Whereas an account manager attends to n customers, a partner account manager attends to n strategic partners that in turn employ m key account managers that in turn attend to k customers, which results in n^*m^*k potentially targeted customers, compared with n direct sales customers attended to. Sales performance measured by sales volume does not increase proportionally, of course, since direct sales involves customers representing large companies with higher potential sales volumes, and since partners also sell and distribute other products. Yet, this is one of the basic positive effects of a partner network: the fact that the partners, by combining products and services provided by various vendors, bundle sufficient sales potential so that they are able to address minor customers efficiently too.

General resellers are not specialized and for most products operate through a distributor who procures product for them from various vendors and often provides business partner sales and technical support because they have the critical mass that warrants doing so. A second tier distributor may sell tens of thousands of DB2 or SQL database licenses per year where an individual reseller might sell only a few. The distributor can afford (particularly if the product vendor subsidizes him) to have a person on staff with specific product skills; the reseller could never afford to. This structure may have made the most sense when product was delivered as physical boxes of documentation and media for each user. Today in the age of high bandwidth networks and electronic delivery it seems a bit anachronistic, even if the skills breakdowns have not changed. We believe there is a trend towards resellers becoming more specialized and wanting to avoid the distributor and amongst distributors for them to take on dealing directly with customers.

VARs (Value Added Resellers or Remarketers) are expected to be experts in a segment or niche that they focus on, perhaps database, or security, or networking. They are often single tier, i.e. they eliminate the distributor. Large vendors may be choosy about whom to accept in this role for multiple reasons: the business partner has to be effective in representing the vendor's products and has to sell sufficient volumes to make it worthwhile to deal with him as a customer with reduced margins (since the business partner needs to retain some margin for his own compensation). Nevertheless, in our experience this is a productive group as a whole and is well worth cultivating. Consider also that VARs may have pull due to their reputation as experts in a field. The general reseller is fine if you wish to procure additional copies of Microsoft Office to add to an existing environment. But suppose that you were a small company needing to create or revamp your applications with a relational database and had no expertise in the field; you would probably prefer to procure your software from a business partner who could say, "Don't worry, we've been doing this for years; here are some names of satisfied customers you can call." "We'll be there if you need help." and "In fact, if you wish, we can provide services to assist you or do the whole job for you."

The pricing aspects for the different partners are covered in section 5.6.

Channel Mix

Of the different sales and distribution channels described above having a direct sales system creates the highest sales costs, but also allows for the most intensive customer contact. Sales and distribution partners can be a much more efficient channel, but as independent companies they can never be supervised as easily as in-house sales resources and they can also sell competing products. Furthermore, sales partners prevent the software vendor from having direct customer contact, which is an essential success factor especially when complex products and large investments are involved. Telesales used as a sales and distribution channel has lower costs, but is suited only for simple transactions. The internet is the most cost- efficient channel, but may not be applicable for more complex software products and with enterprise customers.

Every software company must find out which combination of these different sales and distribution channels, i.e. which channel mix, is the ideal solution for the company itself and for each of its products, and this channel mix must then be put into practice consistently. In general, there is a trade-off between higher risk due to partners and potentially more business.

Successful software companies integrate and coordinate the various sales and distribution channels so that they complement each other synergistically and avoid channel conflicts as far as possible.

Problems can arise if a company tries to assign certain customers or customer groups or even single transactions according to sales volume or value exclusively to one sales channel. The various sales and distribution channels, especially partners, will not accept such a restriction and each sales channel will attempt to handle the transactions involving the largest sales volume, which may lead to major channel conflicts.

Alongside the partners and the sales and distribution channels, and at least as important for a software company are the so-called influencers. These are partners that do not or do not predominantly resell products, but are nevertheless highly influential in customer decision-making. This includes ISVs again as well as system integrators, technology alliances, consultants, and accounting firms.

Consulting as a Sales Support Function

A software company must decide to what extent it wants to provide consulting services to assist its customers in executing projects and implementing software. Experience shows that product-specific consulting services provided by the software vendor in conjunction with a project significantly increase the chances of product success and often accelerate project progress. By providing such services, of course, the software vendor is competing with his most important partners, the system integrators and value-added resellers. A company must thus decide whether it wants to be a software product company only or also a software service company.

A company that sells only software products will strive to achieve a project-related consulting revenue on the order of up to 10% of its licensing revenue. The sole purpose of this is to promote corporate licensing sales through better and faster implementation of its products. A consulting revenue this size will not cause partners to perceive the software company as being a competitor. On the contrary, the partners will most probably be willing to include these services in their offers as an added value.

Management of Sales and Distribution Channels and Incentive Systems

The management and incentive systems for sales and distribution must be consistent with and reinforce the basic elements of the sales and distribution strategy. For a software company, growing the licensing business (or service contract business in the case of SaaS) is the driving force behind greater market share, sales growth and profitability. The sale and installation of new licenses also generates recurring revenue on top of the revenue from license agreements. Therefore, licensing will always be the primary sales objective. Depending on the market situation, consulting or maintenance and support can also be included as sales targets.

A software company must make a fundamental decision regarding its sales and distribution management: should the various sales and distribution channels be allowed to overlap and compete with each other or should each have a well-defined target market and objective? Sales and distribution channels that are to overlap each other are measured by common objectives in order to avoid channel conflicts in so far as possible. This requires objectives which are higher to reflect the sum of what would have been the individual objectives. This may result in the individual channels all pursuing the large opportunities rather than going after the target market which they were intended to pursue. The alternative, assigning specific target markets and objectives, may lead to some squabbles at the boundaries but is often adopted in an effort to focus sales more strongly and avoid unnecessary overlapping. Channel conflicts are almost always counterproductive in practice.

If a software product is sold through the direct sales channel, the software product manager must ensure that his product is favorably positioned in the incentive system since typically this has a significant effect on the motivation and focus of the sales representatives.

4.11 Support and Services

One of the less popular tasks that a software product manager has – which is of eminent importance to achieve customer satisfaction and loyalty, however – is to establish, continually maintain and improve the support structure. This refers to all elements that a vendor or an IT organization introduce and operate to support sales and marketing and to provide maintenance and help to customers.

An important support structure element is product-specific training. This includes training both the company's own sales and marketing, technical support and maintenance staff as well as the customer's staff. In larger companies this requires a multiplier approach, i.e. initial training is conducted by developers and product managers for the training staff ("teach the teachers") that subsequently plans and conducts further training activities. These activities must be planned far in advance. The responsible software manager must ensure that the relevant organizational units allow for and provide in due time the required manpower and budget.

Hardly any software product can be sold without additional services. The services offered can be simple like standard maintenance or of higher complexity across an array of professional services including design and implementation, and can be sold along with the software product as a must or can option. They all require the vendor to establish special infrastructures, have additional resources available, and in part to also assume responsibility and risks that this entails.

Maintenance services for products having numerous customers or users are usually organized on the basis of a three-level structure. A call center on level 1 answers telephone calls or receives input from users. The call center staff generally does not need to have profound technical product knowledge, but should be able to answer basic questions and differentiate between product failures and user errors. On level 2 dedicated product specialists deal with failure analysis and debugging. Level 3 usually involves developers and handles particularly difficult problems. As a general rule, 80 to 90% of all problems arising on levels 1 and 2 should be dealt with on the respective level, permitting only 1 to 4% of all problems reported on level 1 to reach level 3. Significant deviations from this rule of thumb, i.e. a higher percentage on level 3, require thorough analysis, as this constitutes a cost problem and also a resource problem. Level 3, also known as the "change team" constitute a rare resource whose other job may be coding new function. The deviation can be caused by a product quality problem or by level 1 and 2 staff members being poorly qualified, a problem that can be addressed by training.

A number of software vendors have their own professional services organizations to perform necessary services on customer site, or have these services carried out by partner companies or independent consulting firms. These services include:

- Installation support,
- Customization,
- Implementation of additional functions,
- System integration, i.e. integration of one or more products, usually combined with custom development and, if necessary, custom software for an overall solution.
- The latter usually also includes project management and is often offered based on a general contractor agreement at a fixed price and deadline.
- Product training for various user target groups,
- Operational preparations, implementation and support.

Additional services extending beyond single products include:

- Outsourcing, i.e. partial or complete assumption of responsibility for the customer's application development and/or operation. This can even include the founding of a joint operating company and takeover of the customer's personnel.
- Recent developments like SaaS and Cloud Computing expand these services to include a flexible offer and flexible pricing for the "capacities" actually used, taking into consideration a fluctuating demand (capacity on demand) (see chapter 3 and 4.6.2).

All of these services need to be planned and developed, and should therefore be integrated in product management. Drawing up general contracting offers and agreements for system integration and outsourcing in particular requires a great deal of time and effort as well as the availability and assistance of experienced specialists.

4.12   Tool Support

Requirements management is very dependent on adequate tool support that not only provides a document management system for the individual requirement documents, but also contains a workflow engine that manages the flow of the requirements through the process and enables the responsible process owner and product managers to manage and control the process. The selection of a standard software product, however, is not the complete solution to the problem, but only the second step after a company-specific definition of the requirements management process. The selection of the tool must consider the defined process including its information objects plus the overall IT architecture and application landscape of the company. There is a large number of software products worth looking at, like Telelogic's DOORS or Rational's RequisitePro, both owned by IBM now. Helpful information on requirements engineering and tools can be found on the web site of Tom de Marco's Atlantic Systems Guild (www.systemsguild.com).

A major part of the job of a product manager is the coordination of units within and outside of the company that are relevant for the sustainable success of his products. Therefore telephone, video conferencing and a laptop with email software are important tools. The software product manager is permanently endangered by communication overkill, i.e. strict time management (maybe with tool support) and a well-customized filtering and document management system (for emails, electronic documents and paper) can be life saving. In addition standard office software like Word, PowerPoint and Excel are needed. A good secretary can increase the productivity of a software product manager considerably, but cannot save him from working with these tools.

Vendors of Enterprise Resource Planning (ERP) software offer components for Product Life Cycle Management (PLM) which primarily address the manufacturing industry. It is hardly used in the software industry. More interesting are niche vendors like VOConline (www.voc-online.com, formerly BetaSphere) that are specialized in integrating customers in product definition and development. SUN had some positive experiences with this approach in the development of Java.

Since the product manager has to work intensively with a lot of other units within the company, it can be helpful for him to get access to their task-specific software systems. Whether to grant such access will be decided in the context of the company's culture, the organizational structure and defined role of product management, as well as the personal working habits and reputation of the product manager. Project management tools in Development, error tracking tools in Development and

Support, customer relationship management tools in Marketing and Sales and planning and controlling tools of the company or individual units can be of interest. What is really important is that the product manager has timely access to all relevant data in reliable quality that he needs for his work. If this can be achieved without giving him access to the task-specific software systems, everybody will prefer that.

4.13 Software Product Management Summary

In this chapter, we have described and discussed the elements of software product management based on our framework (see fig. 4.2). Our approach is guided by the objective to achieve sustainable economic success over the life cycle of the software product. The software product manager acts as the ringmaster who coordinates all functional units inside and outside of the company that are relevant for this success typically without having managerial authority.

At the core, his tasks are in the areas of Product Strategy and Product Planning with input from Market and Product Analysis. However, he will not be successful unless he manages to orchestrate Development, Pricing, Marketing, Sales and Distribution, and Support and Services. While most of his activities focus on the product or product family level, he also needs to represent his product on the corporate level where his role and influence is highly dependent on his personal reputation.

In the next chapter we discuss the tasks of the software pricing manager and alternative pricing approaches. We advise the closest cooperation between the software product manager and software pricing manager.

Chapter 5
The Elements of Software Pricing

In this chapter we will describe the various ways in which the products of development efforts are converted into economic worth. While nominally this is "pricing," in reality the subject is broader because of all the varied ways in which intellectual property, including software may be converted into financial value today. We will begin with a section on objectives, followed by the role of the software pricing manager and interrelation with the product manager and then introduce the Pricing Framework which will provide the structure for the rest of the chapter. Please note that the role here designated "software pricing manager" may, in some companies, be referred to as "pricer." While we have nothing against that term, it may conjure up the role of someone who simply takes cost parameters, runs them through a financial model and comes up with a price. We have in mind a more comprehensive set of responsibilities which we believe is better conveyed by the title we have chosen. This chapter is written from the standpoint of a large software vendor with broad portfolio and is meant to provide the level of guidance needed for a large and complex environment. Smaller companies, whether selling software or devising charge-back schemes for their own in-house IT, may not have organizations large enough to support the roles of a dedicated software product manager or dedicated software pricing manager. Furthermore, some tasks will not be applicable to all companies, for example, if a vendor does no business outside his own country, he has no need to perform the tasks in the sections on global pricing; the B2C (Business to Consumer) company can ignore the tasks in the sections on selling to large enterprises. While you may feel it's useful to read the entire book, and we certainly encourage you to do so, we have provided a roadmap in section 6.4 to indicate which sections are most appropriate for which readers. Nonetheless, the tasks described which are appropriate to your business are important even if the organization cannot justify having individuals performing each of the roles we describe. For example, the software pricing manager and software product manager might well be the same person in a smaller company.

H.-B. Kittlaus and P.N. Clough, *Software Product Management and Pricing.*
© Springer-Verlag Berlin Heidelberg 2009

5.1   Objectives

As we discussed in Chapter 4, there are many different types of business enterprise which have by their nature varied objectives. However, unless we are considering software product development as a hobby, each of those objectives will have at its core the notion of providing value to a business, an individual, or an institution. In this chapter we will deal with the various ways in which that value can be converted to economic value, either for the software itself or in support of a process which uses the software to create economic value.

As we have discussed several times, including in Chapter 4, our strong bias is towards sustainability of corporate success of the company for whom a product was developed or acquired, so the emphasis in pricing will be towards pricing models which foster such ongoing success, with much less emphasis on short term earnings, short term stock price, and the like.

Once a corporation determines the level of pricing consistency that it needs across its product portfolio and subsegments like platform and brand, it usually falls to the pricing function to enforce those pricing standards. Likewise, terms and conditions consistency also needs to be maintained and the back office infrastructure must be able to invoice whatever price or terms structure is agreed for a product. Offerings which are not supported by the back office systems may lead to problems with failure to deliver to the customer, inability to book revenue due to accounting issues, auditability concerns and the like. Because of this "policeman" role which is expected to maintain corporate pricing standards, as well as to ensure freedom from bias towards any particular constituent, it is wise to separate pricing in this instance from finance. We have seen cases where finance says in effect "rules and consequences be damned, we need an extra $50M this quarter." Such considerations can have highly leveraged future negative results and thus it may be prudent to have pricing and special bids (see 5.7.5) organizationally immunized from such pressures.

Of course, the objectives we are discussing need to be incorporated into the corporate business model to be effective. Where there is conflict in objectives on this point, as when for example there is conflict between product management and other corporate entities seeking a short term goal, suboptimal results for the organization are inevitable. At times, the outcome can be much worse than "suboptimal," perhaps even eroding a whole business segment or undermining the value proposition for an entire product set or class of customers.

Let us take a hypothetical example: a software vendor company has just produced a networking variant of TCP/IP that is fully compatible with existing network installations and which provides 25% faster throughput. Marketing and Sales agree that even with a 10% price premium over competition, the product will sell incredibly well. However, other parts of the corporation, eager to cash in on the new product and perhaps in need of cash, insist on offering a 15% discount "in order to close sales this quarter." First, it is unlikely that such a discount will have any pull-forward effect, since significant benefits are demonstrable without it and any acceptance delay more likely to be due to customers wanting to make sure the product really delivers on its promises. Second, often there is no road back to the reasonable 10% premium. Third, customers may ask why, if the product is as good as claimed, it is necessary to discount it at all, which may for no reason cast a shadow over product reputation from the outset.

Another example might be a hospital surgical accounting application which the product manager wishes to price on an unusual metric for a software product (number of occupied hospital beds, for example). To him, and perhaps to some customers, this may seem an obvious metric for this specific application. Yet the predictability of price may suffer: a hospital might over time move to more outpatient surgery, cutting into vendor revenue, or it might open a large hospice wing whose beds would raise the price of the software while that part of the hospital was not even using the application. Either way, the concern may lead to the vendor pricing organization putting a high price per bed on the product, afraid that they will not otherwise get sufficient revenue to make their ROI (return on investment) objectives. Their fear might well materialize, not because there is anything wrong with the product but because sales may suffer as customers become concerned a) about the potentially erratic nature of price from month to month or b) the product's overall high price. Other reasons to keep metrics fairly consistent include consistency with other metrics in a single sale: if this had been an application on an IBM mainframe, there might well have been products priced based on machine capacity, machine usage, flat priced (not based on capacity), monthly license charged and one time charged with subsequent annual maintenance. It could be that the additional metric was the straw that broke the complexity camel's back.

Rather than repeat the proposition expressed in Chapter 4 that there are inherent conflicts between the long term (and sustainability) view of the product manager and the ability to measure short term performance of individuals, suffice it to say that this same conflict occurs when the pricing goal is long term financial sustainability and the need is to measure short term economic performance. This has broad implications: in addition to deciding whether a product is a success or failure, it often has longer reaching effect on financing of follow-on development, resources assigned to support, advertising, or sales, sometimes creating a self-fulfilling prophesy, most often on the failure side. As we will see in subsequent sections, for sustainability, it is essential that all organizations and individuals have the same understanding of what "success" entails. In that way, if there are to be disagreements, they can be had in the theoretical sphere before the product is developed and money spent rather than after a considerable, potentially non-recoverable, investment has been made. There is a brief discussion in section 6.2 about one possible way to address this.

We attempt to take cognizance in this section of many different types of organization, from pure software vendor companies to corporate IT organizations to companies providing value added services based in some large measure on their unique software or software implementation. As we will shortly see in the framework discussion, there are a number of different product types and corresponding ways (sometimes multiple ways) of pricing each. Our objective is to describe each of the models, to discuss the various ways in which each type of organization may convert its product value into economic worth, and to suggest which methods we have found are most suitable to each situation. In the end, pricing should involve the estimation of an economic value for a product and the setting of corresponding prices and terms which optimize for the organization that offers the product. We will not attempt to dictate what the "right" solution is but rather to discuss the trade-offs in market, in financial, and sometimes in implementation terms so that one may make fully informed decisions for an enterprise.

5.2   The Role of the Software Pricing Manager

Just as the Software Product Manager is the "ringmaster" of bringing a product to market, managing the interrelationship of many different activities on behalf of his product, so too does the Software Pricing Manager have many responsibilities. On the one hand he must oversee all of the financial implications of the product, understanding the P&L (Profit and Loss statement) for the product, the sales forecast, net revenues to be derived after channel expenses, as well as the pricing metric, the implications of pricing different from other products in the family, platform, or channel, the importance to the company's product portfolio, be it all software or not, and so forth. On the other hand he must also understand the market into which the product will be sold, the competitive posture in terms of product content and quality, competitive products and how they are priced, whether alternative pricing metrics will be tolerated, whether differential value can be ascribed to the product and successfully charged for.

The most effective way for all this to be accomplished is for the Software Pricing Manager to work closely with the Software Product Manager from the outset. To optimize for the corporation, they should agree on objectives, how all of the various and sometimes conflicting requirements will handled, what compromises must be made, and how these things will be accomplished.

In the mid-nineties, IBM Europe decided that to provide *esprit de corps* during fairly tough times, a headquarters magazine extolling the work of the HQ was needed. In the inaugural issue, there was an interview of some senior middle level managers with the premise that if they were stuck in an elevator with Lou Gerstner, then CEO of IBM, what would they say to him. One of our colleagues said that he would say "I'm headed for another tough day at the matrix, Lou."

Within any mature corporation there are going to be matrices and none more complex and potentially adversarial than between Product Management, Pricing, Sales, and Finance. Yet this intersection occurs for every single software product and requires the buy-in of each group for success. The best way to accomplish this is by working as a team so that each individual or function feels a sense of owner-ship and responsibility and so that problems and their solutions are jointly shared amongst the team. The alternative, management by contention, seems to turn into contentiousness which is good at blocking but not good at furthering a project.

We spoke earlier of the need for a review of product pricing and terms and conditions with respect to intra-brand and intra-platform consistency, as well as capability to invoice. This review usually falls to the software pricing manager and may reflect contention between "best for product," "best for brand (or platform or corporation)," and "we can't bill it that way without an investment of $5M in back office systems, implemented earliest 24 months from now." Very often there is no "right" answer, with each contingent having perfectly valid reasons for their view. Yet a solution which optimizes for the corporation must be found. This intersection in the matrix may get quite hot and need considerable judgment and conflict resolution, offering good payback for teamwork.

A review like the one described here is likely to be much more necessary in a large organization where there are many products and potentially several dimensions to the product and management matrix. In a smaller company, product term mismatches, price structure and price level problems are likely to show up quickly because all the focus is on a smaller number of products in a well defined and relatively less complex environment. The same is true for in-house charge-back schemes, though IT departments are well served to benchmark their costs periodically lest they discover one day that their users have done the benchmarking and found in-house IT out of line with what is available elsewhere.

As we saw in the job description for a product manager, a breadth of experience is required for that job. The same is true for a software pricing manager (see job description in Appendix B). Often in large corporations, the task of software pricing manager will be assigned to someone junior, who will be given a series of criteria to meet, many products to price, and the setting of price will become a spreadsheet exercise with insufficient regard for the considerations we raise here and in the rest of the chapter. That is not what we mean by software pricing manager who, to do the best job, must understand each of the considerations, their scope and importance, and the implication of decisions in product acceptance terms as well as financial ones. The ideal is to have someone who has had exposure to financial reporting, like I&E (Income and Expense statement), P&L (Profit and Loss statement), and so forth, but who has also had exposure to, if not experience in, sales. If a person with competitive analysis background is available, they might make an excellent candidate. Like finding a product manager, finding someone who meets all of these criteria may not be easy. Yet it's essential if the pricing work is to be well done. We are wont to refer to "pricer's disease" as the firm belief that revenues can be increased merely by raising price or, said another way, that forecast volumes are a constant, price is a variable, and revenue a dependent variable. Clearly real financial projections and pricing will derive from a more sophisticated model.

This leads to a final point which touches skills, education, and organization: to optimize on a financially sustainable product, the pricing manager needs a degree of independence from the product organization and from the finance organization in the sense that neither should be able to dictate price either "for the good of the product" nor "because we need that much revenue." At the time the price for a software product is being set, most development expense has been incurred, so price ought to be set with respect to the value of the product in the marketplace, regardless of the cost of development. (Of course cognizance must be taken of what the product announcement may portend in terms of additional development and customer relationships and impact of price on other products, on the brand and platform.) Finance may well resist the notion of ignoring sunk cost, while Development and Sales may aim for too low a price, assuming they need it for introduction and can raise it later. Thus maintaining independence is important as is selecting an individual whose analytical insights can help him swim against sometimes powerful currents.

5.3   The Software Pricing Framework

Just as we found the product management job and classification of all its responsibilities and activities too complicated to describe as a series of processes and developed a framework for the discussion on the myriad artifacts involved, so we find the various ways of going to market, the considerations for them, the varied ways in which prices are set and evolve with the helping hand of the software pricing manager too complex to describe adequately without an organizational framework. In an article entitled "What Is Strategic Pricing?" first published in Strategic Pricing Group Insights in 2005, Nagle and Hogan describe the Strategic Pricing Pyramid ([NagHog05]), comprising (from the base), value creation, price structure, price and value communication, pricing policy, and price level at the top.

They write in [NagHog05, p. 1]: "A comprehensive pricing strategy is comprised of multiple layers creating a foundation for price setting that minimizes erosion and maximizes profits over time. These layers combine to form the strategic pricing pyramid in [Fig. 5.1]. In keeping with the value-based perspective, value creation forms the foundation of the pyramid. A deep understanding of how products and services create value for customers is the key input to the development of a price structure that determines how offerings will be priced. Once the price structure is determined, marketing can develop messaging and tools to communicate value to customers. The final step before setting price is to ensure that the pricing processes in the company are able to maintain the integrity of the price structure in the face of aggressive customers and competitors."

This concept and many others are further elaborated in *The Strategy and Tactics of Pricing*, the excellent work on pricing by Nagle and Hogan ([NagHog06]). Here they use "The Strategic Pricing Pyramid" as the organizational basis for their work, which we urge you to read: it's the best work on pricing we have come across.

We could not agree more with the strategic pricing pyramid as defined. It applies perfectly to software. Yet when we consider the material we wish to convey, the different nature of software products themselves, the different routes to market and the discrete customer sets, we feel a pricing framework with more software and market specificity will serve better to make the points essential to each product and market segment. Underlying the pricing for each product, we have in mind

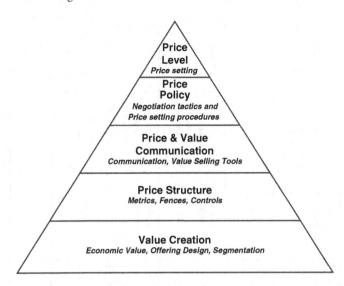

Fig. 5.1 The Strategic Pricing Pyramid, Nagle & Hogan [NagHog05]

building price up precisely as described in the Strategic Pricing Pyramid. To that, we will add an overlay of specific needs for different routes to market and target markets. The Pricing Framework shown in figure 5.2 will serve as the organizational basis for the remainder of this chapter and the discussion of the various ways there are to convert intrinsic value of software products into economic worth for the company that sells the product. The framework begins with the corporation's strategy: what are its goals and how can pricing be complementary to them. Next the framework looks to price structures, e.g. how prices may vary for a single product. The variable that drives different prices for a single product we refer to as a "metric." It can be many things as long as it tracks to increased customer value: quantity, usage, number of transactions, function, etc. The next element of the framework is price policy, e.g. under what circumstances may established prices be changed and by whom. Finally the setting of price level, or how absolute prices will be established, e.g. by calibrating against competition.

From there, we depart slightly from "framework" and describe various different routes to market. While each of these needs the framework elements as described by the Nagle and Hogan pyramid, the actual approach to software sales is distinguished in large measure by the target market, so we have chosen to organize this chapter by defining first a strategy and then the different markets, discussing each in turn: enterprise sales as a separate entity; negotiation as a specific process and skill which is used by software vendors and purchasers as well as by internal IT providers and users; specific considerations for software pricing in a global marketplace and in the business-to-consumer (B2C) market; Software as a Service (SaaS), and finally pricing for in-house IT. We will begin our pricing odyssey with a discussion of pricing strategy.

	Strategy	Structure, Policy, & Level	Pricing in Distribution Channels	Pricing for Large Customer Accounts	Pricing for the Global Market	B2C (Business to Consumer)	SaaS Offerings	Pricing for Enterprise IT Organizations
Corporate level	Set strategy for overall pricing: optimized to short or long term. Determine relationship of Finance, Product Development, and Sales	Single price policy, consistently enforced (may be multiple for different lines of business)	Special needs of each distribution channel	Various approaches to dealing with large customers	Strategic approach to differential prices per country	Strategic guidance on channels to use	Determination of how to position Corp in marketplace: fee, "free", subscription, service	How the IT organization may pay for itself:
					- Currency and how it plays with prices	- Intellectual Property strategy		Profit center
Product/ Family level	Set product family strategies with respect to price structures and	Selection of product price structure, metric, price level, and charge options	Volume programs	Discounts	Approaches to pricing across geos: pro's and con's of each	Tactical decisions on channels	Selection of best go to market vehicle conforming to corporate strategy	
		Provide competitive advantage or optimize revenue	Distributor / reseller / influencer compensation	Negotiation	Relative costs of doing business and effects on price	Price levels compared to competition	Optimize based on same factors but different menu of options	Cost center
		Complete an offering	Market expansion	Special bids		Implementation of IP protection		Service organization
		Incidental to a service	Independent solution vendor	Role of procurement				Make vs buy
		Price over product life	Original equipment manufacturer (oem)	Value selling				Outsourcing
		Cost of implementation						

Fig. 5.2 Software Pricing Framework

5.4 Pricing Strategy

Before a company can bring products to market as a viable business, it needs to establish a business model which understands:

- all potential revenue sources
- costs to manufacture and distribute the concerned products
- its ability to sell them at prices which will allow for profit

Further it must ensure this model is sustainable or adaptable over time so that the company can achieve its objectives. These objectives can be very different from company to company: everything from a small family business which is intended to do nothing more or less than provide the family a livelihood to a Microsoft whose clear purpose is to grow ever larger and dominate the software industry (and perhaps others). We will also discuss later in-house information technology whose purpose is to service the needs of a corporation which has no intrinsic interest in IT *per se* except that it should be responsive to the needs of the corporation, be cost-effective, and perhaps provide some level of competitive advantage through IT functionality not available to competitors. Based on the different objectives strategies will vary widely.

It is our view that such broad strategic directions are the province of senior executives and boards of directors. These directions must be in place before any individual price structures or prices are created, so that the pricing manager knows what his range of options is. For example, if a company which sells both software and hardware were to decide to bundle the price of the operating system into the price of the hardware that would require a very different model than stand-alone prices for hardware and software. A well-known example is Google who decided they would make their money not by charging users per search or per use of each different type of facility but rather offer the search service at no charge to end users and fund it through advertising charged to companies whose ads are actively viewed.

For strategic and sustainable success, a critical point to remember is that these high level strategic directions for pricing strategy cannot be made lightly, cannot be changed easily, and paradoxically need reasonably frequent review to ensure that they are keeping pace with market and technology as well as the actual products that the company is currently producing. For example, in a startup without a great deal of funding, the development team for a new product might only be allowed to continue development if they brought in sufficient revenues to fund the development. In circumstances like these, there may be a need for a large up front license charge to infuse cash into the operation.

But suppose for sustainability reasons the company later wanted a more modest up front fee and more substantial ongoing maintenance stream. In such a case it would be an awkward transition if the initial license fee were reduced and maintenance increased, since the first loyal customers would have already paid a pricey fee for the license and might balk at a large rise in maintenance charges.

In larger companies with multiple products, perhaps covering multiple platforms, perhaps with product portfolios covering multiple disciplines (e.g. networking, storage, security, product development tools), there will usually need to be multiple pricing strategies. The specific strategy for a product or product family may be driven by competition in the market, by financial needs of the corporation, by customer perceptions of value metrics, by the ability to track licenses or usage, or by back office considerations. When targeting a specific market, e.g. the internet, it is important to follow the norms of that market. Alternatively if the norms are not followed the only chance of success is to be able to demonstrate that deviation from the norms consistently yields a lower cost to the customer and is easy to administer. Even in this latter case there is risk: it is always hard to buck a trend, in particular if it makes price comparison difficult. Examples: if every single competitor offers his product with pricing per concurrent user (see section 5.5.2 for an explanation of various charging alternatives), it is unlikely that a unitary price or pricing per registered user will be easy to sell unless demonstrably less expensive in almost all cases (which suggests an unreasonably low price). A company which sells a utility or compiler cannot usually base the price on the same capacity or usage metric that it might use to price an operating system. So different metrics will usually be necessary for different products, yet there will also be a cross-current (the matrix, again) which will want consistent price structures across similar products and/or across products on the same platform. It is the job of the software pricing manager, working with the product managers, to find the optimal solution, which of its nature almost always involves compromise.

Just as the company pricing strategy needs periodic review, so do brand and even product pricing strategies. Periodically, at each level, software vendors need to decide whether their product pricing is successful and ought to continue as is or whether some aspect needs revision. However, simply conducting the review and deciding some products could use a change is not the end of the job. Transition is immensely difficult and is often the reason that price structures and price levels are not changed. As we cautioned earlier, prices cannot be changed frequently or lightly. There is substantial impact on customers, distributors and resellers, the direct sales force. Also, one needs to consider the amount of energy, sales time, and back office time that such a change requires. Often if a vendor makes his existing base "whole" (i.e. protects the existing install bases from any negative effects of the price or structure changes), he makes the overall invoicing unwieldy and suboptimizes revenue into the bargain, perhaps even to the point of being worse off than before the changes. For example, if a vendor increases his prices by 7% but says that the increase only applies to new license acquisitions, that may gratify some existing customers. However, it adds immense complexity: now the vendor is required to know when each license was acquired and to have two sets of prices. In the same customer organization there may be both new and old licenses, creating at least complexity if not chaos in invoicing ongoing charges. Last, the effect of the increase may be to cause some sales not to happen; it would only require a loss of 7% of sales to cause the vendor to be worse off than he would have been leaving price alone, without taking any of his increased overheads into account. On the other hand, if a vendor determines he must raise price, he should ensure that the increase is justifiable in terms of value and that there is no appearance of "gouging" the existing customer base, lest he undermine the goodwill the product has amassed. So price changes, at least structural ones, are best undertaken as part of some larger strategic change when it is really necessary for company or product and can be applied universally.

5.5 Price Structure, Policy and Level

"A foolish consistency is the hobgoblin of little minds," (Emerson). But a reasonable amount of consistency of terms and pricing across products is expected. If a vendor produces only one product, then he often can set his price structure as he wishes, consistent with some of the factors enumerated in the last section. The major considerations are 1) for the customer to be able to predict his individual price for the product and to agree that his costs incurred track with value received; and 2) for the vendor to be able to track and bill the software according to the metric chosen. However, when one has a portfolio of products to sell, the need for consistency comes to the fore, lest the market judge the offerings too complex. Nor does a vendor want his sales force spending valuable time engaging in explanations and debate with customers over why one particular metric was chosen for product A and not for product B when they are complementary products. As a result a software vendor needs to set a policy for the way in which prices will appear; the number of structures and perhaps the guidelines for those structures; and finally the approach to price level: high price value add or low price commodity or somewhere in between.

5.5.1 Price Structure

Price structure is a very important element in marketing and company image as well as for financial well-being of the firm. The way in which prices scale, whether there is built-in discount or not, may have a great deal to do with how a company is perceived. To ensure that we are clear on this key element of pricing, let's begin with a definition; we define

> **Price structure** = the manner in which the prices for a given software product are offered, including the metric by which those prices may vary for the single product (e.g. one single price, price based on number of users, on capacity, on usage, or on volume of licenses acquired).

In our view the responsibility for setting standards and direction in the area of price structure is a "corporate" or possibly divisional responsibility (if one division is reasonably autonomous and is responsible for all the products involved). That is not to say the pricing metrics should be chosen at the corporate level; they should be the province of the pricing managers for the products. However, once established, jointly by the product managers for the family, those metrics ought to be enforced across all products of the family, platform, solution, or whatever grouping has been chosen for consistency. Corporate may also wish to limit the different ways of pricing across the corporation for other reasons: appearance of consistency even between product lines, revenue predictability, revenue stability, cash flow, or other. There ought not to be variations by individual product unless provided for in the standard. Only an overarching entity like "corporate" has the authority to enforce such a standard and thus it is they who must sponsor both the rules and the enforcement.

We have said that it is not easy to change metrics, once established, as it causes disruption from customers through channels and sales force to back office, usually with some loss of sales at least in the short term. Therefore considerable care should be given to the choice of metrics initially. We advocate that early in the development cycle for a product all the product managers and pricing managers who are to be involved in the product family engage in dialog about what pricing metric is most appropriate. The considerations which are relevant are the same as for individual products, except that now compromises may need to be reached when different members of the family have different needs. What is paramount is to choose a price structure which will track with value, or, more explicitly, which the vendor's sales force or channel can convince customers tracks with value. It doesn't really matter how it appears to the vendor if the buyer doesn't accept it. Once the appropriate metric and price structure have been chosen, they should be mapped against the standards set by corporate. If there is a perfect fit, the structure part of the job is done. If there are minor variations, then a decision must be made to seek an exception or to live with the standard. And if there is no price structure which appears appropriate, then a new structure must be devised and requested as an exception. This should all be done within a "consistency grouping" of products for which the corporation deems consistency to be important, not on behalf of a single product.

At this point, the reader may be asking how many metrics could there be? Is this really so important? There can be as many metrics as there are ways of perceiving value: value can vary with number of users who have the product installed, number of registered users, number of concurrent users (see section 5.5.2 for explanations of these terms), number of web users as opposed to in-house users, number of engines in the server, number of licenses installed, number of transactions, amount of data managed, amount of data transferred, transaction size, cycles of processor used by the program, amount of memory assigned, and on and on. But those are only some of the technical measures. The vendor should also consider how his product may be used and anticipate problem situations which his chosen metric does not address. For example, if a vendor has a product which a user is going to want installed on his work desktop, his laptop, and his home desktop, it is unlikely the customer will be willing to pay for three copies when he knows only one will be in use at any one time. In such a case a term which specifies that all three may be installed as long as only one is in use or a nominal price for the two extra copies will both build customer good will and reduce the likelihood of cheating. It is wise when designing any structure to eliminate potential sticking points before they ever become an irritant which needs to be addressed.

Many customers would prefer to base their costs on realized benefit: number of widgets sold, a fraction of a percentage of gross profit, number of fulltime employees or further refined with penalty clauses for failure (downtime greater than "x" minutes, more than "y" unplanned outages per unit time). This leads us to make three comments, the first of which will be repeated over and over in this book: a vendor should 1) make certain the metric chosen tracks to customer perceived value for the product; 2) make certain that the metric chosen leads to predictable costs for the customer and predictable revenues for the vendor; without predictability it is difficult to plan and that can also make the product difficult to sell; 3) not base his price on factors that are outside of his control without extremely careful thought. There are too many things which can go wrong and which have nothing at all to do with the value of his product. Years ago, one company with which we are familiar based its price for all IT services provided to an automobile manufacturer on 3% of gross sales of automobiles. It seemed safe enough, the manufacturer in question was doing well and the economy was strong. But the manufacturer refreshed his product line, the new cars were not well accepted, the economy went soft, and sales suffered badly. The IT provider revenue declined significantly while his contract required him to provide significantly increased hardware, software, and services.

There is one final broad area of software price structure which must be considered: do the products in question provide the requisite data to calculate the price according to the metric and are the back office systems able to execute the proposed price structure in terms of tracking, measuring, and invoicing licenses and ongoing maintenance? If not, is the company willing to make the required investment in both? There is little point in going to all the trouble of finding the right metric, the right price level, having a sales force able to articulate and justify the price based on value of the software if the vendor either cannot determine how many licenses (or other metric) are in use or invoice for that level of use. In terms of advice in this area, the first is for the vendor to ensure that the back office system to support software is flexible and able to accommodate the various price structures which he wishes to use. The second is to ensure that whichever metric he uses to charge, he and his customer are both able to count easily and reliably using that metric. Tools may be necessary or the use of audits, which are used by most major software vendors like Microsoft, Symantec, Oracle, and IBM. But it is of no use to select a structure or metric which cannot be reliably measured and invoiced. This is an area where "trust and verify" is a required strategy. A customer once asked if this philosophy meant we did not trust him. The response was, as it had to be, "We have no reason not to trust you; by the same token, we have no evidence that you will take extraordinary measures to guarantee payment for every single license in use in your enterprise, particularly when you don't have any reliable way of knowing for certain that more than your entitled number of licenses is in use. For that matter, you may be using fewer licenses than we think and paying too much in ongoing maintenance." A far-fetched but illustrative metaphor might be to question whether anyone has ever paid a parking ticket they did not receive for parking illegally.

5.5.2   Charging Alternatives

For software vendors whose objective is to make a profit by developing software, the selection of charging mechanisms presents a challenge, balancing the way customers wish to pay for software with the revenue needs of their corporation. James E. (Jim) Bryant, former chief financial officer of IBM's Software Group and (as of June 2008) executive vice president and chief administrative officer of CA, a large software vendor, once said "Every software company would charge MLC (monthly license charges) if they could afford it." Why would he have said that? That was his view simply because a steady stream of revenue is the most desirable way for a software vendor to get revenue: month after month a steady stream makes earnings predictable and smooth, exactly what investors are looking for. Furthermore the steady flow of revenue is ideal for funding new development; finally, if a customer is really using a product, it is likely he will continue to use it for years and provide the vendor with more aggregate revenue over time than an up front license payment. There are a number of other advantages as well which we cover in this section, but it is important to understand that the driving force behind several of the charging mechanisms we will discuss is to approximate recurring license revenue.

The most common charging mechanism is one time charge or paid up license, prevalent for web sales and for PC and distributed server software.

> OTC = One time charge, a method of charging in which a fee is charged initially for the use of the license and that the customer has the right to use the license in question for the capacity and quantity that it specifies, with no further payments.

OTC rights may not be abrogated except potentially in the case of license violation. Often, maintenance or service is available at a charge and this may include future upgrades as well (see chapter 3). (Some vendors also require continued maintenance payments or the license rights are terminated. Arguably this is more ILC/RLC-like than OTC; it also has implications in terms of when revenue may be booked). It is important when offering maintenance to ensure that the terms and conditions require a customer buying maintenance to buy it for all installed licenses: if not, it is very difficult if not impossible to prevent a customer buying maintenance for one license and using it to supply maintenance to his 10,000 installed licenses of that product. This is even truer if the maintenance includes upgrades. In fact, in the case of upgrades, the customer needs to include even those licenses he may not yet have deployed if he wishes to keep them current. Finally, there needs to be a mechanism for the customer to resume maintenance if he has suspended it. This poses something of a delicate pricing conundrum: the vendor will not want to price this provision attractively enough that customers actually allow maintenance to lapse and resume it later if they have a problem or, in the case of upgrades, if they see a feature they want. On the other hand, the charge to resume can neither be punitive ("punitive" terms almost never work with customers) nor more than the cost of a new license. If it were more costly, the customer would simply buy a new license and thus have two entitlements, one to a current product, a second to a back level product. The customer may be tempted to sell the latter, particularly as he will be resentful at having to buy a new license, and the vendor may lose control of his sales opportunities and his customer base.

Support ("how-to") may be provided at additional charge or is sometimes bundled into the maintenance, as for example in IBM's distributed offerings. Both vendors and customers should ensure that they understand the precise terms of the license and charge mechanisms with OTC: with most vendors the right to use the program as delivered is never taken away. But some vendors require the ongoing payment of maintenance to retain usage rights, while with others there may be a hefty fee for upgrading to a newer version. Such a version might be desirable on its own or necessary to support a new operating system or new hardware. On an individual level we have probably all experienced this with the migrations of Windows on the PC and often the absence of drivers to support new hardware on old software versions. Currently Microsoft is experiencing significant problems getting customers to migrate to Vista (a new operating system) and is setting a deadline for Windows XP (predecessor operating system) technical support to force customers to move. It remains to be seen whether this will be successful, but the problem illustrates one of the difficulties with one time charge.

Nor does one time charge software lend itself well to capacity pricing (capacity pricing is variable depending on the power of the machine or fraction of a machine on which software is executing). If a capacity-based license is acquired, it provides entitlement to a specific capacity and no more. So, if a customer upgrades his hardware, he often is required to upgrade his license as well. This may pose a sales problem if the hardware is being upgraded for performance reasons or redundancy and there is no more work being done by the capacity-priced software. And, there are no refunds if a customer downgrades his hardware, nor may licenses typically be split, although some vendors may sell some form of "points" or "units" which can be allocated by machine.

OTC software has another characteristic which needs noting: when a customer purchases OTC licenses, he will almost always get a better deal buying in quantity. But that entails risk, since at the time of purchase his applications are likely not written, the software he is buying may be largely unproven in his shop and there is no way out if the software later proves unworkable or is unused due to changes in plans. Such unused software is usually referred to as "shelfware" which is frightening to many IT managers as it may represent many millions of wasted capital expense. Vendors have tried to find ways to alleviate concerns about this buy-ahead risk, but under accounting rules one cannot book revenue until the sale is complete, making it quite difficult for a vendor to provide an effective right of return provision.

OTC also entails financial risks to a vendor: IBM at one time converted mainframe operating system VSE from MLC to OTC expecting it to package better with new small, inexpensive hardware. But the business case was predicated on every customer buying the upgrade for each new version at a 40% discount incentive. Customers quickly discovered they could skip versions with little pain, thereby halving the expected VSE revenue. In order to maintain VSE as a financially viable product, it was necessary to convert customers back to MLC, a difficult task.

OTC installed license inventory is almost impossible to track. Typically the vendor will issue a certificate of entitlement for volume license acquisitions. The customer may have an entitlement and his certificate, but that does not mean he actually has deployed that number of licenses. In some cases, the customer may also be entitled to sell unused licenses. So determining actual installed licenses is difficult. This has implications in terms of maintenance sales, future upgrade sales, understanding customer benefit from his purchase, etc.

One time charge advantages are that it is a closed transaction: once it's done, there is nothing for the vendor to keep track of except maintenance entitlement, the revenue is bookable, and the customer has his license. This works well and in fact is almost a necessity when using channels, where sales are not controlled by the vendor. This is especially true for those vendors that use resellers for distribution. Another clear advantage of OTC offerings is that they lend themselves to discounting and promotions, since once the transaction is completed, there is little lingering effect of the discount or promotion (there may be pressure to discount maintenance to the same level as the license, even on an ongoing basis). We define

Software promotion = a temporary product offering with terms or prices that are advantageous compared to regular pricing and terms.

In a moment we will see that promotions are very difficult to execute effectively in a recurring charge environment.

In recent years, most vendors have sought to make their one time charge products into better long term producers of revenue by encouraging people to buy maintenance, including upgrades. This provides a better source of revenue and alleviates the version migration problem. We anticipate that this trend will continue. We also foresee the emergence of a new trend: with the huge increases in processor capacity on distributed servers and the inclusion of multiple cores on processor boards, capacity of individual servers is growing very fast, with server consolidation becoming prevalent in all companies with more than a few servers. Software vendors whose pricing is per server cannot afford to lose revenue with every consolidation, so we expect pricing and charge mechanisms to reflect capacity more and more.

Term License = An entitlement to use a software product over a specific period of time. Such a license is usually offered at a fixed price which often takes the form of annual payments for a fixed number of years, after which the customer must stop using the product, renew his term license, or license the product under other available terms.

Term licensing has some of the characteristics of recurring charge price structures, in that it spreads revenue over the term of the license and if the customer stops paying, he loses the right to use the product. It also has some of the characteristics of OTC with required maintenance in that the pricing often works out to an OTC charge plus about three to four years of maintenance. In some ways this structure is also like MLC due to loss of license right if one ceases to pay for the license. However, at least in IBM's MLC there is right to terminate a license with 30 days notice, whereas with term licenses there is always a commitment to a specified time, often in exchange for some price advantage.

Customers unwilling to commit capital to purchase might prefer this structure, as might those who expect short term use. One customer downside may be the time commitment though that may also be an advantage if product usage is expected through the term. Another potential reason for not preferring term licenses over OTC, for example, is that over time the term license may indeed cost more.

Vendors may prefer term licenses as they "force" the customer to stay current and continue paying for that currency as long as he uses the product. Of course the downside is that there is no acceleration of revenue as there is with OTC, as accounting practice usually requires the recognition of the revenue over the term of the license. However, if it's affordable, it may be a way to build a recurring revenue stream.

> **ILC/RLC** = Initial license charge, recurring license charge: charging method that requires an initial payment and ongoing (usually annual) recurring charges for the license to remain valid.

This is a hybrid license form, one in which the customer must pay a recurring charge in addition to the initial charge, because if these are not paid, he loses the right to use the license. This resembles OTC with mandatory maintenance and is usually disliked by customers. Today it is largely obsolete though still used by some application providers. This may also appear as ILC/ALC, where the "A" stands for "annual." Customers much prefer OTC with optional maintenance, which is in 2008 a quasi-standard industry offering for distributed software.

> **MLC or ALC** = Monthly license charges or Annual license charges are part of a generic recurring license charge group of which monthly and annual are most prevalent. Each charge represents a prepayment which entitles the license-holder to use the program for the period of prepayment.

This licensing method offers advantages to customers in that they have no initial major payment and can usually cancel their use of the product with a period of prior notice, giving great flexibility and no exposure to buying obsolete technology. On the other hand, the long term costs may be greater than OTC, and there is a somewhat greater exposure to price increases over time. Few vendors offer this charge method, since it has a slower payback than other forms of charging and it requires very substantial capitalization to execute, hence the Bryant comment about affordability.

Another difficulty with recurring charge software is that it is devilishly difficult to discount: we made a point earlier about discounts and promotions only being used to change the behavior which would have happened without them. But recurring charges are like rent, they go on forever, so it is impossible to change price in order to influence an event without lifetime commitment to that lower price. Short term forgiveness of a part of the charge is usually not persuasive to the customer as he will do his cost calculations on ongoing costs, not a short time promotional period. What can sometimes be effective is a ramp-up of charges over a reasonably lengthy period of 12, 18, 24, or perhaps even 36 months in extreme cases so that the charges track, at least approximately, to the value received as implementation proceeds. Note that free periods rarely work as the customer tends not to do implementation work until actually paying for the software; there is also the risk that this is seen as a test period with no commitment by the customer.

Customers with large computing requirements used to have little choice besides the mainframe (which is where most of the recurring charge revenue comes from) but with technology advances and improvements in reliability of both distributed hardware and software, distributed computing is more than viable. This change has put pressure on the mainframe platform, primarily at IBM, with customer demands for improving price performance year on year. That creates a painful challenge to those trying to maintain that nice steady reliable revenue stream from the recurring charge software.

Several vendors, IBM in particular, have resorted to structures where as size of processor grows, there is declining price per unit of work. And there are special offerings which we will discuss in the section on pricing for enterprises. The best way to handle the problems described above is to provide discounts for growth which last for a finite period of time and then must be renegotiated: this affords the vendor both a lever to encourage commitment to growth and a mechanism to ensure that the discount thus granted does not become permanent. To the customer it provides discount on growth, which can be a real help with budget increases caused by growth.

Usage charging = charging for a software product based on some measurable defined metric, often the actual measured usage during a period.

The measured usage may be hours times machine cycles, numbers of transactions, amount of storage maintained, pages printed, or any number of different metrics. It may also be based on numbers of users using the program or some variation, with month to month price adjustment based on actual use.

The first such usage of which we are aware was for printer software to support the IBM 3800. After that there were a number of other products available for the mainframe with usage pricing often to afford a lower entry point for light usage and sometimes to avoid situations where the price of a capacity-priced product increased due to a hardware consolidation onto a more powerful processor, even though the workload was identical.

Many customers profess to like this usage charging, and in some cases it does make a lot of sense. But many of them like it because they believe they are light users of some programs and that this will give them a better price. Seldom do they profess willingness to pay more when they are heavier than average users. Strangely, when IBM introduced usage charging as an option for some key mainframe products, there were few customers who selected it. A few said it was "too much trouble" even when there were tens of thousands of dollars at stake per month.

From a vendor perspective, no matter the charge mechanism, the business case demands a certain amount of revenue to close. They are happy to offer usage charging if they can figure out how, but the revenue has to be a credible zero sum game, which suggests that customer expectation of a significantly lower price is unrealistic unless they are an extremely light user.. Developing prices for usage charging is very difficult: there is never reliable data on which to base a usage forecast, so pricing becomes difficult or impossible. As a result of the increased risk, pricing organizations will add a risk premium which may result in overall higher prices, defeating the original objective.

User-based charging = pricing and payment in advance for a fixed number of users.

There are many different forms of "user" and charging may vary depending on which of several definitions is used:

- Registered users: number of people with an authorized logon identity.
- Concurrent users: number of simultaneous users of a program; this may be counted or controlled in terms of logged-in users or in terms of active users vying for system resources
- "In-house" users: number of corporate employees or agents using the program on a routine basis within the company
- "Web" users: casual users outside the company who make sporadic use of the product (one can imagine a portal product which is licensed for "in-house" and "web" users with a different charge for each).
- "Logged-in" users: users actually in a position to use the program resource who may or may not be doing work.
- "Active" users: logged-in users who are actually doing work.

There are many variations and both vendor and customer should be certain that they understand the implications of the charging mechanism; failure to be precise could lead to serious misunderstandings and vendor revenue or customer cost disappointments. Like usage charging forecasting numbers of users is very difficult making pricing very risky.

Flat Price = single price regardless of processor capacity, usage, or other metric.

Most distributed products have, until recently, fallen into this category as well as some mainframe products, an example of which might be compilers. What characterizes these products is the difficulty of finding a metric which both vendor and customer can agree adequately tracks to value. Of course, the difficulty with flat price is that it will seem high to some users and low to others. This may have the effect of pricing so some target customers fall out of the target population while comparatively little revenue is collected from others.

Graduated charges = charges scaled for a program product based on capacity of the machine or environment where the program will run (or has run).

This structure is predicated on the notion that more work can be done (and thus more value delivered) on a large processor than on a small one so that a license price should be higher on a machine with more capacity than one with less capacity. Typically the prices are provided by group, with processors assigned to capacity groups by their manufacturers or industry benchmarks. Alternatively, a specific capacity measure may be created per system in MIPS (q.v.) or MSUs (q.v.) or in terms of "value units" which are also benchmark-derived. IBM introduced OTC "graduated charges" as an option for VM and VSE mainframe products in 1986, in acknowledgement that one single price across a capacity range that exceeded 200:1 (pre-1986) was no longer feasible. In 1987 optional OTC graduated charges were extended to MVS and later graduated charges were made available in MLC for all mainframe operating environments. Many other vendors followed suit with similar or identical structures.

MIPS = throughput of a computer system measured in millions of instructions executed per second.

Because many factors go into determining real throughput, including I/O speed, amount of memory, complexity of instruction set, benchmark workload mix, etc. "MIPS" are often explained jocularly as "misleading indicators of performance." While there have been many attempts to supplant them, they persist as a rule of thumb in the business sector with which many people are more comfortable than newer and potentially more accurate measures.

MSUs = throughput of a computer system measured in millions of IBM zOS service units.

Originally this was a fairly precise measure based on consistent benchmarks which was used to tune an MVS system. To the extent that it was comparable to MIPS, 1 MSU = approximately 6 MIPS, though it hardly tracks consistently with MIPS. If it did it would be no more useful than MIPS. By its very nature it was a measure of how the operating system and the hardware were performing together and was therefore considered a more accurate representation of real throughput. MSUs supplanted MIPS as the basis for IBM (and many other vendor) software charging on the mainframe. However in recent years, IBM has tampered with the MSU measurement to provide a software price advantage for its newer mainframe hardware, which may help hardware sales but breaks the price to value paradigm for the software.

PSLC (Parallel sysplex license charges) = recurring charges for mainframe software based on total capacity of a number of processors which are tied together into a "sysplex."

This form of charging created by IBM early in the 1990s may provide dramatic mainframe software price advantages compared to paying for software on multiple standalone machines. It can be considered as a model for software pricing in parallel-processor environments. This specific term has been supplanted by WLC which requires more modern hardware and operating systems but offers yet more advantages.

WLC (Workload license charges) = recurring charges for mainframe software based on the peak capacity in MSUs used during a month for a particular product.

The invoice is calculated based on usage data collected by the operating system, reported to the customer and provided to the vendor.

Changes to the MSU values aside, WLC is much better aligned with actual usage and therefore tracks better to value if one accepts that value can be based on usage of the software.

To recap: prices will be developed for individual products based on the value which a sales force can get customers to agree to; the charge mechanisms and structures will be those which fit the channel being used for the sale, and insofar as possible, the sale of a new license will be an event which sparks an ongoing revenue stream, either through recurring charges or through the recurring sale of maintenance for the product.

5.5.3 Price Policy

Pricing means very little if it can be changed easily, whether by a product owner or by Sales. Yet there will be situations where price needs to be changed due to circumstances that were not foreseen or that were sufficiently unusual that they did not warrant a discrete price in the original price announcement. To control what may be changed and by whom, most corporations introduce the notion of a price policy. We define

Price policy = a formal definition of the manner in which prices may be altered, e.g. price level (see 5.5.4) or price structure, by whom they may be altered, under what circumstances, and to what degree.

Usually there will be some degree of delegation on price level but little or none on structure, though relationship sales executives have been known to promise things to customers which transcend their specific delegations. Our recommendations are very specific, based on many years of experience.

Structural deviations have such inherent risks that a vendor may well decide they ought not be delegated at all. If corporate wishes to give degrees of freedom to the product manager and product pricer, it is best to have the alternative pricing structures spelled out clearly, along with specific conditions under which the alternatives may be chosen. If the range of deviation is not defined, it is likely that structures will be devised which cannot be supported by fulfillment, correctly invoiced or measured, and for which unforeseen contractual changes are necessary. If structural deviations are allowed with impunity, it is almost a given that pricing will become chaotic over time. As opposed to structural changes, price level delegations will generally be granted by corporate to an entity or entities in line management dealing with the product. Since price levels often tend to fall to the maximum delegation level over time, the corporation may wish to keep permitted sub-delegations modest, and, insofar as possible, established based on a repeatable universal algorithm so that there is no possibility of a 5% discount at one customer for a $1,000,000 transaction and of 20% for $100,000 elsewhere. The exposure is most acute when the dichotomy occurs between two locations within the same customer company. For this reason, Pricing, Sales, and Product Management may wish to set up processes to avoid the possibility. We will go into more depth in this area when we discuss pricing for large customers.

5.5.4   Price Level

Just as we began our discussion of price structure with a definition, we define here:

> **Price level** = the actual amount of charge within the price structure, e.g. if charge per user is $10 or $11, those are price levels.

Once both price structures and policies are established, the next step is to work on price level. The first determination to make is what value level the product has to the customer set. It is probably obvious, but this should be the value that the majority of the target customer population would experience, not the value to some outliers who get exceptionally great or exceptionally little benefit from the product. The market must be examined for competition to see what price levels there may already be for similar function. Added value should carry additional price, but caution: the product manager must be able to identify value that the customer will acknowledge, not just the number of entries on a features list. As a farfetched example merely to illustrate the point, offering support in Romanian for a U.S. federal tax program would not have much meaning for most of the target customers. At this point, nothing matters but value to customer; what development cost, what will be in future releases, what an individual customer has told someone anecdotally, what a developer believes his work is worth are all irrelevant. There is room here neither for emotion nor for cost-based financial rules of thumb. All that counts is what the vendor sales force can convince potential customers the product is worth.

5.5.5   Price Level and Market Tiers

We have used the word "tier" before in Chapter 4, referring to different levels of business partner. "Tier" in this context is quite different. In the interest of clarity, we define

> **Market Tier** = a group of customers with similar needs in terms of price point, level of product sophistication, or level of usage for a product.

Sometimes it will be necessary to consider different market tiers for the same product. There may be an entry tier that needs a small inexpensive product in a particular area and another set or sets of customers who require high volume, high performance, high function and to whom price is not even a consideration until their specifications are met. There may even on occasion be a third tier in the middle. This situation requires in depth understanding and creativity to solve: does the small customer need small function or full function and low usage? Will he be turned off by too many options, bells, and whistles? One of the authors early in his career heard from a prospective customer that his database product was no good because it had too many options and required too many decisions while a competitor with practically no flexibility was ideal. We overcame the objection by tailoring it for this customer (similar to going through the preferences tab on a PC product) to be just as inflexible as the competitor's database. The flexibility which to us seemed an asset to that customer was in fact a liability.

The term is used somewhat loosely in the industry, and we will see in the discussion that follows that the various elements that can define a tier may result in conflict, depending on who is defining the tier. E.g. to a customer full function and light usage may suggest a low price point tier, whereas to a vendor who needs to develop the full function, it may well appear a full function, high price point tier.

If different market tiers are identified, there are several different approaches and tests which may be applied in an attempt to meet the needs and price points of each tier. The pricing manager and product manager must work hand in glove to select the best price level, structure and metric, and even product packaging:

- is there price elasticity, i.e. do volumes of sales increase and decrease inversely to the price level, in some or all of the target markets;
- what is the real market need in terms of functionality;
- does the pricing metric chosen track across the customer set to deliver a price commensurate with value for all segments?
- assuming that there is elasticity and the pricing metric does not segment price sufficiently, the question arises, "Can we package an entry version? What will the additional costs be?"

Packaging an entry version may seem like an obvious solution but beware: entry versions with reduced function aren't effective when the smaller customers require all or most of the function. The reduced function product results in additional cost to the vendor for coding, testing, documentation, and marketing materials, not just initially but on an ongoing basis for service and future development. And, in some cases the full-function product may not get credit for what it delivers as more people talk about the entry product than the full-functioned one. Finally it may take a lot of accepts at the reduced entry level price (net of the additional costs) to offset the profit from the full price licenses that might have been acquired by some of the entry level customers anyway.

If an entry level product doesn't appear to be the right solution, another approach is to forecast what would happen if the target price were to drop to an affordable level even for smaller customers; clearly there might be some loss of revenue from high end customers, but perhaps that can be made up in revenue from a great number of smaller customers, price sensitive high end customers, and by capture of market share. Another test is to consider whether any adjustment of the pricing metric is possible and whether this will 1) be possible without impact on the product family consistency and 2) actually remedy the situation. Yet another solution is to look at some form of usage or capacity-based pricing if this can be rationalized with the base metric and structure chosen.

There is little point in any of this if, in the end, one has arrived at so many compromises that the price fit is poor for all buyers. We have seen product pricing and metrics that compromise between high end, high performance, full function demanded by one type of customer and entry level products with reduced price. If such price changes are not executed carefully, they can result in too low a price at the high end from customers who would have paid more and a price at the low end which is still too high for entry. If a vendor decides to reduce the price from one that is appropriate for high end full function customers in order to capture the low end, he needs to ensure he actually lowers it enough to capture the next tier and does his analysis based on the lower price. Otherwise he "leaves money on the table" with high end customers and gets no or few new volumes because the lowered price is still too high. Despite basic economics textbook graphs, elasticity is seldom linear in these cases and averages do not work; finding a single price or price structure which optimizes revenue and captures the low end of opportunity is sometimes not possible.

At different times the correct resolution may be to forego a market segment, to try one of the approaches above, even occasionally lowering price overall if there is serious danger of market share erosion. These choices must be evaluated carefully case by case based on hard data. It is culturally very difficult to convince a salesman to walk away from a potential sale, even if a sale at a given price or with exceptional terms would damage ultimate welfare of the product. Sales slogans like "never lose on price" and "ask for forgiveness, not for permission" are singularly unhelpful in managing price levels and profitability.

5.5.6 Price Level and Competition

When entering a competitive market, a vendor needs to assess not just the price competition offers for comparable function as he is developing his product and bringing it to market, but what their reaction will be when his product is announced. This will differ depending on many factors: market share, product maturity, product function, ability to package the product with function that one must have (Microsoft Office with Windows, for example). When setting price level, a vendor must anticipate his competitors' actions. For example, if they have a large install base and substantial revenue stream from maintenance, it would cost them a fortune in real revenues and profit to drop price on that big stream, so if a vendor is entering a price-elastic market, pricing sufficiently under the competition to gain customer attention might be an interesting strategy. On this point, a customer once told us that a 10% price differential wasn't worth looking at, that 15% was sort of neutral but was not compelling, but that 20 or 25% differential or more was so substantial that it required a look because it would be impossible to explain to one's own financial management why such a potential saving had not been considered. We have found over the years that this is a good rule of thumb. On the other hand, if no one has significant share, the market is new, then the vendor should be careful about entering with a low price; his competitor is likely to follow suit and then he'll find himself in a price war which, even if he ultimately wins, may leave him as the winner of a market segment with a seriously underpriced product. It is difficult if not impossible to work one's way back, and if this appears to be the vendor's new corporate behavior it may set price expectations for his other products which are impossible to meet.

It has been our experience that coming to market with a more fully functioned product than existing competition often tempts companies to price their products higher than the incumbents. This only works if the function is very much needed and competition does not have it ready to deliver. Having the function and an obvious price differential for it will cause customers immediately to engage the vendor's sales force in a discussion of whether that specific function is worth that price. If it is and that is demonstrable, fine. The vendor must consider, however, whether his sales force is of a caliber to translate the increased functionality into value the customers will recognize and accept. If they are capable of so doing, is that the best use of their time? Or could they generate more revenue and profit in some other way? If the value is not easily demonstrated to the customer set, then high function high price is a dangerous place to be. If there is no competitive equivalent, such a product creates a price function "umbrella" under which a competitor may come. If there is a competitor, both product manager and pricing manager should assess the potential benefit of coming out with a price to match competition, using the additional function as the competitive advantage or the incentive to change products. Role playing sales calls with different scenarios can be instructive on this point as can discussions with consultants or customers with whom a vendor has a close relationship.

5.5.7 Price Level over Product Life

When initially pricing a product, both pricing manager and product manager need to consider the evolution of product price over time. Nominally, for distributed products or even mainframe ones that are priced with an OTC (one time charge) license price and an ongoing maintenance charge, the maintenance will cover product enhancements during the life of the product. That poses a sort of logical dilemma, in the sense that if the product license price remains constant, early adopters, some part of whose maintenance fees are presumably being paid to cover enhancements, pay a great deal more (license + maintenance) than a late adopter for the same level of function. Conversely, the early adopter is paying less for additional seats (or servers or capacity) than he paid in his initial purchase + maintenance when he buys additional licenses. If, on the other hand, the license price is lowered over time, it implies that the license has less value each time it is lowered.

It probably also implies that maintenance price would be lowered to keep maintenance roughly the same percentage of license price over time. This would hurt the recurring stream related to the product. There is no "right" solution to this conundrum, but it must be considered in the context of future product development, whether the product will continue indefinitely with new releases or will be "reversioned" (in IBM terminology) thereby creating a new product. If reversioned this new product would then have its own price level and a transition cost for customers licensed under the old product. Once again the value test should be applied for both the new customer as well as the transitioned customer. Our personal test is: would a candid explanation of our strategy to a customer lead him to agree that it was fair and reasonable? The subject of pricing a product over time may be further complicated by external factors like competition or by currency movement, a particular global market issue we will discuss later in a section on managing price in a worldwide market.

"Reversioning" deserves consideration on its own. Different products (and companies) have followed different strategies: some never reversion but raise prices over time, others create new products which are not necessarily new versions of older products. Within IBM the strategy once was to reversion with architectural or truly major functional change, which a customer once told one of the authors was the only reasonable way to do it. That would be a good strategy but alas reversioning has come to be simply a way to increase price and sometimes change price structure.

Often when there is a new version with a higher price, it doesn't sell well or ramp up installations quickly which leads to byzantine ideas to raise the price of the lower function older products or their maintenance to drive migrations to the new. The best rationale for a new version is still to ensure that the new function is a change that is dramatic or is a major architectural change as mentioned above, that has real business value to many if not most customers. The need for the new function will induce the customers to migrate to obtain it. If many or most customers do not perceive the value, a vendor may get them to migrate but it will be done resentfully, and over time those customers will become disaffected and seek other alternatives or will look elsewhere for future product requirements. There are always two essential steps: ensure that the value is there in the product one wants to sell and ensure that the sales force is capable of articulating the value convincingly to customers.

5.5.8 Price Level – Special Situations

So far we have been talking about a software product whose purpose is to be sold to make a profit. Let us examine some other situations: one case is where a vendor has a series of products each one "OK" on its own but which do not form a coherent solution for want of an overarching structure (sometimes referred to as "glue code"), or which lacks some relatively minor piece to complete the solution suite.

How should a vendor price such a product? First, and most important, he should not overvalue it. We have seen cases where a developer wanted to write a bit of glue code and then price it as though he were pricing the whole solution; that will not work. The rule holds always and is inviolate: a vendor can charge only what his sales force can persuade the customer to accept as the real value of the product. The same is true of the small missing piece. In each case, what is needed is to calibrate the worth of the addition against the value and price of the rest of the components. As in the discussion of entry into a market with a more fully functioned product, a vendor must consider what would happen if he did not charge for the additional function or packaging code. Could that buy market share at very reasonable cost? Would it expand the customer base sufficiently to pay for the development cost? If so, why not consider it? A good thought to hold is that software has a high profit contribution, so increases in revenue translate in large measure into profit. If a vendor achieves more acceptance for his solution, he will bring in more revenue, quite possibly more than selling the incremental product into the existing install base. Through this means he can potentially expand the customer base, and fence out competition for that opportunity. This is in fact what Microsoft has done for years with their operating systems, recouping some cost through an expanding base but also increasing the operating system price over time.

As a vendor takes each step with a product or series of products, the market adds one more impression to the folklore about him as a vendor. Sometimes a relatively minor bit of structuring or providing of additional function at low/no cost can enhance his image of "fairness" and add significantly to customer satisfaction; the converse is also true. We are not advocating giving intellectual property away, far from it. But at each major juncture it may be wise for a vendor to assess the alternatives and decide which may be better for the company, the product family, or the product (in that order). Sometimes price = low or price = zero can be a highly leveraged action to take which can reap significant future rewards.

Another dimension of this is how such an approach may foster the vendor reputation in terms of offering complete solutions. The vendor can reflect on how a customer will feel when confronted with a sales call that says "I have a wonderful solution for you; to solve your complete problem, just integrate two or my products and one from vendor X and you'll be all set. Writing a little glue code and having vendor X's function available will make the vendor considerably more attractive.

A somewhat different case is that of software which is incidental to a service. We are not speaking here of vendor developed software for a specific customer but rather of tools, analysis programs, tuning aids, or applications that are used by a vendor to provide services but which are not of themselves the value add of the engagement as compared to the services. It is our view that software which is part of a service should not be priced separately but made available only as part of the service bundle. While some customers may object to the bundled offering ("We watched your technicians do the analysis last time, so we know how to use the tool, and candidly, our technical expertise is at least as good as yours, so all we want is the tool to be able to do the analysis ourselves."), it is probably better to make only the service available. There are two reasons for this: 1) it gives the vendor control over the analysis and ensures that the tool is used only as intended and that the interpretation of results is consistent with the intent and implementation of the tool and 2) it is very difficult to set value for and price software whose intent is to provide an aid to performing some specific service. Examples of this difficulty are: how does one price a tuning aid which is used once vs. one which is used several or many times? If a vendor has written a conversion aid, for example to convert HTML (browser language) to a particular standard, how can he price that so it relates to value for the small web site vs. the huge one, for the one time user vs. one who is continually converting code? In general it is best to offer and price the service to do these things rather than sell the software independently; in that way one can eliminate the potential issues.

We talked in 4.6.4 about product bundling and why one might choose to sell a bundled solution. While the reasons given are all valid considerations in favor of bundling, there are potential pitfalls. In a bundled solution, setting the price is difficult: it is presumed that the price will be less than the sum of the individual products, otherwise why bother. In order to make the bundle financially attractive, the vendor may need to cut the total bundle price substantially. But that means that if any sizeable group of customers would have bought all the components (or enough so that the total would have exceeded the price of the bundle) the vendor has sub-optimized his revenue (see also [BuDiHe08] and [Biering04]). Further, if one is dealing with companies where there are multiple development groups, combining products from more than one group into a bundle will inevitably start an internal war over how to split the revenue. If the products are available separately then one is liable to get a customer argument for lower price: "I am using only six of the twelve products in the bundle, so I expect only to pay 50% of the bundle price." These problems are not just a one time event at original license sale but continue on with maintenance and support often exacerbated if the bundle support lags the individual product support.

We have two recommendations: if a vendor is tempted to bundle products for any of the good reasons suggested in section 4.6.4, then it is wise to ensure that the result meets the promotion/discount test: the result of the bundling should have a business case which brings in more revenue than standalone product sales. Using this section as a checklist, the vendor can develop strategies to overcome each of the potential pitfalls. Finally, a vendor may find it useful to analyze carefully why he wants to do a bundle rather than integrate the functions into a single product and sell it as a higher-function solution with less granularity and more simplicity.

In a similar vein, there is today a renaissance of the "appliance" concept of a bundled hardware and software offering. The "appliances" today typically perform a single function efficiently and well as opposed to the broader "general purpose computer in a box" of the 1980s. An example is IBM's DataPower appliances which enhance delivery of web pages and improve firewall security. The operating system for such devices can be lean because it needs only support very specific hardware, software and circumstances, the same with the application and the hardware. The reason for singling out appliances is that pricing them has some nuances which require attention:

- The hardware is likely a commodity with low cost and the potential to become more cost-effective over time with technological innovation.
- The software is what is providing the real added value and should not be underpriced.
- Often there is a data component to the solution which requires subscription, e.g. for updating of virus definitions or for changes in browser language; if such a component is a key element of the application, the appliance should be priced to reflect the value of having current data.

We are discussing appliances, so the solution in this case comprises software and hardware (either of which may be manufactured or procured by the vendor). There may well be a temptation to divide the revenues evenly between hardware and software; if that is inconsistent with the way the customer perceives the value, that fact will cause trouble over time. Broadening the discussion to solutions in general, there are several observations to be made:

- If one component of the solution is priced too high compared to its value within the solution, then some other component(s) are priced too low (assuming overall solution price is set correctly).
- That means that over time understating the value and price of those components will cost revenue. For example, the data subscription portion of the solution may be its most valuable part; underpricing it (perhaps as a way of assigning more revenue to an up front license or piece of hardware so as to be able to book revenue earlier) may send a false message to potential clients: that the subscription has less worth than it actually does. Over time irrational correlations of price to value have a way of correcting themselves, almost always to the detriment of the vendor.

Before we move on to the specifics of pricing specific types of software, let's articulate a very important principle which is often overlooked. Both in pricing and in sales incentives: there is never a rationale which supports reducing price for a product, product family, or product portfolio. The only exception to this rule is a credible business case which supports the notion that revenue and profit will both increase as a result of the price adjustment (or perhaps that market share will increase with no loss of profit). In some sense, this is a restatement of our principle of pricing to value. If, by lowering price, one expands the market sufficiently to make up for the per unit profit lost, then one has found a more ideal price point. This represents good value to a larger segment of customers and thus will improve share and increase profit.

All too often vendors design price structures or promotions or campaigns around the idea that there is a minimum of 1:1 elasticity, that is to say that volumes will increase at the same rate that prices decline. In fact, elasticity may exist for some completely discretionary software purchases like games. But for business software, elasticity may only really exist in the context of price versus competition. Businesses usually decide they need a database and go procure one which has the features they need at an affordable price; lowering price is only relevant if it renders the product more affordable compared to alternatives. If a vendor's product is already affordable, lowering price just reduces revenue and profit. Of course, if certain functionality was desirable but too expensive for almost everyone and the price is reduced by an order of magnitude, there will be an expansion of the number of licenses but this is the stuff of major price shifts, not promotions.

Let's consider a hypothetical case: if a vendor has a widget priced at $100 and decides to discount it 10% for some period of time, he is betting that he will get a bit more than 11% more volume at the lower price than he would have gotten had he not discounted. Frequently that notion is a fallacy: the analysis, even if it is done, often overlooks what may happen to the install base. If there is a large base of installed customers, they may choose to buy future maintenance at a reduced price during the promotion period rather than wait and potentially pay more. That affords savings to customers for whom the incentive drove no additional sales and results in a loss of pure profit. Finally, the vendor risks damaging street price. Let us suppose he normally charges 20% of "list" price for maintenance. When later he suggests to customers that they should pay $20 to maintain their license, he may find that their view is that since they only paid $90 for the license, they should have to pay no more than $18 for maintenance, not $20. At best, this becomes a sales inhibitor of ongoing maintenance, at worst it becomes a sales showstopper, resolved only after there has been damage to customer relationship and at the expense of ongoing stream revenue, generally the best kind of revenue to have. Furthermore, the vendor is now underpricing the value of his own product, compared to what it could have been priced at.

The reason we raise this topic here is that we will now enter the world of specific charging alternatives and price structures, where the reader will see a bias on our part throughout these sections away from gratuitous discounts and promotions. Explaining our bias once here will hopefully avoid redundancy in explanations wherever the principle is encountered.

5.6 Pricing in Distribution Channels

We discussed the different sales and distribution channels in section 4.10. Here we want to examine how pricing works for these channels.

5.6.1 Web Distribution

The simplest form of distribution is downloading over the web. In chapter 3 we listed the various types of products suitable for web distribution. Let's examine these in turn. Why would someone publish freeware?

- Some products seem to be available at no charge because an individual has created a utility or similar product which he wishes to share since he knows others have the need, he doesn't anticipate that the economic rewards of selling it would be great or perhaps he wants to give back to the web some value that he has received himself for free.

- In other cases, availability of a free reader, Adobe's PDF reader, for example, or Microsoft's Powerpoint reader, are enablers for a wide audience to access documents created by the proprietary fee products. This in turn raises the popularity and reach of the fee products because anyone can read them at no charge.
- Sometimes it is a way of avoiding erosion and penetration of the core program set by third parties; when Microsoft was challenged by Netscape it bundled Internet Explorer into Windows at no charge, when concerned about RealPlayer, it bundled Media Player at no charge, etc. Making the function available at no additional charge allowed Microsoft to keep control of the Windows environment rather than allowing other companies to gain a foothold within the expanding core functionality the average Windows user would expect to have.
- In a few cases, particularly with small companies on the web, the price of zero is an enticement to use one product and attract the user to examine other for fee products from the same company. "Freeware" may also be supported by advertising and be "free" to the user only in the sense he doesn't pay money for it directly whereas the fee for the product is really exacted in having to watch advertisements. In this latter case, there may or may not be a for fee version which provides the same function but eliminates the advertisements.
- Finally, on the dark side, some make free software available as a way of distributing malware or as an entry point to identity theft.

Shareware represents more of an informal commercial market, where the author believes there is commercial value in the product he's publishing and seeks compensation via specific price or requested contribution. Often continued upgrades and support are tied to registration and payment of the fee. This may work fine for some products, but we offer some caveats: 1) this is not a model for long term sustained revenue 2) often we see instances where the shareware fee approaches or even exceeds fully supported full function commercial alternatives, so it's clear that insufficient work was done on price level 3) there are cases where soliciting contributions might yield a higher return (recently one of the authors of this book needed to find a free zip program with encryption for use by someone not in a position to buy a commercial program. He found one that worked, the file was transferred successfully, and he tried to contribute something to the developer, only to discover that the alternatives were to pay nothing or a $50 shareware fee. $50 was too expensive for a single use so the developer received nothing).

Most PC users will undoubtedly have encountered as much trialware as we: antivirus programs, utilities of all sorts, registry cleaners, etc. We find that these are most useful when one is in the market for specific functionality, perhaps has read a favorable article about a product and wants to try an alternative or two before making a financial commitment. If our experience is typical, then a vendor who chooses to go the trialware route had best be sure that his product will do well in a trial, i.e. not be hard to install and customize, offer function which is fairly rich compared to competition, be robust (to a degree far beyond freeware and shareware alternatives), provide support during the trial period, etc. Other factors to consider include terms and conditions; in a case where by its nature a program is likely to be installed across multiple PCs and laptops in a home, the pricing manager should consider the cost if there is no "per home" license. While it's true that many homes may have only one PC, many others (perhaps the very target population the product is aimed at) may have several. Amongst our friends and colleagues it is not unknown for there to be one desktop and one laptop per person. Considering a comprehensive backup program which for quantity of one use is reasonably priced at $69.95. Will a prospective buyer really consider it if he is required to pay $280 for the four computers (or more) in the household? There are simply too many alternatives at lower price. It might be much more sensible in such a case to price so that the first license is $69.95 (no loss of revenue compared to planned pricing for households with one PC). But then, a reasonable price structure might be not to charge at all for a mobile PC when there is a licensed desktop. To sweeten the deal a bit more, the vendor could charge only $34.95 for the second desktop. Of course, such a pricing hypothesis needs testing for business case purposes, but it might well be that $105 for two desktops and two laptops this product gets the sale while at almost $280 (or even $140) it does not. One must consider that the trial period is the one opportunity the product is likely to get. In our case, if we don't think the product is one we want permanently, either because of functionality or price, it is uninstalled and deleted immediately, not to be reconsidered at least for years. On the other hand, if a vendor has a product with good function and fair price, this way of penetrating the market can work very well. Finally there is "upgradeware." In our opinion, the best way to execute this strategy is to provide a free version of a fully functional program, holding back a few non-essential but still desirable features. In particular, it may be interesting to provide almost all the function but to hold back some ease of use, automation, or additional information add-on. In that way, users can become familiar with the product at no charge and then, once they are dependent upon it, the additional ease of use or other feature available in the "Pro" version may well be appealing enough to spend some money on. Zone Alarm introduced a security suite this way when security usually meant separate firewall and antivirus and spam filter. As they improved the product, the upgrade to "Pro" became automatic for many and they took significant market share in the individual firewall space, despite Norton Antivirus' previous market domination. Several other antivirus and security suites have followed suit, to the point where it seems the norm in that market segment. Symantec's Norton has market dominance, particularly in corporate sales, but Zone Alarm effectively changed the shape of security products.

5.6.2 Business Partner Distribution

We have listed the different categories of business partner in chapter 3 and discussed their importance in section 4.10.

The world of business partners is divided between the reseller model, those who receive a discount on the vendor's retail purchase price and resell at their own price, and the agency model, those to whom the vendor pays a fee for selling the product. Let's look at resellers first. Financially, the reseller model is probably more advantageous to the vendor: expense is avoided, revenue is reduced, E/R (expense to revenue ratio) looks attractive. The downside of the reseller model is loss of control of price and to a large degree the behavior of the partner. A vendor can exercise much more control over his agents, including limiting territory, limiting the products they can sell, controlling price to final customer, and what the partner must do to qualify for participation. The downside of agency is primarily that compensation to business partner becomes expense rather than revenue reduction.

We will now consider each of the potential business partner types, but let's clarify before we begin: the use of any alternate channel is predicated on the idea that one's own sales force cannot reach all the target markets that these alternative channels can reach or that one cannot do so as efficiently as they. A vendor must be prepared to compensate these channels sufficiently so that they are motivated to sell on his behalf and must take the cost (and other implications to be discussed later) into account when building business case(s). We have often heard in the course of working with large software vendors, "It's too expensive for us to get to those customers; we'll get the business partners to do it." It is unlikely that the real marginal cost to IBM or CA or Microsoft to get to one more customer is any higher than for the business partner to do so. It may be so if the business partner already covers the customer in whom the vendor is interested, but one cannot presuppose that. So vendors should use business partners by all means where they are appropriate, but they must be prepared to compensate them adequately (their competitors almost certainly are). And, as we repeat often, they must examine closely the business case, in particular the real cost equation, which will include paying a fee to or discounting the sale price to the business partner for some large transactions which might previously have gone direct. Fundamentally, unless the business partner already has an established relationship with the customer or some expertise that can be provided to attract customers there is no inherent competitive advantage or cost savings in using the business partner channel.

In assessing the business case, the vendor should not be misled by allocated cost, which is often the way that corporations assign cost to software. Under this methodology all Sales, General and Accounting expense is allocated to different brands and divisions and products usually based on revenue. This could lead one to the conclusion that a direct sale from within one's corporation was more expensive than having a business partner make the sale, while the real cost was quite different.

Resellers (may also be called VARs or value-added remarketers) buy either direct from the vendor or from a distributor, upon receipt of a customer order. Generally they buy at price "x" and sell at price "y," with the difference as their margin. Many, if not most, business partners like this structure as it allows them to flow a lot of revenue through their books, making their enterprise appear to be doing a lot of business, even if the rewards are modest. Two exposures the reseller has are creditworthiness of his customer and customer reneging on the transaction.

Agents never buy the software product, they just sell it to the customer on behalf of the vendor at whatever price the vendor makes it available to end users and collects a fee for doing so.

Outsourcers as a customer group will be covered later in 5.7.3. However, there are those who consider outsourcers and companies who host applications as alternate sales channels for software products, i.e. business partners. We will address the potential business partner aspect of outsourcers here, as we treat other potential sales partners. This view is predicated on the theory that by selling his products in volume to outsourcers a vendor can get the outsourcers' customers used to using his products thus expanding sales. Further, if the outsourcer customers were then to decide to bring the work back in house, they would need to purchase licenses for them from the vendor or the outsourcer, further expanding product share. Analyzing this, there are several things that must happen in order for the additional sales to materialize: 1) the vendor must convince the outsourcer to buy and install his product, often to replace one that is already installed; 2) the outsourcer's customer must agree, since the outsourcer will normally only have discretion over a limited number of products that he runs for his customer (elsewhere there is a discussion of risk in changing products and that unlikelihood that this will happen failing some compelling reason); 3) for scenario two to materialize, the outsourcer customer also needs to decide to terminate his outsourcing relationship and bring the work back in house; 4) the customer must decide again that the vendor product is his best choice and buy it, while he may already own the rights to the displaced product. This requires the compounding of a number of events none of which seems overwhelmingly probable.

In our experience, the outsourcer agenda is often designed to do one of two things: 1) get a really low price for the products so the outsourcer can then quote a low price for the function and underbid doing the work in house or with another outsourcer or 2) permit the outsourcer to "sell through," that is to say act as a reseller if the outsourcing engagement terminates. This is desirable for the outsourcer as they will often require the customer to purchase the licenses upon contract termination, reducing their own risk and creating a hurdle to the termination of the services contract.

Many strategic outsourcing contracts have a term that requires the outsourcer, upon termination of the contract, to provide the customer with fully paid up licenses of all OTC licensed products in use. Such a provision requires either sell-through or permission from the vendor to allow license transfer. Consider carefully how to fence this from other customers; in our experience it is not really possible to "fence" outsourcers from other customers.

There are other considerations as well: the impact special outsourcer pricing and outsourcer sell-through may have on price level, on business partner loyalty versus the benefit from potential additional volumes (which may be at substantially reduced prices). We urge a comprehensive analysis before concluding whether to allow sell-through by outsourcers.

ISVs or ISPs (for our purposes, they are essentially the same) are focused on their solutions, not on specific IT technology (at least that is the way it is supposed to work). They may for example need a relational database for their solution. As long as the vendor has one that works that he can provide at a price which is consonant with the overall solution cost, the ISV is happy. From the software vendor's standpoint, there are a number of considerations: will this ISV broaden my reach? Would the customer to whom he is selling have bought the full license as opposed to the discounted version I am providing to the ISV? How do I keep the end user from using the database product for other uses than the simple application from the ISV? If the customer installs the ISV application and my database product, how will I ever collect the full license price if later I try to sell him the database for pervasive use?

Then too, as a vendor, how does one price to the ISV without undermining one's own price structures? Using a simplistic example, let us suppose that a vendor determines that about 20% of the data in the enterprise will use his relational database as a function of using the ISV application. Does that mean it should have a target price of 20% of the normal price when bundled in the solution? Let us further suppose the vendor decides 20% is OK (it may not be); how much does he discount the price to the ISV? Discount it too little, the ISV chooses another database vendor, discount it too much and the vendor may discover that the ISV has held his share of the solution price high while reducing overall solution price at the vendor's expense.

Let's go back for a second to the notion of price reduction because not all the enterprise data that could be stored in the database is actually stored there (a similar discussion can be had for function or number of users or whatever metric). If a vendor chooses to lower price on that basis, how does he then respond to the end customer who says, "well I want to buy your database product but since I'll only be using it for half my data, I want to pay half price?" For that matter, how does he respond if the customer says, "I acquired your XYZ product as part of ISV solution ABC; I want to purchase an upgrade to be able to use the product for other applications as well; what is the upgrade price?"

This litany of considerations is not meant to discourage anyone from using the ISV channel, only to point out that there are many considerations which must be worked out. To complicate matters, the ISVs often have little capital, having just spent a lot of money developing their own product, so they want a) a volume discount based on optimistic expectations for their own product and b) to pay as the solution is accepted. That raises two concerns: normally the software vendor would like to book sales (and treat the ISV as a buyer). Maybe that's not a huge problem if everything else looks good. But what about that volume discount? Suppose the ISV's forecast is wildly inflated; the vendor may have given a discount based on the outright sale of 10,000 licenses whereas in fact he only sells 100. Such a phenomenon risks undercutting the vendor's own sales efforts in those accounts and sets a precedent for a forecast-based discounting model, which is not a good model for reasons we will discuss later.

So what should a vendor do? Be very careful, analyze the options, avoid the forecast discount model in favor of a more "volume-based over time" model, which increases as volumes mount within a specific period. If the solution is the next Microsoft Office and the vendor's product is invited along for the ride, he should not miss the chance. In such circumstances the vendor needs to find a compromise price which satisfies many of the questions we have just been asking without pricing the solution out of the market. He should be cognizant of not having control over the end user price but be sanguine about the likelihood of getting share in the ISV's market without being attached to his product. He can look for "fences" (logical and legal reasons not to permit the same price or terms in other circumstances than bundled in the solution). His licensing of the product should make it clear that the license is only granted for use within the solution so that if there is abuse he can pursue correcting it. The vendor should carefully study the whole proposal; if it seems like a good idea because it extends his reach, fills out available solutions not previously available to him, and poses relatively little risk to his base, then he will want to go ahead. But he should be thoughtful in his evaluation; this is an area where enthusiasm for a new application for one's product can blind one to potential pitfalls.

OEM is somewhat similar to ISV in the sense that the vendor's code is supplied with the solution or product. But in the OEM case, assuming one can keep the relationship strictly to OEM, the end user/customer is not aware of whose code is imbedded (probably doesn't care, and may not have even thought that there must be software driving the OEM product). It's a bit analogous to one's not knowing that a refrigerator which says ACME Refrigerator on it is actually powered by a Westinghouse motor. This has advantages and disadvantages. From a vendor viewpoint, many of the concerns of the ISV model disappear because no one knows it's his code (assuming the code doesn't pop up a logo somewhere, which seems to happen more frequently than one might expect). And, if there are significant additional volumes to be had that don't eat into the full-price forecast for the product, incremental OEM sales may be attractive. On the other hand the vendor company gets no credit for powering the ACME solution, so such sales do nothing to build the company reputation. In our experience the price levels expected in true OEM are much lower than for other sales. However, the risks of having the low price visible are much reduced, and revenue is bookable since the purchase of licenses should always be up front, not deferred. Licensing is usually under the brand name of the OEM device even if the software vendor's conditions are incorporated. To include the vendor's license would be to give the game away in terms of whose product was imbedded.

Influencers (see section 4.10) are generally paid a fee for bringing in a sales lead where they have recommended the vendor's product. They are paid a fee based on the successful execution of a proposed registered (by the influencer) sale. Unlike the other situations described in this section, the influencers are not involved in the purchase and resale of the vendor product and so do not control price, nor can the vendor compensate them via discount of the product; this is strictly an expensed fee payment. There are no special pricing considerations, and presumably the product will be sold for the price that it normally demands in the marketplace.

5.6.3   Channel Conflicts

There are often conflicts between various direct sales forces driven by conflicting objectives, by incomplete market segmentation to correspond to the different sales forces and by different measurements and compensation systems. At IBM, for example, the IBM.com sales force had some leeway in pricing that the direct "blue suit" sales force did not. Passport Advantage, IBM's volume purchase program for distributed software was built off SRP (suggested retail price) price, so discounting by a direct phone or web sales force undermined the apparent value of the discounts inherent in the volume purchasing offering. On the other side of the coin, IBM.com felt they had to compete with web-based resellers who would often reduce their sales price below SRP, using some of their discount as resellers to do so. In building price structures and volume purchase agreements, one must be constantly alert for potential conflicts and fix them before they reach the level of visibility or irritation to customers. Taking this last case as an example, when a "blue suit" sales rep built a presentation for a special deal for a large customer and used SRP as a base of comparison, at times the customer retorted that he was exaggerating the discount because he, the customer, could get 10% discount just by calling IBM.com.

Until very recently numbers of licenses or amount of revenue have been the primary basis for price differentials in distributed and PC software: the premise has been that a large transaction should be discounted more than a small one. To our thinking, this is not always true: it depends how much value is being delivered. For example, Bloomberg, in supplying its financial information terminals, has a price for a single terminal, a slightly lower price per terminal for two terminals, and that slightly lower price per terminal prevails whether the customer orders 10 more, 25 more, or 100 more. While they are an exception to general pricing practice, nonetheless it is a very successful company with a very consistent pricing model that does not discount away value and which has succeeded in convincing their customers that their prices are worth it, based on the value they deliver.

In the software industry, we seem to have trouble convincing customers that one more copy of a program which apparently has zero cost should be priced like the first copy or even the last copy, if in fact priced at all. This is a failure of the industry to construct sales proposals valued on the benefit that the software can bring rather than on an incremental cost metric. It also belies a misunderstanding by customers and often vendor sales forces of how pricing is actually done for software. In fact, one can reasonably argue that the cost of the incremental copy is really the cost of development divided by the number of copies in the forecast, since the costs, apart from support, have largely been incurred by the time the product is sold. But we have never found cost-based price rationales persuasive to customers (just as they are not persuasive to us for the items we buy; it is not our job as consumers to ensure a manufacturer a profit regardless of the efficiency of his cost structures). Much more persuasive are economic arguments having to do with the purchaser: "what is the total worth of this item to you?" Once that is established, the difference between that value number and actual price is the return portion of return on investment. If one can get customers thinking in those terms, the sales process becomes much easier. That is a key reason that later we will talk about getting end users involved in purchases, since they are the ones, not procurement, who understand the real worth of the software to their corporation. Thus, to maximize profits, vendors must ensure that their sales channels can articulate product value in customer terms and never allow the product to become commoditized in the eyes of the customer (or they will suffer the consequences: no product value differentiation, competition based on price alone, and the resulting price erosion.).

Assuming that one cannot make the Bloomberg model work (there are certainly vendors on the web with flat price schemes but theirs are not products bought in the hundreds or thousands by procurement departments of large corporations), somehow the vendor must find a volume purchase algorithm that works for his product(s). Frequently discounts are built into the price structures. For example, in IBM's Passport Advantage once one reaches certain clip levels of purchases during a two year period, one moves to the next price "band." Each band is priced slightly less than the one before, so there is an inherent discount for volume purchase. There are advantages and shortcomings to this scheme. The advantages are:

- because the discount is built in, each deal should not need to be individually negotiated and discounts should be constant and consistent;
- knowing the prices ahead of time makes it easier for customers to see what the cost of certain purchases will be;
- loading prices in business partner databases is easier and so forth.

And now for the disadvantages: unfortunately many of the theoretical advantages listed above can be a lovely fantasy. What has happened over time is that customers have learned to treat the prices derived from such volume purchasing arrangements as "my entitled price" (another way of saying "list price for my corporation"). This is followed inevitably by, "Now, let's talk discount." We will talk more about this in discussing selling to large customers.

There are a number of characteristics required when selling through partners. Many of them are true for direct sales as well, but in the business partner and channel world failure to take these characteristics into account can become a showstopper.

- Each level of the business partner chain must find economic benefit in selling the products.
- The benefits must be constant so that a business partner can develop a workable, reliable business plan with no surprises in terms of economic reward.
- There must be by law (at least in Western Europe and the U.S.) consistency in treatment of similarly situated business partners.
- The vendor cannot by law control end user price in reseller arrangements; they can when the partner is an agent.
- The pricing, sales process, and compensation schemes must be implementable within the systems available to the business partners (They will have multiple vendors' prices, structures, and compensation schemes to keep track of and execute).

To begin with, we favor a discounting scheme for all purchases which reflects to some degree purchases over time (loyalty and commitment to portfolio) but especially one driven primarily by the size of the current transaction and above all the growth it represents. That avoids two phenomena which are less than ideal: 1) that the customers feel an entitlement to deep discounts due to past purchases and 2) that small transactions get relatively deep discounts, making it difficult to provide financial incentive to increase the size of a current transaction. Furthermore, by not "baking in" a substantial discount, the customer will view the difference between what he would pay for a small transaction and what he's paying for a larger one as a real discount. Since in many procurement organizations negotiators are rewarded based on what they manage to negotiate above and beyond entitlement, this way of discounting is far preferable to one with built in discounts largely based on loyalty discount.

Both the algorithm for discounting and the pricing can be made clear to business partners, so that they have line of sight to their own earnings. Insofar as the vendor is concerned, he will probably want to ensure that discounts to each level of the business partner hierarchy are such that the business partner cannot "leave his margin in the street" (meaning use his margin to deeply discount the customer offer) which could have the effect of undermining street price and forcing direct sales to unprofitably low price levels. One may wonder why a business partner would do such a thing; it is simply because the business partner may make a lot of money on services that he sells in conjunction with the software sale, sufficient money that the margin he can make on the software itself becomes largely irrelevant by comparison. For example, in a competitive bid situation where the reseller is simply providing the product and nothing more, $1,000 profit on a $100,000 sale is better than no sale, especially if he feels that this will provide future inroads to the account.

In addition to the price level considerations, there may be compensation beyond the sales discount to a business partner who makes a margin by reselling at a higher price. If a vendor wants to promote a new product, branch into a new business area, or penetrate a new market, he might well feel that his volumes and therefore margin would be small in new areas or with new customer sets. This is especially true with new products, that require investment on his part and volumes and earnings are relatively low. The best way to focus his attention and get him to make the desired investments is to help him financially if he does so. No other scheme works that we know of; we have seen dozens tried.

As business partner compensation and incentives become more complex, one must be careful to keep track of all the possible compensations and discounts offered to business partners for their specific sales. Financially compensation and incentives come out of vendor profit, even though the vendor's accounting system may not make the correlation easy. We have seen cases where 89% of Suggested Retail Price (SRP) was eaten up by channel compensation of various kinds, taking the product below cost. The moral is to ensure that all incentives are figured into the business case before they are ever offered. Another alternative may be to forego some channels or portions of channels that require too much compensation to be economically interesting.

Besides the business considerations, there are also some legal aspects to be considered. Anti-competitive measures are illegal in the United States and in the European Union. We will not give a lengthy analysis of anti-trust, commercial discrimination, or anti-competitive law in either jurisdiction. Much information is available by keying in "EC competition law" (Articles 81 and 82 and merger regulations of the EC Treaty and Articles 53 and 54 of the European Economic Area Agreement) or "Robinson-Patman" or "Clayton act" into one's favorite internet browser search engine. Any practical application of these laws to a specific situation should of course come from qualified counsel. However, there are points which it is important for the product manager and product pricing manager to understand with regard to anti-competition law:

- Any form of price fixing is illegal, whether it comes from collusion between competitors, coercion of business partners, refusal to trade, or other means. (However, in 2007 the US Supreme Court may have signaled some relaxation of certain rules by overturning a precedent case relating to vertical price fixing which is the attempt by a vendor to maintain minimum price).
- Attempts to obtain a monopoly by means of price manipulation, selective pricing, or refusal to trade are illegal (as opposed to having the best product at the best price and a good sales force and developing a natural market dominance).
- In general one must treat business partners equally in like circumstances: it is not permissible to offer the same merchandise to multiple resellers at different prices if they are competing for the same business from the same end customer.
- Payments to resellers for marketing must be fairly proportioned by size of sales, not by any form of favoritism (e.g. "Let's give that business partner more marketing money; he's always a vocal advocate of our products, whereas some of the others are not.") Of course, if one partner is willing to run marketing events on behalf of a product and another is not, there is no reason the vendor cannot help fund the marketing events.
- One may not refuse to trade with a specific qualified business partner, and assessment of "qualification" in this sense must be objective. So "We won't sell to XYZ because they always push brand X's products instead of ours" is not acceptable.
- Subsidizing the sale of one product with another (i.e. using revenues from a well-established lucrative product to enable sales of a second product at below real cost) is illegal as is "dumping" (selling quantities of product in one market below real cost, presumably to offer very low prices in order to undermine a competitor).

The use of the word "illegal" above may be too sweeping for some attorneys and this set of injunctions is probably not comprehensive enough to keep a vendor out of every kind of trouble, so if in doubt they should consult their legal support team. As for the "equal treatment" provisions, a vendor must be very careful how he treats any individual reseller or other business partner, since his only recourse if he advantages one over another is to give the same advantage to all, which may seriously undermine product street price and business case.

Back office invoicing and fulfillment processes may seem more mundane considerations, but the business partner(s) must be able to execute the transactions and collect the money and pay the vendor for their purchases; the vendor must in turn know what he is owed by the business partner. If offerings become too complex, business partners may shy away from one vendor's products in favor of competitors' if they feel they can make as much money and execution is simpler. Looking at Microsoft's most recent compendium of Select (their volume purchasing offering) offerings, there is a great deal of variety and choice, including a few that are akin to rental offerings. Implementation of so many alternatives must be burdensome to business partners and Microsoft alike, not to mention having to be able to explain them all to customers and tell customers which optimizes for them. IBM's Passport Advantage is not so complex in terms of alternatives but has tens of thousands of SKUs (stock keeping units or part numbers), each with a discrete price.

As if the alternatives and granularity of part numbers and prices were not enough, the advent of much more powerful hardware chips and cores is permitting server consolidation. Software vendors are discovering that one license worth of revenue at a flat price for ever escalating chip capacity is not sustainable; in many cases this has meant decline in SW revenue as the customer increases the power of the hardware on which he runs the software products. In order to counteract this phenomenon, prices that scale based on processor size will become the norm for many products adding yet more complexity for vendor, customer, and business partner. Technical and back office support must be there for one to make such new products successful.

Rental offerings (or any periodic offerings like maintenance) are very difficult to run through the channel. Business partners usually make most of their product-derived money from margin, which hardly works well with recurring payments. They also make money on services which are frequently sold with new licenses but rarely with ongoing maintenance. The relatively small revenue and increased number of transactions makes selling maintenance uninteresting for business partners (many partners are willing to take orders if they are paid to do so but not usually to invest much in actual selling), usually resulting in the need for the vendor to undertake this himself. While the vendor incurs some overhead in doing this, he also gains some benefit from increased knowledge of his install base and what is actually running where.

There are two other elements to consider in this context: most business partners will have better looking financial reports if they manage to record revenue in their books against cost of sales as opposed to earning an agency fee for sales execution. It is not always possible to arrange this within the bounds of accounting regulation (the business partner must add value, usually judged to be a minimum of 10%, in order to be credited with the actual sales revenue), but where possible it is well to accommodate the business partner if possible. Business partners may have relatively small capital financial bases which may make it hard for them to obtain credit. We have seen cases where a business partner with two or three (or even one) large transaction reaches his credit limit rendering him incapable of doing other transactions until he is paid for the large one. It is well to have a plan to deal with this, extending credit if need be and the business partner track record warrants it. This not only can go a long way in building a business partner relationship but is in the vendor's best interest also, since it helps him sell his own products.

Final thoughts and advice on distribution channels:

- Business partners are often with small organizations with limited resources; it is not wise to expect or ask them for more than they can deliver.
- Any organization with which one partners expects (reasonably) some degree of consistency and fairness; in order to plan, they must have "line of sight" (clear vision of earnings given a set of sales assumptions) of their potential earnings. A corollary to this: if a vendor is not fair, he will suffer the consequences of a disaffected set of sales partners, just as if he were unfair to his in-house sales force, except that it is often easier for the business partner to "quit".
- It is always best to use each business partner in his area of expertise or for his specific type of market reach.
- Vendors are well-served to set price (and/or compensation) so that each business partner is being rewarded for what he actually does deliver; it does not pay to subsidize the weak nor underpay the strong.
- Vendors will also find benefit in setting product pricing and rewards for business partners and commissions plans for the direct sales force so that they are supportive of each other's sales. It doesn't help success at all if the two forces are undermining each other in front of the customer.

While business partners can deliver very large volumes and contribute meaningfully to revenue, they may not be the best channel through which to sell to enterprises; software vendors often find that dedicated "blue suit" salesmen form relationships with enterprises that result in larger sales, or which may be mandatory simply to respond to the breadth of product and support that an enterprise customer demands. Next, let's examine what pricing into such an environment entails.

5.7   Pricing for Large Customer Accounts

5.7.1   Enterprise – Vendor Relationship

Enterprise sales are often a vendor's largest source of revenue, particularly for products which support businesses (as opposed to games or other products which appeal to end users but not to enterprises). "Pricing" is the art of putting a price tag on, in this case, software products which offers a good return on investment to the customer and also to the software vendor in the form of profit. In addition to specific product prices there are other long-term dependencies of the enterprise on the vendor and of the vendor on the enterprise. A vendor product chosen by an enterprise often becomes a key dependency for the IT operation of the enterprise. To feel the full scope of this, one can imagine the difficulties if one's company had to change mail programs or payroll programs tomorrow because the vendor that supplied the program the company used was no longer in business. We can also consider the converse dependency: a customer who represents a significant percentage of sales becomes a hugely important source of revenue for the vendor.

The enterprise needs a vendor who is stable, will remain in business, will fix problems with his software, and will enhance it over time as needs evolve. The enterprise customer will also want to guard against economic blackmail by a vendor with a proprietary system or unique function upon which the enterprise is crucially dependent. The vendor, not dissimilarly, wants a customer who is stable, with an expanding business, who pays for what he uses, and who increases his use of the vendor portfolio over time. Because of the balance of mutual dependencies, there is ample opportunity for "win-win" transactions and relationships between the two parties. Nevertheless, since these transactions are usually denominated in money, there is also the possibility of sub optimization on each side; the remainder of this section is devoted to explanation of how these relationships work and suggestions on how they can be improved for both parties. There is a presumption throughout that because of their importance to both parties, some or many of the sales will be negotiated.

Enterprise Definition

At this juncture, we need to define enterprise. Why? Offerings for software will contractually apply to any part of the enterprise defined in the contract, so it is important to understand the scope of the organization to which one is extending an offer. We said earlier that in principle one should never offer a discount (or any other price modification) which could not be shown directly to modify behavior and generate more sales to make up for the lost revenue of price reduction. If one allows what is intended to be a specific offer to a particular customer to span more than an enterprise, it becomes an offering or promotion and the business case must be done across the whole market. If the intent is to influence one customer, then the offer must be contractually limited to that enterprise in a manner which causes a change in its buying decision process.

Two scenarios will illustrate the pros and cons of this philosophy. Scenario A: there is a product which sells well in a number of markets and which could be used by the enterprise to which a vendor is selling. The customer asserts that he would like to purchase 100,000 licenses to take advantage of the best pricing but that they wish the right to sell up to 50,000 licenses to other companies.

Clearly, this would have several effects:

1) reduce the effective price per unit to the enterprise from the quantity 50,000 price to the quantity 100,000 price;
2) reduce the price to every customer the enterprise sells a license to (a potential customer would only buy a resold license from the enterprise if the price was lower than buying direct);
3) undermine the channel partners' sales if partners are being used to sell this product;
4) have a tendency to reduce the vendor's street price for the product.

Standard pricing
Quantity of one price / unit   100.00
Quantity 50,000 price / unit   75.00
Quantity 100,000 price / unit   50.00

Scenario A

Customer view of transaction		**Vendor view of transaction**	
(assumes resale of 50,000 licenses @ 75)			
cost = 100,000 @ 50	(5,000,000)	Unauthorized discount	
		50,000 @ 25	(1,250,000)
Extra savings on 50,000 for			
own use: 50,000 @ (75–50)	1,250,000	Loss of revenue on remaining	
		50,000 (on which discount	
		was not earned)	(2,500,000)
Sale of 50,000 @ avg price of			
75 (discounted to customers			
who do not qualify for			
discount)	3,750,000	Revenue from transaction	5,000,000
Out of pocket cost for own		Revenue after losses	1,250,000
use licenses	(1,250,000)	per unit price	12.50
effective per unit price	25.00	effective discount	87.50%
effective discount	75.00%		

Scenario B

Normal business transaction	Scenario B
Sale of 50,000 @ 25% discount	3,750,000
per unit price	75.00
effective discount	25.00%

Fig. 5.3 Effect of allowing resale by commercial customers

Despite the additional 1,250,000 in revenue, this scenario almost undoubtedly has a negative business case for the vendor, since there are so many negatives associated with it. A further downside might come if the customer were unable to resell the 50,000 extra copies even at the reduced price and tried to return them to the vendor. Scenario B: same situation except the vendor refuses to allow resale and the customer backs off to 50,000 copies. Results:

1) customer pays considerably less for the transaction, although more per license for his own use, so there is less revenue although if accounting is on its toes, they may not allow the booking until it is certain that the customer will not try to return any of the licenses;
2) the customer has no risk of not being able to resell;
3) channel and street price are unharmed.

The transaction in Scenario A was the creation of a "buying club;" this can be avoided by careful definition of enterprise in one's contracts, generally to a parent company and subsidiaries it owns by greater than 50%. In some situations the vendor might relax this to 40% if the customer demonstrates control of the Board of Directors and operational control. However, if control by the parent is not guaranteed, then there can be no guarantee that the subsidiary will abide by the terms of a contract signed by a parent. The concern over behavior of the subsidiaries is real; if the parent exercises no true control over the subsidiaries, there is no way for the vendor to protect his intellectual property or enforce protections for himself built into his licenses, since the subsidiary is not a party to the transaction. For a company whose assets are intellectual property, this is probably unacceptable risk.

A Very Special Enterprise: the Outsourcer

In 5.6.3, we touched on outsourcers as a potential alternate channel. We need now to cover outsourcers as a very special type of enterprise about which there is often disagreement in sales situations. Outsourcers have multiple relationships with a software vendor: they are at once (usually) large customers and also competitors as they provide through their outsourcing contracts for the use of products which otherwise would be acquired directly from the vendor. Outsourcers can benefit from consolidation of mainframe workloads (to the extent that these offer price benefits based on size or revenue) and from volume aggregation when purchasing distributed software. Outsourcers often seek several terms and price advantages in addition: they would like a pre-defined low incremental price so that they can bid for additional work with surety of their price levels and flexibility to reduce commitment should they lose customers. It is our opinion that one should be very careful in this area, as those two provisions artfully move risk from the outsourcer to the vendor. The outsourcer is already receiving consolidation benefit which other customers cannot get individually, but future price guarantee with no commitment and flexibility to walk away from commitment simply give price away with no advantage to the vendor. Of course, the temptation is there because often the consolidated business volumes are impressive, but there are a number of effects to consider as illustrated by using IBM as an example:

- There are few if any new mainframe customers, with the consequence that any new mainframe outsourcing customer is a former direct customer. A study done by one of the authors in Europe in the late 1990s, comparing prices available to small customers buying direct with those available to a large outsourcer, suggested that the outsourcers were realizing a 75% savings on the cost of software compared to the prices available to the direct customers (though it seems unlikely that those savings were all passed on to the small customer).
- IBM offers outsourcing services of its own, so by offering special terms to competitive outsourcers it either undermines its own competitiveness or is forced to offer the same terms to its in-house outsourcing arm, providing more competition for direct sales with correspondingly lower revenues to the corporation.

- Often outsourcers' customers use software that is not the vendor's, yet the vendor cannot penetrate the opportunity because the end user company will not tolerate change. The price savings experienced by the outsourcer become profit for him, not leverage for the vendor to sell his own product line. This violates our principle of not reducing price unless it can be shown to have an overall positive impact on business case.

The overarching message of this subsection for vendors is to be very careful both with enterprise definition and treatment of outsourcers. For customers, it is to understand the outsourcer's benefits of aggregation and other economies of scale and ensure that they are receiving some of the benefit as well.

5.7.2 The Value Proposition

One of the most effective sales initiatives the vendor can undertake is to convert the notion of price from a monetary figure related to his "list" or "business as usual" price to an expression of value of his product expressed in terms of its business worth to the enterprise. This has the useful property of avoiding the discount number game ("we never do business unless we get 35% off of the regular price") which ignores whether the price level for the product is already competitive, for example, and has no correlation to value. Conversion to a value-based analysis ultimately benefits both vendor and enterprise; Customer: "Does product X give me good return compared to what I'll have to spend for it?" balanced against Vendor: "Is the price the customer is willing to pay which gives him a good return a fair price for my product?"

The Strategic Pricing Group, of which Tom Nagle and John Hogan are members, suggests positioning product price as a discount off the value to the enterprise, which might translate into something like "The savings we have agreed on that you can obtain from use of this product is $1M. At my price of $250K for the software, you are getting a 75% discount off the worth of the product to you." That might be followed by discussion of payback period and return on investment. This centers the discussion on value, not price or discount level, negotiation of prior deals, or what another customer paid (probably in very different circumstances). The further one gets from value pricing, the more likely it is that the customer will treat one's product like a commodity with no credit for (and therefore no price for) any vendor added value. Thus, demonstrating value in terms of the customer's business is by far the best way to arrive at a negotiated price, since it forces the vendor to demonstrate value in an applied situation, makes the economic transaction dependent on that value, and ultimately forces the customer to implement the software or explain to his management why money was spent and the benefits were unrealized. Since SW takes time to deploy, the vendor can help by ensuring that project success criteria have been established as well as a schedule to review progress and take corrective action as necessary. If the project, in the end, meets the success criteria, trust is established and ensuing sales become easier. Otherwise if no success criteria have been developed or agreed to there is no ability to quantify the existing contract and the procurement department may even ask for larger discounts on future purchases as some sort of compensation or as a risk premium for perceived but unquantified poor performance, product problems, implementation difficulties and the like. Finally, regardless of how the product price was arrived at, failure to establish actual solution value with the customer will often result in a prolonged sell cycle, difficult negotiations, and often mutual dissatisfaction with the result, and difficulty in executing future sales.

5.7.3 Internal Decision Makers and Influencers

Enterprises may have several forms of organization to meet their IT needs: everything may be centralized in one organization with a single budget and centralized decision-making; or individual divisions may control budgets for distributed server and PC software with mainframe software in a central budget, etc. We will cover the alternatives more thoroughly when we cover IT chargeback systems; but germane here is whether those organizations are players in the selection and negotiation process for software acquisition. The answer will change the nature of the sales effort and the negotiation process.

The most important player in any sale is the end user, provided the vendor can engage him: after all it is the end user who will derive business benefit from the software, will have the most contact with it (or at least its results) and thus is in the best position to determine its value in the context of the enterprise. So, regardless of how the negotiations are conducted, a good strategy is to engage the end users as they will probably focus less on price and more on value to their organization. Even when the IT organization holds the budget, the end users will have considerable say in how it is spent, so as a vendor having them as an ally in the sales process is often very helpful.

Usually mainframe software, particularly the operating system and middleware, is centralized in an IT department and commingled in such a way that individual end users cannot be untangled from the whole and thus they are not usually involved in negotiations of mainframe software contracts. Sometimes the end user is the IT department itself where the benefit is expense reduction and productivity increase, which may be inherently less interesting than supporting a new business application because, while expense reduction increases profit, it usually doesn't expand the business. However, once again value to the enterprise can usually be measured, if not in direct business terms, then in transactions per second, fewer outages, management of more data in a database, or in countless other ways that may in fact have a positive effect on the business (with corresponding financial benefit). The common currency to complete the sale is once again agreement on value to the enterprise.

Sometimes benefits may be modest for any individual end user but be quite meaningful at the enterprise level. We will discuss this further under offerings and negotiations, but even in those cases the support of the end users as advocates for the acquisition (or continued maintenance or ongoing license revenue) can be important.

It is well here to remark again that procurement's role is often to get the maximum reduction from base price, from SRP, or from initial proposal price. We will talk about this further as we discuss negotiation, but a vendor or business partner is well-served to have a strategy to deal with this measurement issue. Pitched battles with procurement are rarely fruitful, and the ability to get senior customer financial management to declare the deal a good one for the enterprise may be very useful, for example.

5.7.4   Price Structures and Discount Structures

Enterprise sales vendors will sometimes feel both external and internal pressure to modify business as usual structures, chosen to provide an overall positive business case, on behalf of some specific customer need. It is wise to resist this or at least require a very high level of signoff within the vendor organization. (Another way of dealing with this is to offer to agree but have the price come out substantially higher than BAU, business as usual pricing, which may undermine the appeal of the customized price structure). Aside from the logistical and precedent considerations, if the business case was positive given forecasted volumes at certain price levels and with specific structures, anything done to reduce any of those will have a negative effect on the business case. Furthermore, customer-requested changes to price structures or terms are often ways of shifting risk from the customer to the vendor. While in theory it may be possible to do this and price for the shift, in practice it is usually impossible: once a vendor assumes the risk, he is at the mercy of the customer's performance. In order to price sensibly for risk, one needs to be in charge of the risk factors, which is not the case here.

While price structure changes are rarely a good way to deliver a price point for an individual opportunity, this is not to say a vendor should never discount or have promotions. But the tradeoffs should always balance: more volume compensates lower price, a decision for one's product from a customer who was not in forecast may offset price concession (but this needs to be real and to avoid undermining price points to other customers; it is rare that an initial business case is not optimistic, so the notion that a specific transaction constitutes an expansion of the forecast ought to be viewed with some skepticism). Failure to follow this principle will result in business that is far less profitable than planned when the product was priced. Discounting by sales that undermines the price level and revenue expected is a sure-fire way to render Finance and Pricing conservative over time with across the board high prices to counteract expected discounting, not a good situation.

Discussions on discounting between Sales and Finance often provoke heated debate. Strong opinions emerge from all directions. Some analysis may help to find clarity amidst the emotion. First, our refrain: a vendor should never reduce price without changing customer behavior and ending up with more profit (this assumes that one is dealing with a collection of properly priced products). Next, for enterprise sales, there are always two components to consider, reward for total revenue and reward for increase in revenue; a third element may be to reward product volume transaction size, presumably to accelerate sales, truncate the period of competitive sales exposure, and to avoid the overhead and lack of commitment inherent in many small transactions. Whatever the design, it should cater to those requirements, allow the customer to see the additional benefit he would obtain if he did more volume and yet avoid having the customer feel that the resulting price is his by right and therefore his "list" price. Unfortunately the major tool to achieve the latter is discipline: if a vendor has a discounting structure, he cannot let it be abused without risking long term damage to his profitability and sustainability by offering discounts on top of the structure because "customer X is a huge customer" or, "we need it for the quarter" or, "we know his budget and that's all he can afford" or, our all-time favorite, "if I don't agree to this discount someone else will be sitting in this office next quarter." If the value to price ratio is a good one it is likely that further price reduction is just leaving money on the table (or perhaps the value isn't sold or was never established).

5.7.5 Special Bids

The "safety valve" that most companies have when a special price point is needed is to create a bid for the situation, thus we define

Special bid = a special price offered to a customer due to any one of a number of factors, e.g. volume, total spend, unique circumstances of use, etc.

One way of handling special situations is to have a professional special bids department which reviews the unique sales situations and finds ways of effectively addressing customers' requests (including price and terms) when justified. The key factors here are the "unique" and "when justified." There may be good reasons to grant the terms and/or price if these reasons are limited to a small set of customers (We will cover below what to do if the reasons are pervasive). In granting special terms or prices, a vendor can apply an acid test: "would I be willing to give exactly the same terms to any customer in like circumstances?" If the answer is not "yes," then he probably should stop. The exposure is to do exactly the same thing for all other customers in like circumstances; if the vendor is not prepared to, he should not imagine he will be able to avoid doing it for many if he does it for one. It cannot be kept secret no matter how many non-disclosure agreements the customer signs. Companies acquire each other, merge, form alliances, people move from one company to another, consultants spread news of special deals much as birds spread seeds from the fruit they eat. Consultants will often use their knowledge for arbitrage within the deal and to enhance the worth of their services. Inconsistencies in treatment will cause customers to lose trust in the vendor (and conversely to gain trust in the consultant if it was the consultant who pointed out the inconsistency). Remedies don't exist: as a lawyer once asked one of the authors, "what exactly is your remedy if a customer or consultant violates his non-disclosure agreement? Will you refuse to do business with him in the future?"

Many sales forces are charged with maintaining a "customer relationship." It often forms part of their compensation in fact. Once they learn that some other customer has received a certain term or price, they will lobby like the devil internally to make sure "their" customer gets as good a deal. Add to that the probable compensation structure which will reward handsomely the $5 M sale with only very modest additional reward for $5.1 M, the sales rep has every incentive to sell at a lower price: it makes him look good to his customer and it completes the sale at what amounts to a tiny loss of commission. So the failure to treat customers equitably can even result in negative effects in one's own sales force.

One can also gain significant insights from well-managed special bid departments: if cases come along frequently where the requests appear justified (continually being underbid by the same or multiple competitors, for example), that argues for repricing the product. Or if the situations are won with no concessions only when the development lab intervenes, that might indicate a need for better sales education or marketing materials. Finally, the Special Bids department is well placed to understand if there are specific inhibitors to sales which could be addressed by a promotion or some more permanent change, perhaps tested at first with a promotion. In any case, to be effective the special bids department needs to have real authority, not be subject to whimsical or egregious overruling. If such an organization is well structured and staffed, it is, after all, doing a professional business analysis in the context of the price policies laid down by corporate. There can be many motivations which drive an executive to want to provide an exceptional term or price. Those may range from "a customer with whom we have a special relationship," "this is a situation where the customer is providing us with a reciprocal benefit," to a simple desire to meet short term revenue targets or quota objectives. It is the job of the bids organization to sort all of this out and be thoughtful and articulate enough with their positions to command credibility in both the sales and finance communities. It is our view that this works best if the group reports to Sales at a staff level but with real autonomy and a strong "dotted line" relationship to Finance. In our experience we have not found benefit in having Special Bids report into the same organization that does original product pricing, though there does need to be dialog between them.

5.7.6 Enterprise Offerings

Sometimes in the course of doing numbers of special bids, a pattern emerges which suggests the creation of an offering rather than the repricing of a product or family or platform. In this case we suggest the creation of an offering limited to elite customers, thus we define

Enterprise Offering = an arrangement of terms and special prices, usually valid for a minimum of a year, which offers a customer special prices and / or terms usually as a function of his increased commitment to the vendor's products. Sometimes also referred to as a "Software Relationship contract."

For a vendor with a broad portfolio of software products, the most effective offering may be an enterprise offering with overall price and discounts determined by growth in the total revenue relationship with the customer. This can be a win-win transaction in that a vendor does not wish to reduce the amount of ongoing revenue from a particular customer; the customer on the other hand will wish to cut his ongoing costs and get products to meet new needs at attractive prices. An offering which combines both of these elements is ideal. But all the needs must be there: the ongoing maintenance on previous installed, continued use of rental or recurring charge software, perhaps growth in usage of mainframe or distributed server licenses and possibly of PCs as well. The way this can work is that the vendor secures (usually) a multi-year commitment to a certain level of recurring revenue and some up front purchase of one time charge software in return for an overall better price for a market-basket of products. The most effective form of presenting this is as a single bottom line price (or series of cash flows over contract term) rather than at the line item level. We will see in a moment why this offering will appeal more to senior management than to the individual end user or procurement department. Breaking out the individual line items would put negotiation back to a very detailed level, perhaps showing benefit to only a few users, while in a single bottom line price the benefits actually accrue to the enterprise as a whole. Arriving at a specially attractive price based on higher commitment usually involves some short term sacrifice of, for example, recurring revenue. This sacrifice is worthwhile if it results in a commitment by the customer to grow his recurring revenue during the contract (which usually also spills over into the next contract, since once committed to new products the customer is unlikely to back away from them). Generally a deal advantageous to both parties can be constructed if the growth elements are there, but vendor sales' expectations need to be realistic as no offering ever created demand; demand generation must occur outside and prior to the offering being effective, and the offering becomes the trigger for the expression of the demand. Customer expectations must also be managed: it makes economic sense for a vendor to sacrifice some growth for a longer term commitment; it makes no sense for a vendor to cut price for the renewal of business with no growth.

It is axiomatic that an enterprise offering be consistent between customers of like growth and revenue relationships with the vendor; this can only be accomplished effectively by developing an algorithm or model which takes in the different elements, decides what they are worth, what relationships they must have with each other, and what benefits to provide given certain parameters. To be successful in promoting long term financial health for the vendor, such a model will insist on long term recurring revenue growth and will offer benefit to encourage whatever behavior it is aimed at, for example market expansion or acceleration of period revenue, but it should never sacrifice future revenue for short term advantage; that is a going out of business strategy.

The offering under discussion here is about a whole enterprise deal, not necessarily providing benefit to assist in the sale of any specific product. When one of the authors first presented this to a large UK bank's procurement manager, the customer didn't feel it would succeed. Upon reflection, however, he concluded that it wouldn't work for a negotiation conducted in the usual way through procurement but that the sale would have to be concluded with the CFO (Chief Financial Officer) and senior operations management who were the only ones at a level to assess whether the offer was of benefit to the enterprise as a whole. That bank has now had such a contract in place for a number of years, negotiated just the way the procurement manager suggested.

A CFO will care about overall price attractiveness, not line item detail, hence the single bottom line price we covered earlier will be acceptable to him. The CFO may care about capital purchase versus expense. Under current law and accounting regulation, a vendor may not misrepresent how he is accounting for discounts but he is under no obligation to reveal the breakdown either. Generally the only obligation is to identify specifically what is being financed, if anything, and taxes, as applicable. Avoiding breakout of detail not only keeps negotiation at the right level but helps prevent attempts by a customer to gerrymander allocation of discount.

It may be useful to explain why such an offering needs to be limited; there are several reasons:

- Such offerings are time-consuming to negotiate; they are affordable if there is substantial revenue at stake.
- That not every customer has one adds a cachet which assists in selling.
- The offering as we have proposed it depends on growth. Where the offering may not be attractive due to lack of growth, as in our $20M declining customer below, the vendor can simply not offer it. This would be a better option than having a standard offering which the vendor would have to explain to a large customer along with a rationale for why it did not work for them.

Let's look at a specific example to make clear the implications of requiring growth in the offering.

It may be counterintuitive that what we are advocating is that a customer who does $10M per year of business but who is growing considerably may get more benefit from such a deal than one who is doing $20M but whose business with the vendor is flat or declining. The reason is simple: the objective of the offering is to promote growth in the relationship, not to provide revenue reduction through a fidelity discount in an eroding relationship. Structuring the offering in this fashion also has the benefit that if market prices decline, revenue is hit by decline in prices but not twice in the sense that there is no second reward just because total revenues from that customer are high. The graphs below illustrate the point:

- "p × q" = what the price would be if there were no structural discount.
- "Payment, no offering" is what the payment would be based on entitled price, with no additional discount of any sort.
- "Payment, offering" is a hypothetical of what the payments might be for the growth. shown (represents a 50% waiver on growth amount over three years).

- "Baseline, structural discount" is the starting point at entitled price, so one can get a visual impression of growth and decline.
- "Year 0" represents the inventory in the year before the start of the offering.

Offerings like this one can be very powerful for both vendor and customer. Precisely because of that, they essentially all require negotiation by experienced negotiators sometimes experts brought in from headquarters. Local salesmen are often tied to

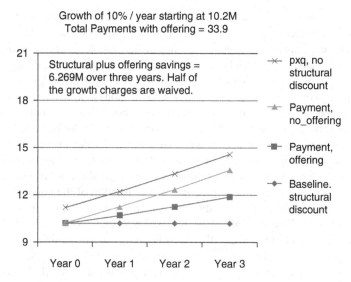

Fig. 5.4 Enterprise offering with growth

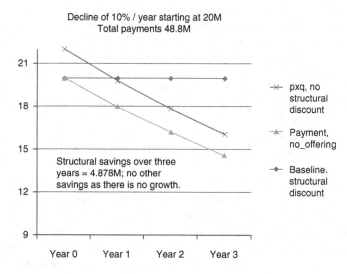

Fig. 5.5 Enterprise offering with no growth

these large customers and generally will not have the independence, experience, seniority or objectivity to negotiate these complex deals. We will cover negotiation as a topic in section 5.8.

5.7.7 After-Sales and Pre-Sales

This section is more about sales than it is about product management and pricing, but the consequences of not following through will impact sooner or later on revenue, affect the acceptance of a product, whether the invoice a vendor sends for the sale will be paid, or dissatisfaction will surface during the next negotiation. A vendor, first must ensure that what is bought is correctly delivered, invoiced, paid for; this much (or at least high probability of collection) is necessary to be able to book the revenue. But a longer term concern is to ensure that the products just sold are installed and in production. This is important for the vendor because the whole economic premise of any sale, especially a large enterprise deal, is that the products will be used and bring value to the customer. The products can hardly bring much value if they are not being used. If the contract just signed is a multi-year contract and some of the products are installed late in the duration of the contract or never installed at all, several unpleasant things will happen at the next negotiation. The customer's view will be "the last deal you sold me was no good," "you need to give me a credit for what I didn't use," "I'm never buying from you again except in small quantities just as I need the products, never ahead," etc. Defensively the vendor can always say, "even without having installed that product it was still a good deal" (if true, OK, but nevertheless it was not as good a deal as it would have been if that product had been installed). One can hint that it was the customer's failure not the vendor's that the product was not put in production, but based on our experience that is hardly a winning argument. So by far the best course is to have the team that sold the deal work with the customer to ensure that implementation takes place

What about the customer? The customer ironically has very similar responsibilities to those of the vendor: to see to it the code is received, the invoice is in order, the product(s) are in order, that the invoice is paid, and that product(s) are installed and put into production. After all, the customer bought the products and spent their money; it behooves them to ensure that their money was well spent. That can only happen if the savings materialize. If there turns out to be a previously unknown product problem, the customer must also ensure the vendor deals with it and rectifies it promptly.

Building for the next sale should start with any projects or products which dropped out of the current sale due to timing or the product evaluation not being complete. That should be augmented by anything on the end user wish list. It is almost never too early to start building the case for the next sale; a vendor is wise to gather as much information as he can, determine what the customer may need to renew in a few months or at the first contract anniversary, start doing "what if" cases based on combining the must-have with the nice-to-have products. By putting together an amendment (augmentation or extension) of the just-concluded deal, the vendor may well generate another substantial sale and give the customer additional product and function for an attractive price. The renewal or amendment of the enterprise deals can become a quasi-automatic process, driven in some measure by momentum and familiarity. This can greatly ease the effort around future sales unless due to a product problem or overselling, for example, the customer begins to doubt whether the arrangement is still advantageous to him.

5.7.8 Global Customers

We will cover in a separate section the difficulties of managing a worldwide portfolio of products and the pricing in different markets, with different costs and ever-changing currency exchange rates. But there are some aspects of pricing to global customers that must be borne in mind: if a customer has many small datacenters or installations spread around the world, it will be difficult for him and for the vendor to obtain detailed knowledge of what is installed, let alone what is needed in each of those locations. After all, a small subsidiary in East Asia of a huge French conglomerate may not command much attention from the local sales force, particularly if sales are largely driven out of France. The converse may also be true: a "huge" local transaction may seem very small to the headquarters sales team; they need to remember that it is huge to their colleagues and deal with it accordingly. And pricing to the global customer must always be logical: a 50% discount for a $200,000 order in India will not sit well if the parent company has just negotiated a $25 M deal at 32% discount. The three important points for a vendor on this topic: 1) it's difficult to get information, so start early; 2) be sensitive to colleagues and their opportunities so that the sensitivity will be reciprocated (and business will optimize for the company); 3) and have in place a mechanism which controls and is able to rationalize the different deals done worldwide with a single global customer.

A vendor might also wish to encourage the centralization of sales if his central site team has a particularly good relationship with the customer headquarters team. This might well allow the creation of larger transactions and decision control at the central location. Careful thought should go into such a decision, however, as local customers may be resentful, the decision process might be lengthened, and there well may be incidental sales that are being gotten today which might have to wait or might even be lost to competition who has only a local relationship with local customer decision-making. Nationalism and pride can sometimes play a significant role in this as well.

If doing business globally a vendor must learn to be sensitive to local customs, and sensibilities. In particular some very direct western mores are alien to cultures in the east, while eastern subtlety is sometimes lost on westerners. We will recount a negotiating experience below which will help make this point. When in doubt seek local advice from someone who can be trusted to know the local culture. Cultural differences can exist within a country as well: the images of the fast-talking New Yorker in backwoods New England or the Neapolitan hustler in Milan are almost caricature.

5.7.9 Sales Training on Pricing

All too often relationship and software product-specific sales forces, heavily focused on product content and customer need (as they should be), do not have the training to perform well in a complex sales situation with multiple software products, complex contracting and financial structures, international sales with multiple tax, import, export, and other regulations. Salesmen should not focus on becoming experts in all those areas; a support infrastructure needs to surround them to accomplish that. But they do need to understand the subjects at least to the point of knowing what they don't know and calling in an expert when one is needed. They also need to support the expert when negotiating with the customer; we are aware of situations where a careless remark to a customer, apparently agreeing, for example, to not require a particular accounting practice, caused a prolonged delay in negotiation because the accounting requirement could not be ignored.

It is also our observation that many salesmen receive far too little training in negotiation, particularly to negotiate with professionals they will encounter in large enterprise procurement departments (see section 5.8). There are two discrete elements involved in solving this: 1) the obvious one is more training, at least to the point of knowing what is dangerous, and 2) bringing in a professional negotiator from headquarters to work the large deals or mentor in the case of small and medium sized ones. The best result is when, after a few such cases, a salesman picks up the skills and can work more easily on his own and eventually mentor others.

5.7.10 Customers with Full Vendor Portfolios

There may come a time when a customer has a full complement of a vendor's products; there literally is nothing left to buy in the vendor portfolio that the customer can use. We have made the point several times that a vendor should never discount unless the discount provides an incentive to change behavior and buy product he would not otherwise buy. In the case just postulated, we have the ultimate loyal customer but limited further opportunity (there will be maintenance renewals and perhaps the odd additional license or licenses for an as-yet unannounced product). Our suggestion is that a vendor extend the principle in this case and provide a reward on ongoing purchases to the customer for his loyalty. This might take the form of continuing a portion of the discount from the last growth transaction. While strictly speaking this may not result in more sales short term, it should be close to revenue-neutral compared to past customer spend. The vendor can rationalize this level of discount, as we do, as a loyalty incentive that changes potential customer behavior by lessening the attractiveness of seeking other products to compete with the vendor's installed products and the ongoing maintenance expense. So in the longer term, such an act will avoid loss of sales. We are not suggesting the compounding of discounts over time, so renewal of maintenance at a 15% discount this year, given as a loyalty reward, should not turn into 25% the following year. Nor should the vendor continue to discount when he is at or below the price of any viable alternative; so if a competitive product is available at 85% of the vendor's price, a limit of 15% discount is reasonable (there will be some conversion cost, so matching price is sufficient). If the vendor's price is already below that of any alternative, then a "loyalty discount" is probably not warranted. But it is much less expensive in terms of sales effort and price concession to keep a good existing customer than to win a new one; there may also be additional payback in public relations benefit that the customer in question could bring to the vendor.

5.8 Negotiation

The word "negotiation" appears many times in this text because it is pervasive in the sale and acquisition of B2B software. It is also prevalent as documents of understanding or contracts are developed between business units and corporate IT organizations. Because of its importance, we have devoted an entire section to it. While the advice is largely in terms of software vendor and software customer, many of the techniques and much of the advice will also apply to in-house negotiations.

Negotiation is both an art and a science. What is a reasonable arrangement between two parties will depend on the value the arrangement has for each party. The vendor must, in addition, ensure that the implications of the negotiation do not reach beyond it in some negative way. For example, a reduction in price should not be construed to be a precedent for deep discounting not just in the single instance but across other dissimilar deals (or for other circumstances or products or other customers). One might be tempted to liken negotiation to a game of chess, with a number of standard opening moves, progressions that are well known up to a point, the occasional deviation, either brilliant or a mistake, and final victory for one side or the other. The metaphor is useful up until the last step. There need not be winners and losers in negotiations; if each party has done his homework, knows his needs, has realistic expectations, and stays within the bounds agreed internally before the start of negotiations, both sides "win" in the sense of agreeing on an arrangement they perceived as acceptable before the negotiations began. Of course, there will be occasions where the vendor and customer cannot reach a meeting of the minds on the value of the software, in which case the transaction should not be consummated (still no winner or loser).

More and more large enterprises rely on purchasing or procurement departments to negotiate contracts. Such organizations are staffed with professionals who may have undergone several years of training and have several years applied experience in negotiation. However, procurement professionals often have little product knowledge and may not value product differences highly (this is sometimes hard to tell because there is often a fair amount of playacting in the negotiation process). There may be other parties involved from the customer side: a finance representative, perhaps an attorney or a professional contract writer, possibly a representative from IT and one from the end user department(s). Finally the customer may wish to hire a consultant to assist procurement by bringing the perspective of someone who has seen multiple vendor and multiple customer negotiations.

The vendor team will usually comprise several members as well: the lead negotiator, a product specialist, perhaps the account sales executive, a systems architect, and an attorney if the customer team includes an attorney.

To provide the best result for their organization, each team should prepare thoroughly: the customer team should understand the needs of each of their end users, the business case for acquisition of each piece of software (which may be part of a complex project with a budget and ROI of its own), prices and terms necessary for the business case to close, what alternatives there are besides the vendor's products, what other projects of interest could be pulled into the negotiation to create a bigger deal so the vendor might be willing to stretch more. It is useful to have a history of past deals done with the same vendor, contracts currently in force, offers made to other customers if such information is available.

On the vendor side, the planning is no less important: the vendor should decide beforehand what the value of the requested software is to the customer and the minimum that he will accept for his products. He should be prepared to forego the business if he cannot obtain that price (hence the term "walk-away" price) and to have his management's prior support to do so. Likewise it should be clear within the vendor team which sensitive terms will not be conceded and which have more flexibility. The team needs the authority of the vendor management to negotiate (to say yes or no to terms and prices without having to check with headquarters on each point which makes the team appear weak). Like the customer team, there needs to be one lead negotiator for the vendor and the team members must be in agreement on the points of negotiation and defer to the lead in case of disagreement or unforeseen customer request.

5.8.1 Negotiation Styles and Gambits

What we present here is largely a western view of negotiation, prevalent in Europe and the Americas. In other parts of the world, different styles prevail and one would do well to use local negotiators when doing business in the Middle East, India, or the Far East as opposed to negotiators from elsewhere, particularly the U.S. and northern Europe. Perhaps one story will make this point: a personal friend of one of the authors went to make what he thought was his closing presentation, the one where he would get the order, to the manager of a large Saudi company.

He was more than surprised to find his chief competitor in the room, seated next to the decision maker, giving him advice throughout the presentation.

Different negotiators will have different styles, and we have seen agreements made between the most antagonistic of interlocutors as well as the most courteous and genial. Our observation is that while there is no "correct" one, an honest and courteous style is the more enjoyable for all and promotes the best ongoing relationship. Some negotiators will signal up front what they are looking for. One very successful negotiator we know will, on his first customer call, in the most literal sense of qualifying the customer, describe to the customer what he understands they are looking for and, assuming they agree with his summary, then describe exactly what he as the vendor is expecting in terms of revenue, commitment to product, short term purchases and recurring revenue. This dialog ensures the customer understands it is a negotiation with give and take on both sides; it also clears the way for serious negotiation, avoiding what can often be time-wasting jockeying for position and posturing at the start of negotiations.

The customer may use a similar approach by issuing an RFP (request for proposal) with many terms, specifications, and prices already defined. This is often used when multiple bidders are invited to bid for the same opportunity, and it does not fit well with an overall relationship offering by virtue of being too precise about specifics thus limiting scope in ways which may not let the enterprise arrangement achieve its maximum potential. An alternative, which falls into the "gambit" category, is a "shock and awe" list of terms like waiver of limitations of liability, freedom to assign the contract, termination at the whim of the buyer; demands for no charge services, interest-free financing, payment at end of contract for excess installations; percentage discount minima, guaranteed ongoing purchase prices, maintenance price guarantees or maintenance at fixed percentages of initial purchase prices, and the like. A recent addition which has become common is the request for service level agreements. Since implementation and operation are in the hands of the purchaser, such an agreement would be very risky for the vendor. Beyond that, it could easily prevent him from booking revenue other than ratably over a period.

From a customer standpoint, this sort of list may be an effective tool to unbalance the vendor with payback almost regardless of the outcome: if you have a list of 300 items (yes, such lists exist), the vendor will not feel he can say "no" to every item even if many items are unreasonable or frivolous. The vendor will not know which the customer truly finds essential making it hard for the vendor to respond. In our experience, the vendor will sometimes make concessions out of defensiveness which the customer did not even expect to receive. There are consultants who are particularly fond of this approach for several reasons: 1) it allows them to demonstrate their expertise and value add by requesting terms that the customer procurement department had not even considered, it may result in an interesting concession for their client for which they can claim credit, and, most important to them, they can record any concession actually granted and know that the vendor in question will allow such a concession; this provides them with very useful information for their next negotiation with the same vendor. Further, if the vendor says "no" to a term granted elsewhere, the consultant may be aware of it and use it as a bargaining chip as well as to impress his customer, non-disclosure agreement or not.

To counterbalance such a gambit, the vendor is well advised to 1) ignore the length of the list and not worry about how many times he says "no;" 2) make concessions only in those areas where he would willingly repeat them for another customer in the same circumstances; 3) make sure he says "no" clearly and consistently to those concessions he does not wish to make; 4) understand the value of the deal to the customer so he can know when the customer cannot afford to have him walk away in the face of unsupportable requests. This is another situation where having the end user on the vendor's side (or at least seriously wanting his product) can be useful: it may be that the term being requested is one which will make procurement look good but is of little or no interest to the end user; they can help keep that element from being a showstopper.

A key negotiation principle is never to make a concession without getting a meaningful corresponding concession. This is sometimes exploited by customers who make extensive initial demands as described above, expecting some of them to be granted with no corresponding negotiating concession on their part. There is also a presentation on negotiation which has circulated amongst procurement departments in various companies and has also occasionally surfaced on the web in the public domain. It makes several points which are germane, but there are two which bear repeating: if you are a customer, don't stop asking until the vendor has said "no" five times (it used to be three) and whether you are a vendor or customer, keep your executives well away from the negotiation. The first bit of advice is designed to allow enough time for someone in the vendor shop to grow nervous, overrule the negotiating team, and grant the concession. It happens. The second is that executives on either side are impatient, have little time, will almost never make time to study the history, fine points, and consequences of conceding a particular term. Executives will want to show their power and decision-making ability, be able to tell their management that they "brought in deal so-and-so," and therefore are likely to pull rank and second-guess their negotiators. Consultants understand this very well: they will do almost anything to get vendor executives involved and keep their customer executives out of negotiations.

In a less adversarial vein, a very useful technique to make sure the wheels of progress ratchet forward and do not slip back is to record each item where agreement has been reached and language agreed to describe the agreement. The forum in which this is done is also a good place to cross off many of the frivolous requests if there are any. For each open item, record the outcome as it is negotiated and have a ground rule that items already negotiated and agreed cannot be resurfaced by one party and be renegotiated later in the discussion. Failure to use this approach often leads to prolonged negotiation with scant progress and no deal in the end.

Styles do differ, but one that has been successful for some vendors is to put the best offer on the table as the first offer. This is the complete antithesis of putting a number on the table and then splitting the difference over a series of negotiating sessions. Why might this method be desirable? Because it honors the notion of arriving at a value-based price and it preserves credibility. If a vendor says, "Look,

I've been as aggressive as I can be on price; from my understanding of your business case(s) this offer gives you great ROI, let's do a deal," it's very disarming. If the vendor has his facts wrong the customer can correct him; if he's lying and the customer can prove it then he's being dishonest and it isn't a good negotiation. But if he's got his facts right and he isn't lying, the customer is pretty much disarmed in terms of asking for more. Certainly there may be a bit of "wiggle room" on a specific term or condition, some content might move in or out, conceivably some minor elements of the deal might change, but the basic framework should have been established. In the haggling method, the vendor is saying first, "my products are worth \$10M." Then he amends that to \$9M and finally agrees to \$8M. What that says is that his first price was 25% higher than what he was willing to sell for which makes any assertion that he was basing his price on value (and that his initial offer was "good deal") an untruth. It sows the seeds for more distrust later in the negotiation and especially in subsequent negotiations. Any concession that is not content-based, after the initial offer, must be construed by the customer as something the vendor was able to do but held back. Absent any way of knowing that he has gotten all the "held back" concessions, the customer negotiator will keep asking, which prolongs negotiation. Conversely, if he says "this is the best I can do" and sticks to it, he builds credibility. Total price can always be adjusted by accelerating or deferring certain projects, doing pilots with reduced numbers of licenses instead of the final license buy for the whole project, etc.

The price point which seems to work best for vendors is the one which is aggressive enough to make Finance or Special Bids very nervous but one which they would be happy with if it were the final agreed price. To the extent that Sales sells a few like this and does not concede further on price after the initial offer, Special Bids, Finance, and Sales Management will all become more comfortable and it will be easier to gain their approval.

It is appropriate here to say a few words about procurement and consultant compensation. From talking to a number of both, we learned that in many cases a significant element of compensation is related to the percentage of additional discount obtained by the negotiator compared to any one (or more) of a number of benchmarks: the prior deal, the initial vendor offer, or the entitled price to which the customer is eligible. It is always good if a negotiator can determine how his counterparts are being measured and compensated and, without compromising the negotiation, give them something that makes them look good. (This is one of the reasons building discount into the price schedule is not a good idea; it cannot be claimed as discount on anyone's behalf).

5.8.2 Negotiations at the End of Quarter

There are a number of milestones in the calendar of a corporation when it is necessary to report the size of the sales harvest. In recent years it has become customary to flail the sales force harder in the hopes the harvest increases. Years ago, this period was during the final quarter of the year to show a good annual report; more recently it has become quarterly to stay in line with quarterly corporate projections for the securities analysts, large shareholders like pension funds, and present and potential creditors. If one allows these considerations into negotiations one risks beating the opportunity so hard that some of the harvest grain (revenue) is lost and the precedent of this decision will last until the decision is not only reversed but there is empirical evidence that it has been reversed. Consider also how ineffective such behavior is: from tens of thousands of negotiations, we only know anecdotally of one or two where an offer made "if you buy by the end of the quarter" was actually withdrawn at the beginning of the following quarter (in such cases, of course, the customer will proclaim his intense anger at the outrageous behavior of the vendor, as well). If the transaction is completed most likely it would have been anyway (and revenue has been lost). More often, it just forms the basis (concession high water mark) of negotiation of the same deal in a subsequent quarter. It would be unusual if the demand were so elastic that a slight price concession could cause it to be pulled forward; the vendor can instead let the customer be the one to articulate it: "I will buy by end of month if you can reduce price by a further $1M." Then the vendor can reduce the price by reducing $1M of content, perhaps making some other small concession, in order to keep his credibility. If one needs to say "no" five times, no better time than the present to start. Customers reading this now know what the vendor tactics may be.

5.9   Pricing in the Global Market

Vendors and customers doing business in multiple countries face difficulties that companies doing business in a single country face much less often: they must balance worldwide prices and costs so that no unit is badly disadvantaged and so that no customer sees price discrepancies that cannot be justified from one country to another. To the degree that such discrepancies appear more frequently in enterprise customers than others, this is a good point at which to discuss international pricing and sales.

Managing prices in different countries presents considerable challenges to the global company. In the case where the customer is also a global company, comparison points of sales done in different countries may surface in negotiation if there are any discrepancies between prices when converted to a common currency. There are two reasons that prices may differ: 1) that the vendor has applied some sort of adjustment, usually an uplift, to his native country price when doing business abroad and 2) that since the product and price announcement the currencies of the prices being compared have changed in relative value. (We are presuming that most of the pricing work is done in one currency in one country and we are referring to it as "native country price.") While clearly the currency issues are the same, one time charge and recurring charge products present somewhat different problems, so we will deal with them separately. We will deal with price uplift first.

Throughout this discussion we will refer to "price harmonization" by which we mean keeping prices within a reasonable, explainable margin one to another.

5.9.1 Price Uplift

A vendor may impose price uplifts on top of his native country price when he does business in certain other countries for a variety of reasons: to ensure that currency never hurts his financial reporting in his home country, because the actual costs per unit of revenue of doing business in the uplifted country may be higher than in the home country; or some combination of the two. There are also countries in which the traditional discount percentages are high which the vendor may address by raising announced price so that net price, with higher discount percentages, remains at desired levels. Of course this must all occur at price levels which remain competitive, but the chances are good that if the need is there for one vendor it will also be there for another

5.9.2 One Time Charge Products

One time charge products with a price differential to any other country present the risk that the customer will try to source from the lower price country. The internet and electronic delivery have made this threat more real. Aside from the loss of revenue (in "real" monetary value), there are other issues associated with the products being procured from another country: the sales force who actually convinced the customer to buy the product perhaps not being compensated, possible problems with local tax authorities who believe VAT or sales or use tax is due, potential problems with product fulfillment and support (in order to provide support locally, there generally needs to be local revenue to fund the support), and the development of competition within the sales force to sell software to global entities. So it is best if the prices can be kept in relative harmonization from one country to another. Before we discuss a suggested methodology for keeping price in line, let's address maintenance.

Maintenance may appear at first to resemble recurring charges. However, that is deceptive because unlike recurring charges software, maintenance is a periodic purchase good for a specific period with no loss of license rights if maintenance is not renewed. The implication is that the decision of where to purchase occurs each time maintenance is purchased. The vendor may attempt to control this with terms and conditions but the ability to enforce such terms is tenuous and probably cannot be done without moderate to severe risk to customer satisfaction. Maintenance too argues for fairly reasonable price harmonization.

There are two reasonable approaches to harmonization of which we are aware (of course there are more approaches, including harmonizing to the lowest price worldwide, or to the highest price, but those are hardly "reasonable.") The two methodologies are actually quite similar except for starting point. The first involves picking a base country (usually the native country of company headquarters) and using its price as the base price. The second method sets a base price using an average of prices from all countries, weighted by the amount of revenue in each country. In the example below we have chosen to use the currency in Country "B" as the common currency.

Once the base price is set, the vendor can then define a bandwidth around that price that is tolerable deviation by country. The reason for doing this is that currencies will shift continually and the bandwidth allows for some movement so that it is not necessary to change every price at every review.

Assuming for a moment that Country "B" is the home country, we could use the price of 100 as the base price. This is a typical approach with U.S.-based companies. However, selecting any specific currency entails risk that the currency becomes too strong or too weak, which distorts prices and revenues. When the U. S. Dollar and the Euro were close to parity, selecting either one as base was acceptable for both Europe and U.S. With a weak U.S. Dollar, that may not be the best approach. (It may be obvious, but artificially pegged, i.e. not freely traded, currencies like the Chinese Yuan, or those that are very volatile, as the Brazilian Real has historically been, are not good candidates for a base currency).

Let's examine the second approach, which has at its core the notion that the worldwide base price ought to be the price that is charged in each country times its share of worldwide revenues. In order to make any sensible comparison or calculation all the prices and revenue numbers need to be converted to a common currency. This is done by choosing the common currency and then applying market rates to convert local currencies to the common currency. The data and results appear in columns two through four of the table below.

Then, in the same table we have for each country:

(Local country revenue in common currency) *
(Local country price in common currency) /
(Total worldwide revenue in common currency)
= (Revenue-Weighted Base Price contribution for that country in common currency)

The sum of the revenue-weighted base price contributions column gives us the final weighted price in common currency. By calculating percentage tolerance (in this example, we are using 3.5%) above and below that number (the bandwidth referred to above) we determine maximum and minimum allowable prices in common currency terms. The prices after adjustment to those limits are shown in common currency in the next to last column. Finally, in the last column, are the new local currency prices with the changed ones circled. The paragraphs and graphs below will describe the limits and how the calculations are done in detail.

Country	Initial Local Currency Price	Common Currency Exchange Rate	Price in Common Currency	Revenue in Common Currency	Weighted Average Common Currency Calculation	Common Currency Price After Adjustment	Final Local Currency Price
A	14.45	8.44	122.00	1,500,000	3.10696	105.61	12.51
B	100.00	1.00	100.00	25,000,000	42.44482	100.00	100.00
C	81.58	1.14	93.00	5,000,000	7.89474	98.47	86.38
D	120.69	0.87	105.00	20,000,000	35.65365	105.00	120.69
E	15.17	6.79	103.00	7,400,000	12.94058	103.00	15.17
Total				58,900,000			
Base Price					102.04		

Fig. 5.6 Price Harmonization

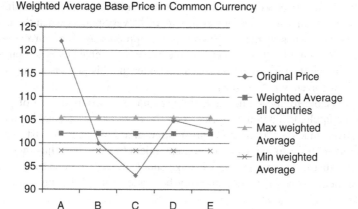

Fig. 5.7 Common currency prices, weighted average, maxima and minima

The same exercise shown graphically makes clear that prices in countries A and C are being pulled within the acceptable bandwidth.

Using this methodology, each country influences the final price in proportion to the amount of revenue it brings in; this means that the customers who provide the greatest amount of revenue feel less price dislocation. The revenue used for the proportioning usually must be across the vendor's whole product set as product revenue is too volatile by time period to be useful for the exercise. The weighted average base price calculated by this formula for this hypothetical case is 102.04.

The second part of the methodology is to decide what reasonable harmonization amounts to. In some pricing circles, a 7% band from high to low was used, and this seemed to work reasonably well in practice. Such a bandwidth in this case would mean a price between 98.47 and 105.61 in common currency. Looking at the prices above that would imply that the Country "A" needs to reduce its price from 122 and Country "C" needs to increase its price. That raises the question of how much one should raise or lower price. The answer depends on how fast currency is moving. In our example, two countries are considerably out of line; if that were the result of neglect of price harmonization for a long period of time, it might be wise to moderate the adjustments and bring the prices into line over several quarters. However, if it were the result of a few months currency change, then large adjustments to bring the prices back within the bandwidth would be called for. After all, if the currencies are moving quickly apart, being too moderate in the adjustment simply makes the next adjustment more difficult. Such was the case with the falling Rand in the 1990s and the U.S. Dollar since 2002. Assuming full adjustment back into the acceptable bandwidth, the price changes look like this:

The only difference between the methodology we chose and the first methodology which simply would have taken the native country price, yielding a base price of 100, is that the range of acceptable prices in that case would have been between 96.5 and 103.5 and Country "D" would have needed adjusting as well. Of course the average price level would have been lower than the second methodology. The downside of the first methodology is that it works very poorly when the base currency goes soft, whereas the weighted average approach is more currency-neutral and thus more durable. It is also easier to explain price changes based on average worldwide price than it is to explain to a customer that his price is going up due to changes in a currency not his own.

It is advisable to apply this methodology quarterly. Some degree of judgment needs to be applied: if a country price is on the edge of the acceptable bandwidth, hasn't moved much since the previous quarter, and there is a forecast that it may reverse course in the following quarter, it is prudent to avoid the adjustment, largely to avoid the disruption that any price change entails to sales force, business partners, and customers. An adjustment can easily be made in the following quarter if the currencies drift further apart.

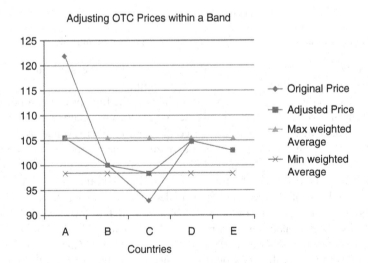

Fig. 5.8 Harmonization within a price band

5.9.3 Recurring Charge Products

Recurring charge products are quite different and much less susceptible to a good harmonization methodology. That is because of the ongoing nature of the charges and the fact that a price change affects all users, not just future purchases. Supposing that, as a result of currency movement, a local product price needs to be increased by 10% because the currency in that country has weakened; how does a vendor explain to the customers in that country why their periodic charges need to increase by 10%? They have done nothing to cause the increase, they may do business only in their own country and earn all of their revenue only in local currency. Surely they will not understand why their price needs to increase. (To get some feeling of the emotional impact of such an action, one can imagine that one is renting an apartment in New York City for $5,000 a month and the landlord, who happens to be Belgian, calls to tell say that he is increasing the rent to $6,000 for no other reason than that the U.S. Dollar has declined in value 20% with respect to the Euro).

The best approach for recurring charge products that we are aware of is to announce at a fixed price in local currency and, with very rare exceptions usually due to major currency realignments, never alter that local currency price. The result over time of course is disharmonized prices. However, as each successive version is announced as a new product, new prices can be announced as harmonized prices. This has the effect of never letting the prices get too far apart, as reversioning typically can take place every 2.5 to 4 years. The downside of this approach is to make version migration difficult if there are serious version price increases in local currency terms, but it seems to be the best system devised to-date. Unfortunately, it takes considerable courage to raise prices in one's home country in one's home currency, particularly if that home currency is the U.S. Dollar, so it has been difficult for companies to maintain this strategy since 2002 as the Dollar has depreciated more than 50% against the Euro (and many other world currencies). The alternative is demands from customers in stronger currency countries access to the price of the weaker currency countries. Concessions to those customers will reduce prices worldwide, with considerable loss of revenue and profit in real currency terms and with little possibility of later recovery: not recommended.

5.10 Business-to-Consumer (B2C) Software

With the exception of some of the web-based sales models mentioned earlier, most of this chapter deals with Business to Business (B2B) software. B2C is very different, so let's spend just a bit of time talking about the differences before moving on:

- Most of B2C sales are delivered via the web or through business partners, though some vendors like Intuit (Quicken & TurboTax), Symantec (Norton products), and Adobe do quite significant direct business as well.

- Most consumer software tends to cluster around price points independent of the kind of value we have been talking about. For example, most games currently (July 2008) seem to be selling in the $39.95 to $59.95 range in the U.S. There are other ranges for the UK and the European Union Euro countries; nonetheless they are relatively fixed. Office suites which straddle B2B and B2C sell at higher prices but also in a range pretty much dictated by Microsoft Office (competitors, in order to have a chance, must sell underneath Office).
- In short, much of the consumer software has been commoditized, like games, which even while unique will not gain acceptance if they price themselves out of the commodity range. Even games with considerable innovation like Wii games are currently selling for $49.95 at discount stores.

To be successful in the B2C space, a vendor needs an interesting product: why switch to Corel if everyone with whom one interfaces uses Office? A vendor needs good distribution channels: some people will buy from bricks and mortar retail stores, others from specific web retailers, one can't expect to get to everyone direct on the web; and based on empirical evidence one needs to price the products in the range with competition. Joel Spolsky's "Camels and Rubber Duckies" [Spolsky04] provides a good basic overview on developing an optimized price for software. We refer to it for that reason; unfortunately Mr. Spolsky goes on to suggest that a product may carry several price points for several market segments, a notion that we reject. In our experience if a vendor tries to have several price points for the same software product, he will discover that customers who paid more than the minimum price are or become resentful, that his average sales price converges on the low price, while his service costs increase with increased volumes. Further, the people who would not buy except at the low price still don't value the product while he has reduced the perceived value of the product with all other customers by making it available to some at a low price. Nonetheless, the first part of the article does take one through a good initial price-setting exercise.

The area of B2C is also an area with the same sorts of intellectual property protection issues as music and video. While researching prices, we found several sites in India advertising well known titles at a tiny fraction of their suggested retail price. In parts of Asia counterfeit copies (at various levels of quality) are available on the street for a pittance. One of our friends, visiting Beijing was offered a "real Rolex" at $8 U.S. A local colleague counseled against it, saying he would take him to a neighborhood where he could buy a "genuine counterfeit Rolex" for only $12 U.S. If reasonable facsimiles of Rolex watches can be manufactured and sold at a profit for $12, it's not hard to imagine what easily copy able software can sell for.

To summarize: to make money selling in this space, a vendor needs a good product, good distribution that covers the various ways people may buy, and some form of intellectual property protection (or perhaps an alternate model like that suggested for SaaS in the next section).

5.11 Software as a Service

Software as a Service (SaaS), as defined and described in chapter 3, has existed for some time and is significantly growing in revenue numbers. From a time when the two references were Google and Salesforce.com, we now see expansion of SaaS into SAP, Oracle, and Microsoft as well as many other less familiar names. SaaS comes with a broad range of pricing models:

- Fixed price per month (which is similar to the traditional monthly or annual license charge and annual maintenance fee)
- Usage-based price per month (which is similar to attempts of usage-based pricing in traditional license models, but easier to implement and administer since the software runs under the control of the vendor)
- No cost, but with embedded advertisements that create the revenue for the vendor. Examples of the latter model are the Google search engine or the Google office products called Google Docs.

The one common thread in the popular view of SaaS is that software provided in this way will somehow provide a less expensive solution for the customer than other forms of provisioning answers to his IT requirements. We offer as evidence the definition of SaaS from Wikipedia as of July 2008. This is not meant as a substitute for our earlier definition of SaaS but as an illustration of the emphasis in the popular domain (Wikipedia) on supposed cost savings:

"**Software as a service** (**SaaS**, typically pronounced 'Sass') is a model of software deployment where an application is hosted as a service provided to customers across the Internet. By eliminating the need to install and run the application on the customer's own computer, SaaS alleviates the customer's burden of software maintenance, ongoing operation, and support. Using SaaS also can reduce the up-front expense of software purchases, through less costly, on-demand pricing. From the software vendor's standpoint, SaaS has the attraction of providing stronger protection of its intellectual property and establishing an ongoing revenue stream. The SaaS software vendor may host the application on its own web server, or this function may be handled by a third-party application service provider (ASP). This way, end users may reduce their investment on server hardware too." Wikipedia, July 2008.

Some pundits add to this an intersection with cloud computing which implies even more savings. While SaaS provides investment avoidance to the customer for software licenses, infrastructure and the like, as described in the Wikipedia article above, it does not eliminate any of those investments or activities: they still must be undertaken by someone else and may reappear to the end customer as expense rather than investment. There may be economies of scale and exploitable efficiencies for the SaaS provider which he can pass on in the form of low prices. There may also be structures in which the SaaS vendor's costs are not being paid directly by the end user. On the other hand, the SaaS provider does incur all the cost elements that a customer supplying his own software from a vendor would incur plus he must provide an interface to his customers, and make a profit on the sum of those elements which the individual customer typically does not have to do. Thus the trade-off is between the economies of scale that such a supplier can provide balanced by his need for profit and by who pays for the service and how. If economies win, then the price of the service can be lower cost than customer implementation. If the economies are not great, or considerable work is needed on the part of the customer to interface with the SaaS service (extra software, local storage of data, high speed communications, integration of results with the rest of the customer's IT, etc.) SaaS may not provide good economy. If the applications that the SaaS vendor provides compete with proprietary in house systems which offer competitive advantage, e.g. Walmart's or Amazon's retail systems, it is unlikely that a SaaS offering at any price can displace the in house applications. From the vendor viewpoint, those products or solutions which tend to stand alone or need fewer interfaces to other customer systems appear likely to provide the greatest customer acceptance and therefore the best opportunity.

Actual pricing of the SaaS service will be based on the standard elements of pricing: a forecast, value provided to customer, analysis of competitive alternatives, cost of development, desired return on investment, all of which will be used to develop a business case as described in chapter 4. Only with SaaS the equation is more complex: it needs to deal with hardware, cost of software, floor space, cost of servicing, power, communications lines, operations costs and the like. The return on investment will need to include all of those items in addition to the fundamental cost of development. Prevailing charging schemes for SaaS are on a usage model, often with variable metrics, where one pays a rental fee. This provides exceptional flexibility, which is part of the economic appeal to the customer. On the other hand, that means the SaaS vendor must forecast usage, never easy, customer retention rate, and duration of end user contract in order to predict his revenues and set price.

In many ways the description above could fit the pricing of any outsourcing company. Based on our experience, the most important term an outsourcer can obtain when acquiring software is the ability to have a defined cost when taking on a new customer and to shed cost when they lose a customer. The same is true of SaaS providers, yet they have a number of capital costs which it may be difficult to shed. When one examines the competitiveness of SaaS versus the in house IT department, there may be puts and takes in the price equation: The corporate IT shop may not be a profit center, in which case it can charge lower prices, and it is less likely to have to pay penalties to users if it fails to meet service level agreements. It may have the disadvantage of not being able to provide quickly the same functionality that the SaaS vendor can provide. The SaaS vendor by contrast may well have economies of scale and application expertise that the in house IT department cannot match. But he does have to make money, which implies a profit and probably a risk premium must be added to price, he may have to incur potentially costly service level agreements to convince customers to sign on, and, most difficult of all, he may be forced to continue to innovate to maintain business viability as his original offering becomes commoditized in time. Of course, the exception could be that the SaaS vendor may provide a unique service not available elsewhere. If so the SaaS vendor has leverage in maintaining a customer once signed on, since there may be no alternative for him. That is a case where value is high and price can be too because of that value. Such situations cannot be common and often attract a crowd of competitors if the opportunity is lucrative.

Online advertising is gaining more and more market share in the advertising market. Since most attempts to ask viewers for payment for online information contents have failed, advertising has become the dominant revenue generator for publishers on the internet. With Software as a Service (SaaS) some companies like Salesforce.com manage to generate revenue through payments for use. Others like Google apply their successful search engine business model to SaaS, i.e. they do not charge per use, but display advertisements that generate revenue thereby financing the software offering. There are several pricing models for online advertising:

CPM (Cost Per Mille): Price per thousand page impressions. This model is directly derived from the traditional advertising pricing model. It is typically used for banner advertising. The number of times is counted when the banner is shown to a viewer which is called page impressions.

CPC (Cost Per Click): Price per click-through. The price has to be paid for every time a viewer clicks on the ad, i.e. a link to a specific web page of the advertiser. This is the model primarily used by Google.

CPA (Cost Per Acquisition): Fixed or relative price when a click on the ad leads to a buying transaction. The advertiser only has to pay for a click when it leads to revenue. The price can be fixed, a percentage of the revenue or a mix.

All three models require trust in the relationship between the publisher and the advertiser. With CPM, the advertiser is dependent on the publishers' numbers since he has no control over the number of page impressions. With CPC, the advertiser can compare his numbers with the publisher's numbers, but can hardly detect if the publisher has someone generating fake clicks. With CPA, the publisher is dependent on the advertiser's numbers since he has no control over the number and revenue of buying transactions.

Google's business model has proven to be an unprecedented success based on CPC. However it remains to be seen if the model works for SaaS in general. With the search engine, the keywords entered by the user provide an almost ideal input for matching ads to them that reflect the user's interests and thereby get high click rates. This will not work in the same way for SaaS in general. In the case of word processing software or calendar software, what is the basis for matching ads? The more unspecific the displayed ads are, the fewer clicks they will result in. So the SaaS provider may end up with a CPM model that is generally less lucrative than CPC. Despite the attractiveness of the ad-based models, however, they do not seem to be proliferating as rapidly as the direct charge to consumer model, possibly because advertisers want to see a clear return on their investment and there are not a lot of applications where consistent use will yield continued regular sales through advertising. Thus the prevailing model is direct charge, with charging schemes tuned to actual value provided which means usage-based or user-based charging as defined in section 5.5. Since the vendor has total control over the actual usage, a more fine-grained price differentiation regarding the functions used becomes possible.

Because of its characteristics, SaaS can offer low cost of entry into a solution. Customers considering this would do well to consider the long term cost and interface costs and not limit analysis to entry cost. SaaS can provide some high value services to end users on the web at no cost while advertisements to support the service are still providing some income to the SaaS vendor. We expect direct-charged SaaS solutions to be dominant which may offer some economies of scale to customers for highly standardized applications like U.S. income taxes or simple payroll. But because of the fundamental cost equations (as well as security issues, interface between applications, and desire for added-value proprietary subsystems), we cannot see SaaS or cloud computing eliminating IT departments at large corporations as Carr ([Carr08]) claims. As is often the case in the IT market, new business models and technical possibilities broaden the number of options for both vendors and customers, but do not replace existing options completely.

5.12   Pricing for Corporate IT Organizations

In this section we will confine ourselves to the means of pricing the IT services provided to lines of business with little reference to paying for application development for the line of business application "products." In our view, those should be handled similarly to a commercially developed product, except that there is only one customer and the price should probably equal cost, unless IT development is a profit center. One caution: we have seen many cases where grandiose development was to be covered by eventual sale of the product to a general market. We are hard pressed to remember even one or two of these that were successful.

5.12.1   Classic Allocation of IT Costs

Where there are costs in an organization, those costs must be allocated back to the users of the facilities for which the costs are incurred. There are few more controversial and difficult allocations than those of IT costs back to the IT users. In our experience it is difficult to find users who do not feel that they are paying too much or IT organizations who do not feel that their budgets are being unfairly squeezed. Let us begin by looking at some of the traditional approaches, identify some of the problems, and conclude with suggestions for how to approach this issue; there are no silver bullets, but hopefully we can help with some guidelines to support a considered decision.

Originally computers tended to be "accounting machines" acquired to help with invoicing, keeping track of inventory and the like; they then became mainframes and their costs in the 1960s and early 1970s was usually borne either by the finance department or on a special expense line dedicated to infrastructure support. There was little or no purchase of equipment or software, so there were hardly any capital expenditure issues. We only recount this 50-year-old history because it is the departure point for IT cost accounting and there is still inertia in many organizations which slows total divergence from that original approach.

By the middle of 2008, many things have changed:

- Capital expenditure accounts for a significant portion of IT budgets. So almost all hardware is purchased or leased, and most distributed server software is purchased.
- Only maintenance, services, and some mainframe software is recurring charge.
- Personnel and software are likely the two largest segments of the IT budget; it is often extremely difficult to reduce either.
- Virtualization and shared environments make it ever more difficult to know just who or what is using which resource. A trivial example: six simultaneous executions of the same identical program may take much more than six times the resource of one execution due to additional system overhead; to be fair, how should that overhead be allocated? Should user six incur greater cost than user one? Should user one incur more cost because there are additional users?
- IT departments now range from captive in-house IT centers with fully allocated costs in the traditional model all the way to wholly owned profit center subsidiaries which look like outsourcers.
- Recent legal and accounting focus is on making certain that costs are correctly allocated to products.

The way in which IT expenditures will be paid for begins as a strategic corporate decision. We will not debate here the merits of various corporate structures or whether IT should be a profit center or an expense item. There are pros and cons of each approach; for example:

- A profit center may focus more on its own profit objectives and less intently on the needs of the corporation.
- Good management may be taken to run the profit center as a business which may not be the core business of the company.
- Profit centers may be inclined to cut expense by providing minimum acceptable IT as opposed to encouraging innovation.
- Costs may be lower if IT is at arm's length from the lines of business and charges them market prices. By the same token the lines of business can compare directly their costs and quality of service with what an outside outsourcer would provide.
- Allocation of costs may be easier if there is a global contract with the lines of business as opposed to a chargeback scheme.
- A profit center can take in outside work to help fund corporate IT.
- There may be tax or other advantages to having a profit center subsidiary own the capital assets.

There are several decisions that "corporate" must make and give as direction both to IT and the lines of business.

1. Will IT be a profit center or cost center?
2. Is it necessary to do a precise accounting of all costs and ensure that each line of business pays exactly for the costs it causes the company to incur or will price be used to influence the direction of IT usage, for example from mainframe to distributed?
3. What level of granularity is to be charged back to what level of the organization? Is there infrastructure cost that simply cannot be allocated back on an accurate basis so is best left in an infrastructure expense line and paid for by corporate or allocated based on revenues? Or is there to be allocation down to the department level?
4. If IT is to be a profit center, will it be allowed to take in outside work? Will the lines of business be free to shop around or will they be obliged to use the corporate IT profit center?
5. If IT is a profit center, what return on investment (ROI) or return on assets (ROA) are they expected to achieve?

Once these principles are established, IT pricing can begin. There are a number of challenges: as distributed servers have made inroads into the once exclusively mainframe world, IT management has tended to lay off some of the costs of maintaining the distributed systems onto the mainframe. They have done this to ensure that the costs they charged for distributed were lower than the lines of business could get on their own, so that they, the IT organization, could maintain (or in many cases, gain) control of distributed processors. (Often end users and lines of business underestimated those costs for a very good reason: they wanted autonomy and so never counted items like, for example, the 25% of a senior engineer that it took to maintain the system). It is often hard to keep an accurate count of deployed software. We have known many customers who could not tell within 20–25% how many servers or desktops they had deployed, let alone what software was on them; this makes charging IT to lines of business difficult. Draconian chargebacks and budgets may make the organization bureaucratic and slow to react when the business needs fast changes in IT. Inappropriate allocation of expenses may cause incorrect decisions to be made.

Using the example above where six users are all running the same application, let's make the extreme assumption that the way the chargeback scheme works is that the most recent user takes the economic hit for all the overhead in the six identical program example above; if the sixth user happens to be the department developing the company's newest product, such excess costs could kill the product before it is launched.

That example may seem far-fetched, so let's take a more subtle but more realistic example: there is a large mainframe with costs fully allocated to five equal-sized users; a sixth user, exactly the same size as the existing five, is added for an incremental cost of 10%, totaling 110 for the entire system. What is likely to occur is that each user will now be assessed 1/6th of 110 or 18.33. That may seem fair, but from an incremental cost point of view, the newcomer is paying 8.33 above the actual incremental cost that he has caused and each of the prior users is now being subsidized by 1.67 compared to what they were paying before. In addition to the risk of burdening a new product with cost, this phenomenon may also or instead create distortions in terms of choice of platform for incremental workload and may suboptimize for the company: if the new workload will also fit on a distributed processor whose cost is 15, then the owner of the new workload might decide to go with that solution rather than spend 18.33; the result is that the corporation spends 5 more overall (incremental cost of 15 versus 10) and may lose some benefit of having the workload in a single IT complex with centralized management.

5.12.2 Allocation of Usage-Based Charges

Users often feel they are charged too much and want to pay only for "usage." Few ever explore beyond the word to define usage of what. Let us take another extreme example to illustrate the point: let us suppose that we have a COBOL compiler and hardware that is capable of doing 1000 compilations an hour. "Usage" might mean (many users would love to have it so) that for the three compilations they do in a 24 hour period they pay 3/24000 of the monthly cost of the compiler divided by 30. It is unlikely that charges at that level will pay the cost of the compiler. Other users may be willing to pay for average usage over time when that may not be appropriate either. Let's consider a case where a user uses half of the IT resources "on average" for the month. It would seem reasonable that they pay for one half the cost of those resources. But if we add one more data point and say that that same user at month end requires a system ten times larger than the peak monthly utilization of all the other IT users, then to ask those other users to pay for half is unreasonable.

When IBM first considered usage charging for software, the Santa Teresa Lab (now Silicon Valley Lab) was concerned about their revenue and not at all happy with DB/2 pricing that was going to depend on peak MVS system resource usage for the part of the machine that was running DB/2. They looked at approximately 35 different algorithms for data base charging, amongst which were database size, number of accesses, number of records, number of relationships in the relational database, combinations of the above. In the end, they agreed to the original proposal: to measure the system overhead as measured by the operating system devoted to servicing each product. Simply put, the mainframe operating system is in charge of providing machine services to each program running under the auspices of the operating system. A good rough indicator of how much capacity is being used is to see how much of the available system capacity is being used by each logical partition (LPAR in IBM-speak) where a product is running. After considerable analysis it appeared that peak resources used in DB/2's MVS partition tracked as well or better to value than any other algorithm. They agreed because nothing else was "better" and because to do otherwise would have made them the sole defenders of a different algorithm. In the same timeframe some customers wanted to pay by transaction. Suffice it to say that there are CICS transactions which are over in nanoseconds and others that can run for days; it would be difficult to maintain they carried the same value and should carry the same charge.

We introduced the word "peak" into the DB/2 example. Why peak instead of average usage or cumulative usage? The answer is largely to deal with the ten times example cited above: there is value in being able to handle the business peak; failure to do so presumably has some adverse business consequence. This is not unlike electrical utilities who charge different rates for electrical peaks at different times of day. But another analogy may better help to illustrate: supposing one calculates that the average number of people per trip in his automobile during the course of the week is 1.5 people. When he decides to buy his next vehicle, he rounds up to 2.0 seats which sounds fine until he considers that on Saturday mornings he is responsible for getting his two children and six of their friends to soccer practice. No other vehicle is available. Now he is compelled to buy a nine passenger vehicle to deal with Saturday morning. Having sufficient capacity to handle the user peaks in IT is similarly an investment that needs to be made. It seems to us that the extra costs of the peaks should accrue to those who cause them to be incurred.

5.12.3 Characteristics of a Good Chargeout Scheme

The problems in allocating IT costs are myriad. There are no easy answers; let's look at what might be a good set of objectives for and characteristics of a cost allocation system (we also recommend reading both the Mark Raphael META Group whitepaper [Raphael03] and the Philip Goldstein ECAR paper [Goldstein05]):

- Full chargeout based on true costs, so that all IT expenditures are accounted for (in a profit center structure, this would have profit objective added to it).
- Predictability, so that both lines of business and IT can plan reliably.
- Simple enough so that it can be explained and understood (and assessed as fair) by lines of business as well as corporate management. The simplicity must not compromise accuracy to any significant degree, however. The invoices should not require a huge department to create or verify, nor should they be the subject of monthly (or more frequent) meetings to hash out.
- As usage-based as possible, in the sense of usage that drives costs, usually peak usage. If the peaks between lines of business do not overlap, and largest peak is similar for different lines of business, then the cost of the peak can be spread amongst the lines of business, to the benefit of all.
- Spread infrastructure costs which are hard to separate and allocate by line of business in one of a number of ways, depending on objective: in proportion to overall usage-based charges, in proportion to number of users or number of employees, in proportion to line of business revenues, etc. (This may be useful as a means to have some of the cash cow lines of business subsidize the new businesses, for example).

- Related to service levels, so that the lines of business have quality guarantees to ensure they get what they are paying for.
- Periodic (annual or semi-annual) negotiations for additional services, budget planning, etc.

Some things which are probably not desirable:

- Allocation down to the application level or too deep within the line of business (e.g. department). In fact it is probably best if allocation is at the line of business level. Too much granularity could inhibit innovation and IT usage even when it was needed.
- Charging in ways that do not reflect actual costs of the IT provided.
- Allowing one user or line of business to use more resource than he is paying for.
- Calculating usage charges in such a way that they inhibit the use of IT, unless of course one user or line of business is driving costs which must be paid for.

5.12.4   Corporate IT Conclusion

Much has changed since IT first became a corporate reality expensive enough so people thought to allocate the charges. The trend over fifty years has clearly been to achieve a closer link between those causing certain expenditures and those paying for the costs of IT (which helps in the analysis of value versus cost); in short, to make the process of paying for IT "more fair." A chargeback scheme which adheres to the principles outlined above and is generally transparent to corporate management and the lines of business will provide economic facts from which to make better business decisions. It will also make the process of paying for IT easier.

5.13   Pricing Summary

In this chapter we had as objectives to discuss an overall pricing strategy for software products and then to describe the necessary elements to consider for each broad segment of opportunity and go-to-market strategy. We discussed the inherent contradictions from competing objectives and alternatives, the difficulties to be encountered, not least of which is finding the skills and personalities necessary to excel as Pricing Manager amidst the competing constituencies within the company producing the software and the market acquiring it. We hope we have made clear that there are no "silver bullet" answers where a specific solution can be applied to fix all problems, address all channels, and satisfy all markets. In fact, what we hope instead is that having read this chapter, all readers will have gotten an appreciation for alternatives, tradeoffs, pitfalls, and know better now what to consider as they go about taking their companies' creativity to the marketplace to exchange it for financial value, or conversely trading some financial value to acquire products which further the aims of their enterprises.

We also discussed the importance of working synergistically with the Product Manager on behalf of products and the importance of independence to act unencumbered by company politics if one is to achieve success for the product set. And we have discussed a range of specialized topics from global price management to internal IT chargeback schemes. We hope these are of use whether you as reader are a vendor or consumer.

The trends we see are towards greater concern with "usage pricing" even if, carefully analyzed, this turns out to be repackaging of the prices that were already in the market. SaaS and cloud computing will have their place and will be the successful means of providing some functions (but few mission critical and no competitive advantage ones); on the other hand, we expect many legacy applications to continue as they have been, especially where close ties to customer data, customer infrastructure, or concerns over security outweigh the financial benefits of larger critical mass pricing and lower cost permanent infrastructure.

To the degree that a company wishes to leverage its IT, the implementation of specialized applications giving unique insights into their business or executing it in a special or productive way may be the differentiator between successful and "also-ran" companies in the early 21st century. Vendors seeking to be successful selling software should aim at intercepting those opportunities and providing the tools to allow customers to leverage IT, giving them fair return on their expenditures while permitting vendors a good profit for their own companies.

Chapter 6
Software Product Management and Pricing in the Company Structure

After having discussed the elements of software product management and pricing in detail in chapters 4 and 5, this chapter deals with the organizational aspects of vendor organizations as well as of corporate IT organizations. In 6.1 and 6.2, we look at how software product management and pricing, respectively, cooperate with other units of a company. 6.3 covers the integration of software product management and pricing into the organizational structure. In 6.4 we discuss the different priorities and the implementation alternatives of software product management and pricing dependent on the type of company and product set.

6.1 Software Product Management in the Internal Environment

For a software company, short, mid and long term success primarily depends on the success of its software products which can be expressed financially as well as indirectly via customer satisfaction or customer loyalty. This suggests the establishment of an organizational structure that is fully focused on this product success. This is exactly what software product management is about. Ideally the software product manager is a virtuoso who plays masterfully with all parameters within and outside of the company that are relevant for product success short, mid and long term. And the parameters are manifold. They go from product definition and market definition through management of or at least influence on marketing and sales to pricing and requirements management including customer involvement. This broad spectrum was described in chapter 4.

This broadness makes software product management attractive and challenging at the same time. There is no other position in a software company in which the holder is so closely in touch with all relevant topics of the company. Unfortunately, there are hardly any employees in a company that have such a broad skill base. Richard Campione, SAP's Senior Vice President of Suite Solution Management, says: "If you try to find a person who fulfills the complete list of requirements you end up with the null set." Typically a product manager has made his career in one,

H.-B. Kittlaus and P.N. Clough, *Software Product Management and Pricing.*
© Springer-Verlag Berlin Heidelberg 2009

maybe in two areas, but not in all of them. That is why he is competent in these one or two areas, in all others he is no expert. Most often this leads to acceptance problems or neglect of these other areas. Education programs that could prepare an employee for product management rarely exist though leading companies like SAP have established such programs. Often, however, learning by doing is the only way someone can learn.

It is part of the concept of an "enterprise" that people with different abilities, experiences and skills work together as employees in order to reach common goals. Typically this cooperation is governed by division of work so that the individual strengths of each employee can be optimally utilized. The task of management lies in the definition and communication of these goals – strategic to operational – to create organizational structures that lead and support the cooperation, to check the progress towards the goals frequently and to intervene whenever necessary. In this sense software product management is a comprehensive management task to its full extent focused on one or several software products.

Division of work for a software company usually means that there are separate organizational units for Development, Marketing, Sales, Services and Consulting. Controlling, HR and Legal are usually staff units that report directly to the executive management that often sets corporate strategy. Corporate IT organizations more and more are organizing themselves like software companies, often without differentiating between Sales and Marketing. Here the existence of HR and Legal depends on the degree of independence from the parent company.

Whether Software Product Management is a separate organizational unit or not, its task is to optimize the cooperation of all other units with regard to product-related goals. This task is conflict-laden in several dimensions. If the company has more than one product or product family, there is competition, not in the market, but internally regarding the limited resources. In this competition that is carried out in strategy discussions and planning processes, each product manager represents his product. He is expected to take a strong position and be biased. On the other hand, it may not help his career if he questions the executive management's strategy (see also section 4.6.1). These inherent conflicts are the reason the product manager not only needs broad competence, but also a high degree of diplomatic dexterity when dealing with conflicts of goals and culture, human factors, and corporate politics. This aspect is well described from real world experience by Condon [Condon02]. Executive management can and must help here by clear definition and separation of tasks, responsibilities and competencies (see [Gorche05]), and by acting as referee in case of escalation.

Units like Sales and Development differ in their cultures in all industries, but nowhere as severely as in software. While sales people usually have an orientation towards short-term goals and individual customers, developers tend to have a long-term abstract perspective. Denning and Dunham state in [DenDun03], p. 141: "Information technologists are trained to view worldly objects as potential abstractions to represent inside a computation. Customers collapse into abstractions in this world. Abstractions do not have concerns or make assessments." On the other hand, sales people tend to make a sale at almost any price even when customer requirements have to be committed that endanger the focus and consistency of a software product. Condon tells in his book [Condon02] how the software product manager has to act as mediator in conflicts like this one. Very rarely has a software product manager the right to give orders to all relevant organizational units. Typically he needs to sell and persuade which is easier if he is considered competent in the subject under discussion. But since nobody can be equally competent in all areas, leadership in a non-hierarchical sense is required. However, often the product manager does not act as leader, but as Jack of all trades. In those companies, executive management as well as the managers of the other organizational units tend to misuse the product manager as caretaker for any problem that comes up and does not clearly belong to one of the units. As a consequence, the product manager is forced to give higher priority to the urgent tactical problems than to the important strategic ones which often means that he cannot deal with the important ones that influence the mid to long term success of his products at all. Executive management is not well advised to allow such a situation. What can help are clear mandates which delineate separations of responsibility between the product manager and project managers who are responsible for a development project or the launch of a new product.

In bigger companies, product managers can be organized in a team in which the different skills of the team members can be fully exploited by an intelligent division of work. In smaller companies division of work in a product management team is usually not possible. In addition the success of the company is so tightly connected to the success of the one or the few products of the company that executive management wants to take care of the most important product management tasks themselves, in particular the financial ones. However, the holistic product view is most important for smaller companies as well. Since an executive cannot cover the holistic approach for time and skill reasons, some core elements are often neglected.

6.2 Software Pricing in the Internal Environment

Software pricing is equally conflict-laden as software product management as we have already pointed out in chapter 5. So a lot of the considerations in 6.1 apply as well. There are several different jobs which must be fulfilled by Pricing in a software company: original price setting, approval of offerings, approval of pricing for special situations with individual clients, long term product profitability. No matter where organizationally Pricing reports, there is the danger that one or more of its different roles will be unduly influenced by the organization to which it belongs. What is important, then, is to maximize the independence of Pricing so they can do their job(s). While the independence is important, the same devotion to product is as important here as it is with Product Management: the pricing manager must have as his first priority the long term profitability and success of the product. That will ensure responsiveness to Sales, to Marketing, to Development or whoever is making requests, with a keen eye also on longer term financial welfare.

It is difficult to find a single individual who has the experience to understand the tradeoffs in financial as well as product welfare terms of acceding to or refusing a particular request, e.g. for a promotion or special bid. There is no training for such jobs except years spent in Sales, Marketing, and Pricing, and few people build a career in such a way. Even if one is fortunate enough to find a person with the skills, to be truly successful, they must also possess strength of conviction and be able to persuade their various constituents of the correctness of their position. Since that will not always be possible, they must have strong political backing within their company and support from top management.

One may, of course, organize along specialist lines as described for product management. But that does not relieve the need for the Pricing organization to have the collective persona described above. To achieve such a collective persona, there must be the same degree of cooperation and coordination and communication as amongst the specialized product managers as described in 6.1. In the next section, 6.3, we discuss some organizational alternatives for both product management and product pricing.

As we discussed in Chapters 4 and 5, there may be conflicts which arise over what constitutes "success" for a product and especially over the measurement of short term results. One approach, which may be useful for major products is one that IBM used to employ. There were "interlocks" between development and sales on projected sales, with each side committing to certain actions and with a set of agreed volumes as a result. At the time these were decided in small meetings and recorded on flipcharts by a Business Management organization. One director of Business Management had an interesting technique: once agreement had been reached, "Assumptions," that is to say the commitments by each party on behalf of the product, were recorded on one flipchart and "Volumes" on another. A photograph was taken of each chart and these were distributed to the participants. His injunction: "If at any time you wish to discuss the achievements with respect to this product, bring your copy of these photographs and be prepared to discuss your performance with respect to the assumptions which were your responsibility." This process, while it has largely fallen into disuse, helped ensure that there were no fantastic assumptions or major misunderstandings between parties. Similar processes can be useful to ensure that there is consensus between parties on specific products or product families.

This sort of process may not cure organizational priority differences, but it can be of assistance in getting facts on the table for discussion to ensure that the real problems are being understood and addressed. Commonality of priority and purpose must, ultimately, come from the top of the corporation.

6.3 Organizational Alternatives

Most of the core elements of software product management and pricing (see chapters 4 and 5) have to be handled in any company dealing with software, but software vendors and corporate IT organizations have different priorities (see 6.4). Therefore the question of organization of software product management and pricing is not "if", but "how", i.e. how is the organization to be structured so that the tasks of software product management and pricing can be done in an optimal way. As usual for organizational questions, there is no commonly valid answer. Influencing factors are size and culture of a company, the structure of the rest of the organization, the product structure, and last but not least the acting persons and their likes and dislikes.

In general a company must recognize that it has software products before software product management and pricing and their organizational alternatives become a point of consideration. This recognition is usually trivial for a software vendor, for corporate IT organizations this understanding has been gaining ground (see section 6.1). We assume this understanding for the following discussion.

Software product management and pricing have an inherent entrepreneurial component that manifests itself in the objective of sustainable product success. Therefore it is no surprise that in smaller companies executive management takes care of a large part of these tasks. The larger a company grows, the more executive management has to delegate responsibilities and competencies. Since executive managers tend to continue to make all important product decisions by themselves, it seems like a waste at first to dedicate valuable resources to product management or pricing. That is why software product management or pricing do not exist as separate organizational units in a lot of companies. The tasks are partially done by executive management who utilize the functional units of the company for some tasks. However, for reasons of time alone executive management is typically not able to pursue them continuously and holistically. Therefore we advocate establishing dedicated software product managers as soon as the economic situation of a company allows that. At the beginning one person can be responsible for several or all products of the company including the pricing responsibility. Later that can be separated as the products become more specialized or the workload too great for one person.

The previous chapters, in particular chapter 4 and 5, have emphasized the enormously broad spectrum of tasks and considerations in software product management and pricing. In 6.1 we discussed the problem that an individual product manager cannot have equally deep skills in all elements of software product management. Either he has to restrict himself from managing in areas that are outside of his skill profile and rely on the specialists, or, if the software product management unit is big enough, the product managers can specialize according to their respective skills. In smaller companies this second alternative does not exist, i.e. if software product management is done holistically by a single person his management abilities are especially important. When there is specialization in a bigger unit, there must be sufficient attention to the individual product, i.e. the product focus must not suffer due to specialization. Otherwise the software product management unit runs the risk of making itself superfluous since it only mirrors the specialization that the other units of the company represent anyway. Further, the products will suffer from lack of an overall manager. In 6.2 we discussed the pricing side. While pricing is typically done by the product manager in smaller companies, there are good reasons for separation as soon as the company size allows that. In particular when a company has several product managers for their various products, a pricing manager as their counterpart can ensure that common standards are defined and observed.

The holistic entrepreneurial component in software product management suggests structuring the company so that the organizational unit is close to executive management, i.e. as a staff function. This is what SAP recently implemented. The probability of success of this structure depends to a large degree on the company's culture and the attitude of the people involved, in particular of executive management. The staff function has a lot of responsibility without the right to give orders to those who have the majority of the resources and need to contribute a lot for success. If the company's culture is in conflict with non-hierarchical cooperation and any escalation to executive management is interpreted as a personal attack as is common in a lot of companies, the software product manager is in a losing position. This organizational structure can only work if executive management defines, communicates and lives the rules of the game such that the software product management unit is openly supported.

What are the alternatives? Let us first assume a functionally oriented organizational structure (see fig. 6.1), i.e. underneath the corporate executive management there are the areas of Development, Sales, Marketing and Services plus administration and staff functions, e.g. Finance and HR. The software product management unit could either be integrated in Development or Marketing. An integration in Sales is not recommended since the short term goals of Sales create too much of a conflict with the Software Product Management's goal of sustainability.

Integration into Development often seems more plausible and so is implemented. This is driven by the idea that Development can best foresee where technology is going. The experience of IBM that used this organizational structure for a long time shows the disadvantages. Developers are typically far away from the market and the customers even when closer customer contact is supported by diverse initiatives. Due to the cultural difference between Development, Sales and Marketing, a product management unit that belongs to Development cannot really fulfil its role as mediator since it is not considered as (and probably isn't) impartial. The responsible

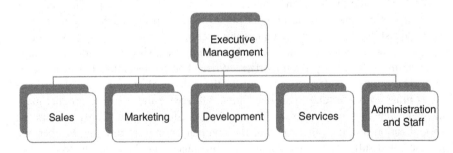

Fig. 6.1 Functional Organization

Development manager will typically avoid being escalated by his own Product Management unit.

The same disadvantages appear in part when one considers making Software Product Management a part of Marketing, but Marketing is closer to the market and the customers. Marketing is usually a smaller unit whose self interest is better aligned with sustainable software product management although its goals are more short to medium term. So we argue for putting the Software Product Management unit into Marketing if executive management does not want it as a staff function in a functionally oriented organizational structure. However, this is only valid if Marketing is clearly separated from Sales.

When software pricing is not part of the tasks of executive management or product management, but an organizational unit of its own, it can be a staff unit for executive management. SAP's overall pricing strategy is with Corporate Strategy with Product Management making proposals on standard price levels and Sales making final decisions based on strict rules. Alternatively, Pricing is often part of the Finance organization which can lead to conflicts with short-term goals of Finance. In some companies, it is a staff unit to the Head of Sales which tends to be a road to disaster unless the Head of Sales is a unusually disciplined person.

A lot of companies have migrated from a strictly functionally oriented structure to other organizational structures that are better aligned with the necessities of cooperation across the company. It is not the subject of this book to discuss the pros and cons of these organizational structures from matrix to business process orientation. But we want to emphasize that given the diverse forms of cooperation and communication within a company, no organizational structure – whatever it looks like – can make non-hierarchical cooperation superfluous. Exactly the management of such non-hierarchical cooperation is a major task of product management.

Let us look at the current organization of IBM as an example. It is a multi-dimensional matrix organization with the dimensions product, function and geography. Function means an organizational entity, for example Sales or Development. Underneath the corporate executive management there are several divisions that are responsible for certain product groups, e.g. servers or software. In parallel there is a Sales and a Services organization. All employees in a country belong to the respective country organization from an HR perspective, but are functionally assigned to one of the divisions. Within the product divisions, the product portfolio is further divided into smaller product groups. In the Software Division for example there are product groups for middleware or database products. The respective leader of the product group has the complete product responsibility for his products that is assumed by a staff function for Product Management and Marketing and another one for Finance that includes Pricing. The development resources in the worldwide labs are assigned to the divisions and the product groups with the respective leader of a product group having the right to give orders. In most cases a lab works for several divisions and product groups. Between the product divisions and the sales organization, there are contracts related to time periods for dedicated resources and target revenues for each product unit that in the next step are broken down by geography and product. The main disadvantage of this structure is that due to the rigid centralization of Product Management and Marketing, the country- and region-specific requirements are often not sufficiently recognized. Plus there are the problems of reaching consistency between the product groups and divisions unavoidable in an enterprise of this size.

Each product group is expected to run its own business that is managed by the Product Management unit. This includes the right of the leader of the product group to give orders to dedicated sales representatives which is an advantage from a product management perspective, but has the disadvantage of competitive situations between IBM's sales representatives. It makes it very difficult for a sales organization to follow the rule of presenting "One face to the customer".

IBM is an example for product management and pricing in a huge enterprise. The current structure with its pros and cons can be adapted to considerably smaller companies. Corporate IT organizations can also learn from this. Traditionally they have no marketing and sales units, but this is increasingly changing. Especially when the business units are allowed to buy IT products and services from the market without the IT organization, the necessity for marketing and sales becomes obvious. But even without this, it can help the IT organization to approach the business units with its products and services and its contribution to the success of the company from a sales perspective. According to our experience it is helpful in this context to position the software components as products, i.e. as assets of the company, because this corresponds to an entrepreneurial view on IT. The logical next step is an explicit management of these assets, i.e. software product management. What we described above regarding the organizational structure applies to the corporate IT organization as well. The role of Pricing depends very much on the degree of independence of the corporate IT organization from the corporation.

6.4   Scenarios

In this chapter we position the elements of software product management and pricing for different types of companies and products and give recommendations about which elements are important for which situations. This can also be used as a roadmap to chapters 4 and 5 for readers who only want to read the parts that are directly relevant to them. In order to do that we will analyze some typical situations without claiming completeness:

- **Scenario A**: a big software vendor that develops application software, e.g. SAP, or system software (operating system, database, middleware) for the business-to-business segment (B2B), e.g. IBM.
- **Scenario B**: a midsize or small software vendor with a high number of small and medium-sized companies (SMEs) as customers.
- **Scenario C**: a midsize software vendor with a high number of customers in the consumer market (B2C), e.g. a vendor of PC games.

- **Scenario D**: a mid-size software vendor that offers SaaS, e.g. Salesforce.com.
- **Scenario E**: a corporate IT organization.

In the following matrix, the priorities of the elements of software product management are shown for these scenarios:

Element	Section	A	B	C	D	E
Objectives	4.1	++	++	++	++	++
Role	4.2	++	++	++	++	++
Framework	4.3	++	++	++	++	++
Market Analysis	4.4	++	++	++	++	+
Product Analysis	4.5	++	++	++	++	+
Portfolio Management	4.6.1	++	+	+	+	++
Fundamental Decisions	4.6.2	++	+	+	+	o
Positioning	4.6.3	++	++	+	++	+
Business View	4.6.4	++	+	+	+	+
Ecosystem	4.6.5	++	+	+	+	o
Legal Terms	4.6.6					
License Models		++	++	++		+
SLAs		+	+	+	++	++
Protection of IP	4.6.7	++	+	+	o	o
Corporate planning processes	4.7	++	+	+	+	+
Roadmap	4.7.1	++	+	+	+	+
Release Planning	4.7.2	++	++	+	+	++
Requirements Management	4.7.3	++	++	++	++	++
Development	4.8	++	++	++	++	++
Marketing	4.9	++	++	++	++	+
Partnering	4.9	++	+	+	+	o
Sales and Distribution	4.10					
"Blue Suit" sales		++	+	–	o	+
Reseller						
• Distributors		+	++	++	–	–
• VARs		++	+	o	–	o
Telesales		o	+	+	++	– –
Internet Sales		o	+	++	++	– –
Influencers		+	o	+	+	o
Support structure	4.11					
Maintenance		++	+	o	+	+
Education		++	+	– –	+	++
Technical services		+	+	– –	o	+
Professional services	4.11	++	o	– –	–	+
Tools	4.12	+	+	+	+	+

– – not relevant; – less important; o should be considered; + important; ++ very important

In the following matrix, the priorities of the elements of software pricing are shown for these scenarios.

Element	Section	A	B	C	D	E
Objectives	5.1	++	++	++	++	++
Role	5.2	++	++	++	++	++
Framework	5.3	++	++	++	++	++
Pricing Strategy	5.4	++	++	++	++	++
Price Structure	5.5.1	++	++	++	++	++
Charging Alternatives	5.5.2	++	++	o	+	+
Price Policy	5.5.3	++	++	o	+	+
Price Level	5.5.4-8	++	++	+	+	+
Pricing in Channels	5.6	++	+	++	--	--
Pricing for Large Customer Accounts	5.7	++	+	--	o	-(+)
Special Bids	5.7.5	++	++	--	o	-(o)
Enterprise Offerings	5.7.6	++	o	--	o	-(o)
Negotiation	5.8	++	++	+	+	++
Pricing in the Global Market	5.9	++	+	o	+	--
B2C Software	5.10	--	--	++	-	-
SaaS	5.11	++	+	o	++	o(+)
Pricing for Corporate IT Organizations	5.12	+	+	--	--	++

-- not relevant; - less important; o should be considered; + important; ++ very important

For corporate IT organizations (column E), the entries in parentheses are relevant for readers involved in vendor negotiations.

A big vendor of software (scenario A) will always require the full spectrum of all product management and pricing activities. Such a company needs a broad sales approach with direct sales and partners. In addition it needs partnerships for implementation on different levels due to the complexity of its products. That is why most such vendors run partner programs.

License conditions are centrally managed for worldwide use with adaptations to local law. Pricing models (one time charge, monthly license charge, capacity- or usage-dependent models) should be quite flexible in order to apply the appropriate model in each of the different customer situations.

For requirements management in this scenario, the product manager will rely on the full spectrum of sources for requirements including user communities and customer surveys. Due to the multitude of usage scenarios and the customer-specific customizing, the involvement of potential customers (for new product development) or existing customers (for further development) in early phases or in pilot tests is recommended. In this scenario, the introduction of product families and platforms must be considered and implemented early-on since it creates synergies, e.g. in Development or Support, and supports Marketing and Sales through a convincing product strategy. In these situations, the product manager will work in a family or platform team with intensive and permanent harmonization of plans and activities.

Big software vendors usually have standard development processes that the product manager cannot really influence. Still the product manager should try to get development processes and environments that are efficient, state-of-the-art and competitive with shortened development cycles.

We see the involvement of software product management in the corporate planning processes as important and absolutely required in all scenarios. Decisions on budgets and resources are typically made a year in advance. Here the software product manager is in internal competition with his colleagues, i.e. he always needs a good "story" about why the company should invest in the development of "his" product. A cynical but also insightful salesman once quipped, when confronted by a colleague's comment that it was clear a certain product was strategic because it was being significantly enhanced, "Nonsense. That is not a measure of its strategic importance; it is testimony to the effectiveness of its product manager!"

A midsize or small software vendor that sells to SMEs (scenario B) will typically rely less on direct sales and more on distributors and partners and be very dependent on them. This needs to be considered when collecting requirements as the involvement of customers is more difficult than in scenario A. Professional services are not important, i.e. these vendors usually do not have professional services organizations of their own.

A company that only goes after the consumer market – like a vendor of games software (scenario C) – will probably not establish a "blue suit" sales team of its own, but rather sell its products through distributors or the internet. For feedback and requirements the product manager can go to the partners and – in case he has access – to his customers via surveys. Such a vendor will aspire to high brand recognition. So the product manager will give his games the same look-and-feel and organize them as a product family, not only for marketing reasons, but also to reduce development cost, achieve reuse and improve price and/or margin. For games, pure SaaS is typically not an option because of the performance requirements of games. For other types of B2C software, SaaS may become interesting.

Another group of companies that we want to analyze are the companies offering SaaS (scenario D). The "products" offered by these companies are primarily online services that are based on a complex bundle of hardware and standard software (system and application software), operations and other services. Partnerships are not focussed on sales, but rather on technology with hardware and software vendors. The contracts are usually not based on license agreements, but increasingly on service level agreements (SLAs) that govern which services are to be provided when, how fast and with what level of quality. An escalation process is defined for any deviations from the SLA. Pricing in channels is not an issue here.

In principle, a corporate IT organization (scenario E) that offers products, i.e. self-developed applications or modified standard products, needs all core elements of software product management, but compared to a software vendor with some different priorities and implementations. Let us look at IT organizations that provide services for both their parent company and external customers. Usually Sales and Marketing as well as alternative channels and partners are not as important as with a vendor. Dependent on how the company approaches the market and how urgently new customers are to be won, marketing, a direct sales force, alternative channels and partnerships gain importance.

A well-designed support structure with a call center and a central contact point for problems of internal and external customers can be a competitive advantage for a scenario E organization. The requirements management process has key importance in all scenarios. A corporate IT organization has to collect, analyze, evaluate and implement its requirements (from both internal and external customers) as well as a vendor. This process alone justifies the establishment of a product management unit – even if other elements of software product management get less attention. Most important is the focus on long term strategic aspects. How will the market develop, which products and services are to be offered in the next three to five years. These questions are tightly intertwined with the IT strategy of the corporation so that the product manager needs to cooperate closely with the strategy unit or become part of the IT strategy board of the corporation.

These examples demonstrate that most of the elements of software product management and pricing as described in this book are commonly valid for the most diverse software companies – both vendors and corporate IT organizations – with some differences in priorities and weights. Common to all types of companies is the importance of requirements management as the central process in software product management. The implementation of the right requirements at the right time within the available resources in connection with the right marketing and sales strategy are key to the success of the product manager and of his product.

Chapter 7
Summary and Outlook

Companies are usually founded in order to participate in the economy successfully in the long term. Therefore – in spite of all modernistic focus on the short term – it must be a key objective of any executive management to make the company's success sustainable. Based on this concept of sustainability, this book emphasizes the importance of disciplined software product management and pricing for the success of companies that have software products in their portfolio. The term "software product" is defined as a product whose primary ingredient is software. This definition holds for both vendors and corporate IT organizations.

In general, there is no single magic recipe for the definitions of responsibilities and the organization of software product management and pricing. These questions have to be answered dependent on the objectives of the company, the existing organizational structure and the company's culture. We argue that Software Product Management has the responsibility for the sustainable success of a product in the market. Success depends on allowing the software product managers to focus on the important items and not be overwhelmed by the urgent day-to-day necessities. Some care needs to be put into defining the right measurements. Holistically seen, software product management is a continuous activity, only parts have the characteristics of process or project. Product management encompasses the positioning of a product in a market over time including the potential establishment of a product platform or family, the representation of the product in all corporate planning and decision processes and the management and coordination of all parties within and outside of the company that are relevant for the sustainable success of the product, in particular Development, Sales and Marketing. The most important process in the responsibility of the product manager is the requirements management process. Specific tool support for software product management is only available for requirements management, but office and business intelligence tools are also helpful.

Most core elements of software product management are relevant for both software vendors and corporate IT organizations, but with different priorities and weights influenced by the number of customers and the type of product. While software product management has been broadly utilized in vendor companies, it is rather new for corporate IT organizations. This book covers software product

H.-B. Kittlaus and P.N. Clough, *Software Product Management and Pricing.*
© Springer-Verlag Berlin Heidelberg 2009

management and pricing from all angles and for both vendors and corporate IT organizations.

We are convinced that the increased focus on software product management and pricing will enable the vendor companies and IT organizations to cope with future business and technological challenges in a better way. And challenges will abound. Prices have been going down so much that processor and storage capacity and communication bandwidth have already become commodities. The trend towards cloud computing furthers this development. These capacity considerations are no longer the limiting factors that they used to be. This opens the door to a new phase of innovation with software as the key component.

In the consumer business, we expect major innovative changes in the area of mobile services, e.g. location-dependent services. The vision of ubiquitous computing will become reality over time providing an environment for a wealth of new applications not yet foreseeable. While these developments will keep software vendors busy, they also give significant challenges to corporate IT organizations. These challenges not only stem from new business processes that are enabled by these new technological possibilities. The discrepancies between the IT capabilities employees have at their workplace and what they have at home have been increasing in most companies. With the entrance of so-called "Digital Natives" into enterprises, these discrepancies become a major disadvantage. The term "Digital Natives" refers to the generation that has been used to PC games and the internet before they could even talk. They will not join a company that does not support their work style adequately. Plus a company cannot benefit from their abilities to the full extent if it does not provide the appropriate environment. What changes in the workplace their entrance will bring cannot yet be foreseen; but one can be sure that the demand will be for accelerated use of new technology to increase company effectiveness in the marketplace as well as improve productivity.

Another significant change comes from the hardware side. "For a variety of technological reasons, manufacturers have embraced multicore CPUs for the mainstream of desktop computing," writes Mark Oskin in [Oskin08]. That means that performance improvements are primarily achieved by extending the number of CPUs packaged on one chip. In order to benefit from these performance improvements, software vendors need to move to the more complex parallel programming model. Most commercially available software today is not prepared for this, nor are most of the programmers. So this development can easily change the competitive landscape in some software market segments drastically.

The technological changes will also lead to innovative new business models. We can already see that with the growing interest in SaaS and cloud computing. As we have pointed out, this means that there is more choice which makes life for both software product managers and pricing managers more interesting and demanding, as well as providing them with new opportunities. It also requires them to cooperate more closely and continuously than ever before. Their roles will become even more important for developing creative new business models and continuously bringing together technology and business anew, both in software vendor companies and corporate IT organizations. As SAP's Richard Campione states: "I expect the software industry to become significantly more mature over the next 10 years. The increasing focus on and professionalization of software product management is not only a major driver, but also an indication of this trend."

Appendix A
Job Description of Software Product Manager

Title: Software Product Manager of product (family) X

Reports to: Director Product Management

Responsibilities:

- Responsible for the sustainable economic success of his product (family) X in line with the corporate goals and the corporate strategy.
- Develops the product strategy for all products in his family and the family itself.
- Cooperates closely with Pricing.
- Negotiates the long term marketing plan and the marketing and sales strategy for the market segment including the short to long term marketing mix that leads to maximum growth of revenue and profit of the product family (e.g. advertising, publicity, product image).
- Monitors the achievements vs. goals and plans for all products of his family in cooperation with Controlling and reports the results to executive management.
- Responsible for the requirements management process and make-or-buy decisions for further development of the product (family).
- Responsible for the release planning for all products of his product family.
- Represents his product (family) within the company in all relevant processes and participates in the development of the product portfolio of the company, in particular with regard to additions of new products to his product family (including analysis of competition, market and new technologies, business case with ROI (Return on Investment) calculation).
- Coordinates all relevant units of the company, in particular Sales, Marketing, Services and Development with regard to his product family, including orchestration of product announcements and similar public events.
- Represents his product family outside of the company, i.e. with influencers, press, customers, trade fairs, conferences etc.

Qualifications:

- Diploma in Informatics or Marketing,
- At least seven years experience in at least two relevant areas of the company,
- Broad knowledge of the market,
- Proven ability to communicate convincingly on all levels inside and outside of the company (written, oral, presentations) and to negotiate,
- Ability to work on a broad spectrum of tasks with changing priorities in parallel,
- Masters all relevant business processes and business measures,
- Deeper knowledge regarding contract and license issues.

Appendix B
Job Description of Software Pricing Manager

Title: Software Pricing Manager of product (family) X

Reports to: Director Pricing

Responsibilities:

- Cooperates closely with Product Management for his product set.
- Develops the product pricing strategy, the choice of charging methodology, and the specific prices for all products in his family and the family itself, in cooperation with the Product Manager.
- Understands and supports the long term marketing plan and the marketing and sales strategy for the market segment including the short to long term marketing mix that leads to maximum growth of revenue and profit of the product family.
- Responsible for the sustainable economic success of his product (family) X in line with the corporate goals and the corporate strategy.
  - Continuously monitors product during its life and is sensitive to new competitive threats, install base erosion
  - Plans for and executes pricing changes required to support migrations to and from his product
- Works with tax department (or whoever manages tax issues) to minimize tax expense and maximize profit.
- In the case of an international company with products sold in multiple countries, works to maintain reasonable harmonization of prices both within regional economic areas (e.g. Canada & U.S., European Economic Union). Participate in development of and be sensitive to a strategy to meet the (probable) need to repatriate profits from foreign sales.
- Whether international or not, understand the ramifications of various price, royalty, transfer pricing, and tax alternatives and advocate for the optimal at product, family, and corporate level.
- Understands and works with corporate to optimize funding for development divisions; this may involve several means of moving money from sales companies (or divisions) to development via mechanisms like corporate funding

or transfer pricing. Is able to support funding requests with hard market forecast data.

- Cooperates with Product Management in monitoring the achievements vs. goals and plans and the financial consequences of those results for all products of his family and assists in reporting the results to executive management.
- Responsible for the overall profit and loss of the product and the financial considerations related to the requirements management process and make-or-buy decisions for further development of the product (family).
- Represents an independent financial view of his product (family) within the company in all relevant processes and participates in the financial aspects concerning the development of the product portfolio of the company, in particular with regard to additions of new products to his product family (including analysis of competition, market and new technologies, business case with ROI (Return on Investment) calculation).
- Ensures that prices are available as needed to support announcements, sales, and back office processes of the company.

Qualifications:

- Diploma in Informatics or Finance, or a Masters in Business Administration,
- At least five years experience in at least two relevant areas of the company,
- Broad knowledge of the market,
- If an international company, background in tax, transfer pricing, international sales is a real plus,
- Proven ability to communicate convincingly on all levels inside the company (written, oral, presentations) and to negotiate,
- Ability to work in parallel on a broad spectrum of products and tasks with changing priorities,
- Understands the financial consequences of chosen prices with respect to all relevant business processes and business measures,
- Understands the financial consequences of pricing as they interact with contract and license alternatives.

Appendix C
Views on Software Product Management and Pricing in Literature

While there is still hardly any literature neither in English nor in German on Software Pricing, some material has been published during the last five years that is related to software product management. There is a lot more literature on product management in general, but it is just as differentiated in its approach to the subject as the content and organization of product management itself. There are authors who attempt to explain product management without respect to industry or product. Other authors differentiate more strongly. Obviously, a different type of product management is required for a service product, e.g. a cleaning service, than for capital goods, e.g. a digger, or consumer products, e.g. a toothbrush. Other authors concentrate on one or more aspects of product management. Depending on the backgrounds of the authors, you can find a marketing focus, for example, on brand management, product naming or advertising, or a focus on the production process, or new development.

This book is written by experts for experts. For this reason, we confine ourselves to naming only those literary sources we consider to be useful for anyone interested in software product management and pricing. We make no pretenses of academic completeness, nor would we rule out further useful sources unknown to us at present.

There is one excellent book on pricing written by the consultants Thomas T. Nagle and John E. Hogan ("The Strategy and Tactics of Pricing", [NagHog06]). It is not focused on a single industry and covers the subject following their Strategic Pricing Pyramid. We are not aware of any books devoted to software pricing.

A book that specifically deals with software product management is by Dan Condon [Condon02], an expert who has acquired experience working for various American software manufacturers. His account is thus limited to the management of standard software. He sees the product manager as a coordinator for all internal functions that contribute to the development and commercial launch of a product. He points out the conflicts occurring in practice and tries to achieve a better understanding of the various views and cultures of the people involved. Even if the presentations are sometimes a bit simplistic, they are very practical and readable for someone who has not yet gained experience in software product management. The experienced expert is more likely to profit from the excellent description – at the end of the book – of how the system software business evolved from the use of expensive proprietary products to open source software. The author does not attempt to predict future developments, however. Overall the book does not aspire to treat the topic of software product management comprehensively.

The "Product Manager's Handbook" [Gorche05] deals with the topic irrespective of the type of product and industry. It was authored by the American Linda Gorchels, who is currently active in consulting and training after acquiring practical experience in product management in various industries. The headings for the main parts of the book are somewhat misleading as they all refer to skills. The book is actually structured according to project management tasks and areas of activity. These tasks are very skillfully and comprehensively described as far as this is possible without reference to industry and type of product. Few, yet detailed, examples prove her practical experience. This is the best book that we know of about product management in general.

In his book with the title "Product Strategy for High Technology Companies" [McGrat01], the experienced management consultant Michael McGrath discusses strategic topics affecting the work of product managers. The title of the book is slightly misleading, since McGrath is less concerned with individual products than with overall business strategy and its application to product platforms, product families and individual products. He details strategies for market differentiation, competition and growth and delves into the topic of portfolio management. The book is replete with so many case studies based on the high-tech industry that it is sometimes no longer generally applicable. However, this is really the only aspect of this otherwise brilliant book that we would criticize. Since the content of this book reflects our own views and experience to a large extent, we will quote it several times in chapter 6, in which we highlight the integration of product management in the company as a whole.

One of the few subtopics of software product management that is discussed exhaustively in the pertinent literature is requirements management. Yet this topic is usually viewed in relation to a specific development project. We believe that Bruno Schienmann has a groundbreaking idea, which he elucidates in his excellent book "Kontinuierliches Anforderungsmanagement" (Continuous Requirements Management) [Schien02]. His suggestion is to view customers, products and projects separately, which corresponds to our approach in section 4.7.3.

The American consultant Robert Cooper describes the process of identification, development and commercial launch of successful new products across many industries in his book "Product Leadership – Creating and Launching Superior New Products" [Cooper00]. Even if his war metaphors may be rather hard to digest for some readers, the content otherwise proves definitely useful. He focuses exclusively on top management, however, and completely ignores the human factor, which plays a particularly important role in go/no-go decisions concerning projects and in portfolio management in general. This factor is discussed very convincingly in the book "The Smart Organization: Creating Value Through Smart R&D" [MatMat98] written by the Matheson brothers, who also give considerably better examples. [Cooper00] dedicates a chapter to a summary of portfolio management, which is presented in full detail in [CoEdKl01] and is of relevance to product managers, since they usually have to champion their product in the portfolio management process (see section 4.6.1). Cooper uses the term "innovation" quite indiscriminately for anything new. It does appear to be quite important, however, to differentiate between evolution and innovation particularly in the software field (see also section 4.6.1). Innovation is a rather radical type of change, e.g. a change in technology, involving much greater risks and opportunities and requiring a different management approach than evolutionary development. William Miller and Langdon Morris describe this in their book "4th Generation R&D: Managing Knowledge, Technology, and Innovation" [MilMor99] which is worth reading.

Consultant Mark Butje wrote the book "Product Marketing for Technology Companies" ([Butje05]) that is actually an introductory text for product management. It demonstrates that the terms "product management" and "product marketing" are often not clearly separated. In Alyssa S. Dver's "Software Product Management Essentials" ([Dver07]) less than half of the short text deals with software product management and pricing as we have defined it in this book. The rest is focused on development, beta test and product marketing including product launch. Similarly Brian Lawley focuses on product roadmaps, beta programs, product launches and review programs in his short book "Expert Product Management" ([Lawley07]) which does not live up to its title. The book "Software-Produktmanagement" ([SnHaTe04], in German) is mistitled since it covers maintenance and continuous development of large application software systems only.

There are some books covering the software industry. MIT's Michael Cusumano looks at "The Business of Software" ([Cusuma04]) both from a business and technical view that proves his extensive experience consulting software companies. In [BuDiHe08] (in German) Buxmann, Diefenbach and Hess analyze the economics of the software industry with special emphasis on their research areas. They discuss economic principles like network effects, strategies for software vendors and globalization. In "Software Ecosystem" ([MessSzy03]) Messerschmidt and Szyperski describe software and the software industry from the perspectives of several involved parties. Though the book provides some good summaries, the authors seem to have attempted more than is possible in one book. The title seems to have been attached to the book after it was finished since the "ecosystem" is not really covered in the sense as we have defined it in this book.

Unfortunately, there is very little research in the academic realm on software product management and pricing. We consider the work of Sjaak Brinkkemper and his team at the University of Utrecht very promising and have discussed their article [WBNVB06] in section 4.3. They will hopefully publish a more comprehensive book on the subject in the near future.

In view of the economic significance that software has achieved over the last few decades, it is amazing at first glance that there is so little literature available on the topics of software product management and pricing. Upon closer examination, however, the reasons for this become apparent. It is difficult to cover the entire topic in full breadth in this extremely dynamic, i.e. rapidly changing, market. Secondly, market leaders consider the topics as highly relevant competitive factors. They are not at all interested in giving customers and fair trade authorities too much inside information, and often forbid their employees to publicize such information. This is also the reason why researchers at universities have very limited access to this information.

Appendix D
Glossary

The glossary contains all terms formally defined throughout the book.

Software Product Terms

Product = Combination of (material and/or intangible) goods and services, which one party (called supplier) combines in support of their commercial interests, to transfer defined rights to a second party (called customer).

Software product = Product whose primary component is software.

Embedded software = A piece of software that is not sold as a stand-alone software product, but is integrated in a non-software product.

OEM software product = software product of software vendor A that is used by company B as a component under the covers of one of B's products.

Product Platform = the technical foundation on which several software products are based.

Product Family = A group of software products which for marketing reasons are marketed as belonging together under a common family name.

Product Line = A group of software products which are variants of a base product governed by a common software architecture.

Cloud Computing = An IT service provision model by which IT infrastructure is provided based on an architecture that ensures a high level of scalability and reliability, and accessed through the internet.

Software as a Service (SaaS) = business and delivery model that allows customers to use software over the internet without having to install it on their own computers.

Software Ecosystem = Informal network of (legally independent) units that have a positive influence on the economic success of a software product and benefit from it.

Business Case = Comparison of the costs associated with a product or project to the quantified economic benefits or value to be derived from it.

Product Bundle = Set of products that is sold as one product with its own price.

Maintenance = product fixes, often including new releases.

Support = help in getting the product to do what its specification says it is supposed to do.

Upgrade protection = similar to maintenance but sometimes offered discretely from maintenance, it offers only the right to upgrade to the next release(s); the number of upgrades may be limited.

Subscription = generally used to describe an offering which combines maintenance, support, and upgrade protection.

Software Pricing Terms

Price structure = the manner in which the prices for a given software product are offered, including the metric by which those prices may vary for the single product (e.g. one single price, price based on number of users, on capacity, on usage, on volume of licenses acquired).

Price level = the actual amount of charge within the price structure, e.g. if charged per user the price is $10 or $11; those are price levels.

OTC = One time charge, a method of charging in which a fee is charged initially for the use of the license and that the customer has the right to use the license in question for the capacity and quantity that it specifies, with no further payments. Nor, after purchase, can the license be terminated unilaterally by the vendor.

ILC/RLC = Initial license charge, recurring license charge: charging method that requires an up front payment and ongoing (usually annual) recurring charges for the license to remain valid.

MLC or ALC = Monthly license charges or Annual license charges are part of a generic recurring license charge group of which monthly and annual are most prevalent. Each charge is for a prepayment which entitles the license-holder to use the program for the period of prepayment.

Usage charging = charging for a software product based on some measurable defined metric, often the actual or peak capacity used during a period.

User-based charging = pricing and payment in advance for a fixed number of users.

There are many different forms of "user" and charging may vary depending on which of several definitions are used:

- Registered users: number of people with an assigned logon identification.
- Concurrent users: number of simultaneous users of a program; this may be counted or controlled in terms of logged-in users or in terms of active users vying for system resources
- "In-house" users: number of corporate employees or agents using the program on a routine basis within the company
- "Web" users: casual users outside the company who make sporadic use of the product (one can imagine a portal product which is licensed for "in-house" and "web" users with a different charge for each).
- "Logged-in" users: users actually in a position to use the program resource who may or may not be doing work.
- "Active" users: logged-in users who are actually doing work.

PSLC (Parallel sysplex license charges) = charges for mainframe software based on total capacity of a number of processors which are tied together into a "sysplex."

WLC (Workload license charges) = charges for mainframe software based on the peak capacity used during a month for a particular product.

Flat Price = single price regardless of processor capacity, usage, or other metric.

Graduated charges = charges scaled for a program product based on capacity of the machine or environment where the program will run (or has run).

Term License = An entitlement to use a software product over a specific period of time. Such a license is usually offered at a fixed price which often takes the form of annual payments for a fixed number of years, after which the customer must stop using the product, renew his term license, or license the product under other available terms.

Software promotion = a temporary product offering with terms or prices that are advantageous compared to regular pricing and terms.

Special bid = a special price offered to a customer due to any one of a number of factors, e.g. volume, total spend, unique circumstances of use, etc.

Enterprise Offerings = an arrangement of terms and special prices, usually valid for a minimum of a year, which offers a customer special prices and/or terms usually as a function of his increased commitment to the vendor's products. **Sometimes also referred to as a** Software Relationship contract.

MIPS = throughput of a computer system measured in millions of instructions per second.

MSUs = throughput of a computer system measured in millions of IBM zOS service units.

MFLOPS = millions of floating point operations per second. This is a measure used largely for scientific systems, but it may be part of benchmarks used to determine raw hardware speed which then may be used in determining the capacity of the hardware on which software is running and thereby influence the price.

Bibliography

[Arthur96]   Arthur, W.B.: Increasing Returns and the New World of Business, Harvard Business Review July 1996

[Balzert00]   Balzert, H.: Lehrbuch der Software-Technik: Software-Entwicklung, Spektrum Akademischer Verlag, 2. Auflage, 2000

[Balzert08]   Balzert, H.: Lehrbuch der Software-Technik: Software-Management, 2. Auflage, Spektrum Akademischer Verlag, 2008

[Baseline07]   Baseline Magazine : The 4Q Fastest growing Software Companies, www.baselinemag.com, 2007-06-11

[Besaha03]   Besaha, B.: Bounty Hunting in the Patent Base, Comm. acm vol. 46, no. 3, March 2003, pp. 27–29

[Biering04]   Biering, S.: Preis- und Produktstrategien für digitale Produkte, untersucht am Beispiel des Software-Marktes (Dissertationsschrift), Haufe, Freiburg, 2004

[Brynjo03]   Brynjolfsson, E.: The IT Productivity Gap, Optimize Magazin, Issue 21, July 2003

[BSAIDC08]   BSA/IDC Global Software Piracy Study: global.bsa.org/idcglobalstudy2007/pr/pr_us.pdf, 2008

[Butje05]   Butje, M.: Product Marketing for Technology Companies, Butterworth-Heinemann, Burlington, 2005

[BuDiHe08]   Buxmann, P., Diefenbach, H., Hess, T.: Die Software-Industrie – Ökonomische Prinzipien, Strategien, Perspektiven, Springer, Heidelberg, 2008

[Carr08]   Carr, N.: The Big Switch: Rewiring the World, from Edison to Google, W.W. Norton, New York, 2008

[Carr03]   Carr, N.: IT Doesn't Matter, Harvard Business Review May 2003

[Condon02]   Condon, D.: Software Product Management: Managing Software Development from Idea to Product to Marketing to Sales, Aspatore Books, 2002

[CoEdKl01]   Cooper, R.G., Edgett, S.J., Kleinschmidt, E.J.: Portfolio Management for New Products, 2nd edition, Perseus Books, Cambridge, 2001

[Cooper00]   Cooper, R.G.: Product Leadership – Creating and Launching Superior New Products, Perseus Books, Cambridge, 2000

[Cusuma07]   Cusumano, M.: The Changing Labyrinth of Software Pricing, Comm. acm vol. 50, no. 7, July 2007, pp. 19–22

[Cusuma04]   Cusumano, M.: The Business of Software, Free Press, New York, 2004

[Cusuma03]   Cusumano, M.: Finding Your Balance in the Products and Services Debate, Comm. acm vol. 46, no. 3, March 2003, pp. 15–17

[DenDun03]   Denning, P.J., Dunham, R.: The Missing Customer, Comm. acm vol. 46, no. 3, March 2003, pp. 19–23

[Dver07]   Dver, A.S.: Software Product Management Essentials, Anclote, Tampa, 2007

[FeFiHL05]   Feller, J., Fitzgerald, B., Hissam, S.A., Lakhani, K.R. (eds.): Perspectives on Free and Open Source Software, MIT Press, Cambridge, 2005

[Fenn08]   Fenn, J.: Understanding Gartner's Hype Cycles, 2008, Gartner, Inc., Research Document G00158921, June 2008

[Gartner08]   Gartner Group: Gartner's Top Predictions for IT Organizations and Users, 2008 and Beyond: Going Green and Self-Healing, Gartner Group, Stamford, ID Number G00154035, Jan. 2008

[Goldstein05]   Goldstein, P.J.: Chargebacks and Information Technology Funding, ECAR, 2005, www.educause.edu/ecar

[Gorche05]   Gorchels, L.: The Product Manager's Handbook: The Complete Product Management Resource, 3nd edition, McGraw Hill, New York, 2005

[Hawkins08]   Hawkins, S.: Magic Quadrants and Market Scopes: How Gartner Evaluates Vendors Within a Market, Gartner, Inc., Research Document G00154752, January 2008

[Hayes08]   Hayes, B.: Cloud Computing, Comm. acm vol. 51, no. 7, July 2008, pp. 9–11

[HoRoPL00]   Hoch, D.J., Roeding, C.R., Purkert, G., Lindner, S.K.: Secrets of Software Success, Harvard Business School Press, Boston, 2000

[IanLev04]   Iansiti, M., Levien, R.: The Keystone Advantage – What the New Dynamics of Business Ecosystems Mean for Strategy, Innovation, and Sustainability, Harvard Business School Press, Boston, 2004

[IEEE99]   IEEE Standards Software Engineering, 1999 Edition, Volume Four: Resource and Techniques Standards, New York, The Institute of Electrical and Electronic Engineers, 1999

[JohGus00]   Johnson, M.D., Gustafsson, A.: Improving Customer Satisfaction, Loyalty, and Profit: An Integrated Measurement and Management System, Jossey-Bass, 2000

[KatSha85]   Katz, M.L., Shapiro, C.: Network Externalities, Competition, and Compatibility, American Economic Review vol. 75, 1985, pp. 424–440

[Kittlaus08]   Kittlaus, H.-B.: Software-Produkt-Management, in: Herzwurm, G., Mikusz, M. (ed.): Industrialisierung des Software-Managements, GI-Edition Lecture Notes in Informatics, Bonn, 2008

[KiRaSch04]   Kittlaus, H.-B., Rau, C., Schulz, J.: Software-Produkt-Management – Nachhaltiger Erfolgsfaktor bei Herstellern und Anwendern, Springer, Heidelberg, 2004

[Klemens06]   Klemens, B.: Math You Can't Use – Patents, Copyright, and Software, Brookings, Washington, 2006

[KotArm07]   Kotler, P., Armstrong, G.: Principles of Marketing, 12th Edition, Prentice Hall, Upper Saddle River, 2007

[Lawley07]   Lawley, B.: Expert Product Management: Advanced Techniques, Tips and Strategies for Product Management & Product Marketing, Happy About, Cupertino, 2007

[LeKaVä07]   Lehtola, L., Kauppinen, M., Vähäniitty, J.: Strengthening the link from business decisions to requirements engineering: Long-term product planning in software product companies, Proceedings of the 15th IEEE International Requirements Engineering Conference (RE'07), New Delhi, India, Oct 2007

[LerTir05]   Lerner, J., Tirole, J.: Economic Perspectives on Open Source, in [FeFiHL05], pp. 47–78, 2005

[MatMat98]   Matheson, D., Matheson, J.: The Smart Organization: Creating Value Through Smart R&D, Harvard Business School Press, Cambridge, 1998

[McGee04]   McGee, K.: Heads Up – How to Anticipate Business Surprises and Seize
                 Opportunities First, Harvard Business School Press, Boston, 2004
[McGrat01]   McGrath, M.E.: Product Strategy for High Technology Companies, 2nd
                 edition, McGrawHill, New York, 2001
[MessSzy03]   Messerschmitt, D.G., Szyperski, C.: Software Ecosystem – Understanding
                 an Indispensable Technology and Industry, MIT Press, Cambridge, 2003
[MilMor99]   Miller, W.L., Morris, L.: 4th Generation R&D: Managing Knowledge,
                 Technology, and Innovation, John Wiley, New York, 1999
[Moore93]   Moore, J.F.: Predators and Prey: A New Ecology of Competition, Harvard
                 Business Review May 1993
[Myers00]   Myers, J.H.: Measuring Customer Satisfaction: Hot Buttons and Other
                 Measurement Issues, American Marketing Association, 2000
[NagHog05]   Nagle, T.T., Hogan, J.E.: What Is Strategic Pricing?, originally published
                 in Strategic Pricing Group Insights, a member of Monitor Group, 2005
                 (www.monitor.com/Portals/0/MonitorContent/documents/Monitor_
                 What_Is_Strategic_Pricing.pdf)
[NagHog06]   Nagle, T.T., Hogan, J.E.: The Strategy and Tactics of Pricing – A Guide
                 to Growing More Profitably, 4th edition, Pearson Prentice Hall, Upper
                 Saddle River, 2006
[NagHog06d]   Nagle,   T.T.,   Hogan,   J.E.:   Strategie   und   Taktik   in   der
                 Preispolitik – Profitable Entscheidungen treffen, 4. Akt. Auflage, Pearson
                 Studium, 2006 (deutsche Übersetzung von [NagHog06])
[Oskin08]   Oskin, M.: The Revolution Inside the Box, Comm. acm vol. 51, no. 7,
                 July 2008, pp. 70–78
[PragMark08]   Pragmatic Marketing, Inc.: Pragmatic Marketing Framework: on www.
                 pragmaticmarketing.com
[Raphael03]   Raphael, M.: Principles for Equitable Chargeback: the Economics of
                 Utility Computing, Meta Group White Paper, 2003
[Reichh96]   Reichheld, F.F.: The Loyalty Effect: The Hidden Force Behind Growth,
                 Profits, and Lasting Value, Harvard Business School Press, Cambridge,
                 1996
[RobRob06]   Robertson, S., Robertson, J.: Mastering the Requirements Process, 2nd
                 Edition, Addison-Wesley, New York, 2006
[RuhSal05]   Ruhe, G., Saliu, M.O.: The Art and Science of Software Release
                 Planning, IEEE Software, vol. 22, no. 6, 2005, pp. 47–53
[Rupp07]   Rupp, C.: Requirements-Engineering und –Management: Professionelle,
                 iterative Anforderungsanalyse für die Praxis, Hanser, Munich, 2007
[RusKan03]   Rust, R.T., Kannon, P.K.: E-Service: A New Paradigm for Business in the
                 Electronic Environment, Comm. acm vol. 46, no. 6, June 2003, S.
                 37–42
[SalRuh07]   Saliu, M.O., Ruhe, G.: Bi-Objective Release Planning for Evolving
                 Software Systems, Proceedings of the the 6th joint meeting of the
                 European software engineering conference and the ACM SIGSOFT sym-
                 posium on The foundations of software engineering, ACM, 2007, pp.
                 105–114
[Samuel08]   Samuelson, P.: Revisiting Patentable Subject Matter, Comm. acm vol. 51,
                 no. 7, July 2008, pp. 20–22
[Samuel03]   Samuelson, P.: Trade Secrets vs. Free Speech, Comm. acm vol. 46, no. 6,
                 June 2003, pp. 19–23
[Schien02]   Schienmann, B.: Kontinuierliches Anforderungsmanagement, Addison-
                 Wesley, München, 2002
[SnHaTe04]   Sneed, H.M., Hasitschka, M., Teichmann, M.-T.: Software-Produktmanage-
                 ment: Wartung und Weiterentwicklung bestehender Anwendungssysteme,
                 Dpunkt Verlag, München, 2004

[Spolsky04]   Spolsky, J.: Camels and Rubber Duckies, 2004. http://www.joelonsoft-
                   ware.com/articles/CamelsandRubberDuckies.html
[Stand06]   Standish Group: Chaos Report 2006, http://www.standishgroup.com/
                   chaos/index.php
[TapWil06]   Tapscott, D., Williams, A.D.: Wikinomics – How Mass Collaboration
                   Changes Everything, Portfolio/Penguin, New York, 2006
[Tukey58]   Tukey, J.W.: The Teaching of Concrete Mathematics, The American
                   Mathematical Monthly, vol. 65, no. 1 (Jan. 1958), pp. 1–9
[VähRau05]   Vähäniitty, J., Rautiainen, K.: Towards an Approach for Managing the
                   Development Portfolio in Small Product-Oriented Software Companies,
                   Proc. of the 38th Annual Hawaii International Conference on System
                   Sciences (HICSS'05), 2005, pp. 314–323
[Waldo08]   Waldo, J.: Scaling in Games and Virtual Worlds, Comm. acm vol. 51, no.
                   8, August 2008, pp. 38–44
[WBNVB06]   Weerd, I. van de, Brinkkemper, S., Nieuwenhuis, R., Versendaal, J.M.,
                   Bijlsma, A.: On the Creation of a Reference Framework for Software
                   Product Management: Validation and Tool Support, Proc. of the
                   International Workshop on Software Product Management (IWSPM'06 -
                   RE'06 Workshop): Minneapolis/St. Paul, Minnesota, Sept. 2006

Index